Palgrave Studies in the History of Childhood

Series Editors
George Rousseau
University of Oxford, UK

Laurence Brockliss
University of Oxford, UK

Palgrave Studies in the History of Childhood is the first of its kind to historicise childhood in the English-speaking world; at present no historical series on children/childhood exists, despite burgeoning areas within Child Studies. The series aims to act both as a forum for publishing works in the history of childhood and a mechanism for consolidating the identity and attraction of the new discipline.

More information about this series at
http://www.palgrave.com/gp/series/14586

Miriam Müller

Childhood, Orphans and Underage Heirs in Medieval Rural England

Growing up in the Village

palgrave
macmillan

Miriam Müller
University of Birmingham
Birmingham, UK

Palgrave Studies in the History of Childhood
ISBN 978-3-030-03601-0 ISBN 978-3-030-03602-7 (eBook)
https://doi.org/10.1007/978-3-030-03602-7

Library of Congress Control Number: 2018960500

This Palgrave Macmillan imprint is published by the registered company Springer Nature Switzerland AG
The registered company address is: Gewerbestrasse 11, 6330 Cham, Switzerland

Acknowledgements

I am immensely grateful to friends and colleagues who kindly read and commented on earlier drafts of the chapters in this book. Without their support, encouragement and critical eye, this book would have turned out undoubtedly much poorer. Particular thanks have to go to Prof. Chris Dyer, Prof. Chris Wickham and Prof. Naomi Standen. I am also very grateful for the comments made and questions asked by various audiences to whom I presented papers based on this research at the Medieval Congress of Leeds, at seminars at the University of Kent and the University of Birmingham, the *Childhood Conference* at the University of Edinburgh, and the *Seen but Not Heard* Childhood Studies Conference at the University of Sussex. I also wish to thank numerous friends and colleagues who suffered me going on and on about medieval village children, and offered their thoughts, ideas and criticisms. In particular, I would like to thank Aysu Dinçer, Richard Goddard, Mike Evans, Jean Birrell and Cordelia Beattie. This book could also never have been written without many hours in two archives in particular; the Wolfson Centre for Archival Research in the Library of Birmingham and the Archive in The Hive in Worcester, and I am very grateful for the help and assistance of the staff there. I would also like to thank the Marc Fitch Fund for their generous grant which facilitated the use of images. Finally, I am thankful to my students at the University of Birmingham, who asked me about the fate of village orphans a few years ago, which set me off on this rather unexpected journey into researching village children. I hope this offering goes some way to answering at least a few of your brilliant questions, and please keep asking them!

Contents

1 **Introduction** 1
1 Village Children 1
2 The Child 7
3 Sources: via Orphans and Underaged Heirs to Village Children 13
Bibliography 28

2 **Vulnerable Members of the Community** 33
1 Communities and Lordship 33
2 Growing Autonomy 45
3 The Age of Majority 58
Bibliography 73

3 **Inheritance, Rights and Goods** 79
1 Heirs, Rights and Communities 79
2 Chattels, Buildings and Material Culture 86
3 Heriots and Livestock 98
4 The Tenement 104
Bibliography 114

4 Looking After Underaged Heirs 119
1 The Children 119
2 The Peasant Guardians 130
3 The Roles of Lords; Guardians and Profiteers 140
Bibliography 153

5 Plotting Out a Living 157
1 Kinship Networks and Match Makers 157
2 Learning to Make a Living: Education at Home, Independence and Service 166
3 Attending Grammar School 174
4 Problems and Conflict 182
Bibliography 194

6 Conclusion 197
Bibliography 204

Glossary 207

Index 211

List of Figures

Chapter 2

Diagram 1	Relationships between tenant, lord, land and communities	58

Chapter 4

Chart 1	Sex ratio of heirs at the manors 1270–1400	123
Chart 2	Proportion of male and female heirs in per cent	124
Chart 3	Recorded number of underaged heirs at the manors of Winslow, Norton, Halesowen and Walsham le Willows 1290–1400. Note that records for Winslow only commence in 1322, and for Walsham in 1308. No underaged heir is recorded for the remainder of the fourteenth century at either manor post 1385	129
Chart 4	Guardians recorded at Winslow, Halesowen, Walsham le Willows and Norton from 1290 to 1400 in per cent	132
Chart 5	Incidents of 'Other' and 'Unknown' guardians at the manors of Walsham le Willows, Winslow and Halesowen	134

Chapter 5

Fig. 1	Royal 2AXXII f.220v. 'The Westminster Psalter', Westminster or St. Albans, England mid-thirteenth century. St. Christopher carrying Christ child in a sling (© British Library Board. All Rights Reserved/ Bridgeman Images)	168

List of Tables

Chapter 3

Table 1	Details of inheritance proportionally mentioned in custody agreements from 1270 to, and including 1348	87
Table 2	Details of inheritance mentioned in post-Black Death custody arrangements	89
Table 3	Household goods recorded in inventories of underaged heirs across all manors	94
Table 4	Tools recorded in inventories of underaged heirs across all manors	96
Table 5	Livestock recorded in inventories of underaged heirs across all manors	96
Table 6	Other items recorded in inventories of underaged heirs across all manors	97
Table 7	Types of heriots given at Winslow in per cent	100
Table 8	Types of heriots given by underaged heirs at the manor of Norton in per cent	100
Table 9	Cattle heriots by underaged heirs at Winslow	101
Table 10	Average values of livestock and other possessions given in heriot payments at the manor of Winslow by underaged heirs	101
Table 11	Average and individual values of livestock and other goods given in heriot payment by underaged heirs at the manor of Norton	102

Table 12 Average value (where more than one animal was given) of livestock given in heriot payments at Halesowen, note that in the later period only 3 animal heriots were recorded at the manor 102
Table 13 Livestock heriots given by underaged heirs at Halesowen in per cent 103
Table 14 Average value of livestock given as heriots by underaged heirs at Walsham le Willows 103
Table 15 Heriot given by underaged heirs at Walsham le Willows 103
Table 16 Landholdings of underaged heirs compared to general landholding at Winslow 105
Table 17 Landholding and inheritance at Walsham le Willows 106

Chapter 4
Table 1 Ages of wards upon arriving at court at the manors of Walsham le Willows, Halesowen, Norton, Brandon and Winslow, from 1270 to 1400 in per cent 121
Table 2 Ages of wards at Walsham, Halesowen, Norton, Brandon and Winslow in per cent across the period 122
Table 3 Allocated guardians according to gender at Winslow, Halesowen, Norton, Walsham le Willows 137

CHAPTER 1

Introduction

1 Village Children

I blame my students for this book. A few years ago some of my students were discussing the possible effects of the Black Death on family structures, and they asked me what happened to all the children and young people left orphaned by the first, and most devastating arrival of the Black Death in mid-fourteenth-century England. I felt that I was not able to answer their questions satisfactorily and at the same time my own curiosity was awakened. This book is the fruit of the resultant research.

At the heart of the research for this book are the societies and communities of later medieval rural England, a world I know most about. While research on childhood and adolescence in medieval urban contexts has increased in recent years, we still know very little about childhood in the villages and hamlets which housed the vast majority of the medieval English population. Most medieval children would have grown up in villages. Their experiences would have been defined by the seasonal changes in the agricultural year, fields growing with crops, livestock farming and the complex social dynamics of rural communities, their kinship networks, neighbours and parish structures. Their horizons would not necessarily have stopped at the crossroads outside their villages to the next town as we shall see, but for most children the vast majority of their young lives would have been spent within fairly small, and often tight-knit communities, centred around a manor and a parish church as the most important institutions of local authority.

M. Müller, *Childhood, Orphans and Underage Heirs in Medieval Rural England*, Palgrave Studies in the History of Childhood,
https://doi.org/10.1007/978-3-030-03602-7_1

To many modern ears this may sound romantic. We live in a world which is increasingly anxious and concerned about how much time our youngsters spend indoors, playing on a whole host of electronic devices, instead of climbing trees, hunting for butterflies and pond dipping. A few years ago Richard Louv tapped into these worries with his book *Last Child in the Woods* where he described a phenomenon he called 'nature deficit disorder', childhoods bereft of nature, leading to mental ill health and unbalanced young people.[1] More recently, a petition was making its way across social media, including Facebook demanding that nature-related words, such as cygnet, bluebell and acorn should be reinstated into the Junior Oxford English dictionary. The petition, once again, echoed concerns that rising childhood obesity and mental illness must surely be related to a declining engagement of children with nature.[2]

Perhaps because academics like to think in binaries, rural childhood has often been presented in dichotomous terms. Commentators have been inclined to pit images of rural idyll against the alienated dirty landscape of inner cities, from the left such stereotypes were underpinned by the conceptualisation of the brutal vagaries of industrial capitalism against an often romanticised, and backward-looking imagined golden age of the village community, which rural historians of medieval England in particular are only too familiar with.[3] The imagined idyll of the rural child is also intimately bound up with imagery of the natural child first set out by Rousseau in his famous book *Emile* in the eighteenth century.[4] Indeed the link between ideas of nature and childhood can be traced back to medieval times. In the twelfth-century, Life of St Anselm its author Eadmer describes how in discussion with an abbot about the education of young people St. Anselm likens children to trees which need care and freedom from fear to develop well with good morality.[5]

Yet while the concept of the ideal childhood is intertwined with nature and often contrasted with the unnatural—hence harmful—urban sphere, within the exploration of rural childhood one can also locate another dichotomised image. Literature and the media is dominated by images of children in the countryside engaged with nature, playing alongside streams and in flowering meadows. As Powell et al. are at pains to point out, however, the study of modern rural childhood has worked hard on the deconstruction of this idyllic and nostalgic view.[6] The flip-side of the positive images are defined by social and economic factors. Boredom for young people, prying neighbours, lack of educational opportunities, a significant element of rural poverty, and a life which could be harsh and unforgiving, especially in the past.[7]

As researchers of the past, it is impossible for us to escape the present. As a result, I researched this book, enmeshed in these concerns of modern life with the aim to find out more about the rural children of the later middle ages. While the impact of crises like the Black Death and the early fourteenth-century famine were at the forefront of my mind, my main concern was also to find out about contemporary, medieval attitudes to children and young people, what those attitudes tell us about the communities they lived in—including the adult world, and to what extent young people of the middle ages were able to decide their own paths in life. Were young people oppressed and exploited—as has been intimated in some studies—were they treated as adults? Did they have rights and were they considered to be vulnerable? In asking these questions, a number of problems soon became apparent. Firstly, I felt that I was asking the wrong questions, as they were too grounded in our contemporary conceptualisations of childhood; the root problem of this, I felt, was that I was still hampered by the debate caused by the publication of P. Ariès' seminal study *Centuries of Childhood* in 1968, which effectively threw the proverbial gauntlet at medievalists with the now famous assertion that the notion of childhood did not exist in medieval society. Instead, it is important to move beyond such earlier discussions about historic, especially medieval childhood sparked by Ariès, as they seemed to be addressing the wrong questions, and thereby answering them in a rather unsatisfying way. (The discourse typically went something like this: Was Ariès right? No, he was not, there were concepts of childhood in medieval society.) The attempt to show that there was a concept of childhood in medieval England in refuting Ariès is useful and important. However, the analysis of the question can only lead one philosophically speaking up the garden path, a pretty and interesting one, but one with serious limitations. The danger is that in focusing on Ariès and thereby allowing him to set the research agenda, it becomes difficult to seek answers beyond the parameters set by him.

Ariès absolutely has to be credited with opening the field of childhood studies for historians. His work was of importance, not just in arguing—quite rightly—the now widely accepted view that the concept of childhood itself is a construct; but also in daring to look at the topic of the history of childhood in the first place. Still, while medievalists have successfully shown that in the middle ages children were not so integrated into the adult world that children were treated like little adults, a slightly different approach is required now which looks at the topic of medieval childhood in a more holistic manner, which moves beyond Ariès' concerns, asking not whether an idea of childhood existed, but rather how childhood was conceptualised on the ground, how communities interacted with young people, how medieval people conceptualised learning and training, and even more importantly, how young people themselves fed into these structures and made them their own. With this in mind I wanted to look at the young people themselves; and attempt to view their world not merely through the eyes of their adult contemporaries, a highly challenging, and perhaps almost impossible task, as our extant documentary sources were all written by adults.

Ariès' genius was that he rightly pointed out that, in essence, childhood as a concept is specific to particular social and cultural contexts. As such, Heywood has argued that childhood can be seen as an 'abstraction'.[8] Ideas of childhood are at variance according to cultural, social geographic and chronological contexts. Ariès' grave mistake was his subsequent application of a presentist perspective which sought to define childhood in past European societies according to definitions of childhood prevalent in the 1960s. Of course, this led to the ludicrous conclusion that there was no concept of childhood in medieval times. The reaction by medievalists is understandable, yet also somewhat problematic. The aim—quite rightly—was to show that Ariès was wrong. It was pointed out that he looked at the wrong sources, that he neglected sources, that his view was too narrow, that he did not consult a wealth of material which did, in fact, show that a concept of childhood did actually exist in medieval society. They argued and demonstrated that childhood was perceived as a separate stage to adulthood and that children—at different ages were associated with different characteristics.[9] The result of all this important research, as Heywood succinctly summarised in a recent publication is that 'among those active in the field the argument that "in medieval society the idea of childhood did not exist" is assuredly dead in the water'.[10]

Satisfying as this might be, we are only beginning to understand medieval childhood in its own right. Many of the excellent studies on medieval childhood have concentrated not just on urban environments, but also the better off in society.[11] As a result, we have learned that medieval thinkers divided childhood into different developmental stages, there was also advice for childbirth, the nursing of infants as well as successful weaning.[12] We know that there was a culture of childhood and children played with toys, and a substantial amount of literature has explored the experiences of growing up in urban contexts, including the nature and regulation of apprenticeships.[13]

The key objective for this book was the examination of the lives of rural young people. The children who grew up in peasant communities. Some in hamlets and small villagers, others in large villages with markets and perhaps even urban traits, but still functioning under a system of feudal lordship, rather than growing up within urban borough contexts.

Socially, as well as economically, this group of people would have constituted the vast majority of the later medieval English population, and estimates place the extent of the rural population at between 80 and 90%. The medieval peasantry can be understood to have constituted a distinct social class. In Marxist terms the relationship between peasants and lords was a defining aspect of the peasantry's socio-economic identity, constituting part of the feudal mode of production, whereby with the backing of the force of law and hence also local manorial custom, lords were able to extract surplus produce from their peasant tenants.[14] Social class influenced profoundly then—as now—the experiences of children and adolescents. Additionally, social class also influences the construction of the concept of childhood itself.[15] It is therefore important to explore rural childhood and adolescence distinctly from urban experiences. A child growing up in urban environments would have been exposed to quite different social and economic as well as legal stimuli. Towns saw a wider variety of crafts practiced than villages. There would have been regular markets, perhaps even annual or bi-annual fairs, and while the stereotyped image of medieval villagers as experiencing little outside their villages is now known not to hold true, it is certain that urban children would have seen a much busier coming and going of strangers, and cultural interactions which went far beyond the confines of their neighbourhoods. In larger towns like London or Norwich there would have been several regular markets, prisons, the public spectacle of royal announcements, executions, performative public punishments, alongside a regulatory system linked to the powers and influence of guilds, which also helped to regulate not just the quality of their respective crafts, and their training in apprentices, but also the care of orphans.[16] We hear about attempts in towns to regulate building practices to make houses less prone to fire damage, attempts were made to regulate waste disposal and the location of trades which were notoriously foul smelling like tanneries. Children growing up in these environments often had to content with quite crowded housing conditions and dangers associated with busy streets.[17] At the same time, urban young people were likely to have some sort of access to formalised education, be that in schools or as formally regulated apprentices to crafts found more readily in towns. Rural life, was in many respects less busy, cultural experiences lacked the variety associated with urban spaces as well as the regulatory systems and powers associated with guilds.

Such factors raise some important questions, in particular regarding the training and education of rural young people. How were children trained in their villages? How did they acquire skills and how did they learn to make a living? While it is certainly the case that some urban societies were run like lordships and in the hands of private lords, like, for example, the town of St. Albans, which famously was in an almost constant battle with its lord, the Abbot of St. Albans, generally speaking, urban society experienced regulation through borough courts and guilds, rural societies were dominated by the jurisdictional powers of private lordship. Such differences mattered, and as such the socio-economic contexts young people found themselves in influenced almost every aspect of their lives. As a result, the decision to focus almost exclusively on the experiences of rural children was not only deliberate but yields results which are not always directly comparable to urban research.

Despite such broad differences, and of course, these are broad brushstrokes, every urban context had its very own peculiarities and specificities, just as a hamlet in a remote part of Wiltshire will show different characteristics to a large thriving village in, say Norfolk, it is important to bear in mind that peasant does not equal peasant. Peasants did not constitute a homogeneous mass.[18] Historians working on medieval English peasants generally divide these into the poorer, the middling and the wealthier strata of rural society.[19] As far as possible it has been the aim to bear such differences and stratifications in mind, and explore the experiences of family life and childhood according to variations in social and economic strata. In particular, it has been the aim to explore the impact of crisis like the Great Famine and the Black Death had on the life chances and experiences of rural young people.

We should certainly not be tempted to romanticise the rural lives of young people. While research indicates a significant degree of freedom among village children, we also know that life could be harsh and dangerous. Infant mortality was high, and children could die from illnesses which are now easily treatable. The authority children fell under, the church and the state, represented most directly via the local, private jurisdiction of the manorial lord, similarly exerted powerful control over their communities. Their lives were also complex, some of the children we encounter in this study were legally free, others were unfree, the sons and daughters of villein tenants who fell under the customs of their manor, sometimes referred to as serfs of bondmen. Some had parents who held both free and unfree land. Their parents—and later they themselves—had to perform various customary servile duties for some of the land held in villeinage and only pay cash rents to their lord for the free land they owned. Mixed marriages between the free and unfree were far from uncommon in some manors, and young people had to learn to navigate the resultant complex legal and social ramifications. Village life with all its economic and political dynamics was demanding and could be hard work, socially as well as physically. To a degree survival was intertwined with successful mutuality; successful networks and alliances could make or break families. Young people had to learn how to become effective operators in these social groupings with rural communities on the one side, and seigniorial as well as ecclesiastical jurisdiction on the other. Accordingly, the experiences of rural childhood have been placed firmly within the context of the rural experience of lordship.

2 The Child

The study of childhood, and indeed the history of childhood, seems to be an inherently paradoxical pursuit. On the one hand, everybody thinks they know what a child is. The expectation is that when an adult sees a child they are able to identify its child—like nature and inherent essence of characteristics which make it other than adult. When I ask my students to define a child, they are readily able to list a whole set of generally understood characteristics. Children, it is accordingly noted, are smaller than adults, they are less mature, they are younger, often silly, reckless, more creative, copy adults, tend to have a circumscribed vocabulary, especially when very young, are vulnerable, are dependent and need to be looked after, are easily manipulated, can't look after themselves, need to be educated and so on. Of course, such definitions not only rely on perceptions of the adult as of average adult size with average mental and physical capacities, but they also betray the underlying problem of attempting to define the 'child'. Herein lies the first paradox, as any attempt to define childhood in and of itself runs fundamentally into the problem that the child in much of western society is always defined as against the stereotypical adult. The child is 'other' than adult, it is what the adult is not, and as such the child becomes 'othered'. The child is not adult, the adult is not child. Further dissection of these concepts always runs into problems—what about very mature young children? What about mentally disabled adults? This dichotomy, positing adult against child conceptually in not only prevalent in common parlance and the media, where the wellbeing of the child is regularly agonised over, but, as Alanen has pointed out, it has also been identified—perhaps rather unsurprisingly, in a similarly dichotomous manner in sociology.[20] The problem is not only that the child is posited against the adult, but conceptually the child is seen and defined almost entirely negatively, as Alanen argues, while the 'child cannot be imagined excerpt in relation to a conception of the adult', the perspective is not focused on 'what the child is', but rather on what the child is 'subsequently going to be'.[21] In other words, the focus of attention is on the adult, the adult defines the child, whereby the child is reduced to a status of a small person waiting to become an adult—by implication a superior and more important being.[22]

This dichotomous conceptualisation of childhood against adulthood lies at the root of some of the problems in our research of the history of childhood, and I would say, the history of childhood in medieval society in particular.

Essentially, a view of children as subordinated, as well as, by implication, inferior to the adult world is created. Corsaro has more recently echoed Alanen's concerns, noting that while we might be able to identify a significant, yet fairly recent growth in studies on childhood, in sociology as well as in history, the relative marginalisation of children in sociology in particular can be explained through their subordinate position in society, where childhood is merely focused on a period of socialisation into the adult world.[23] This top-down perspective encourages us to view children as secondary to adult concerns, by implication their agency is seen as non-existent or extremely circumscribed, their raison-d'être, reduced to learning how to become an adult.[24] The view of children as of secondary importance was not confined to sociology. In an important new archaeological study of late medieval children in southern England Heidi Dawson has recently lamented the neglect of childhood in archaeology. She noted that while children have always made up a significant proportion of the population, archaeologists have been slow in focusing on the archaeology of childhood.[25] Indeed, while researchers, like Sally Crawford have significantly advanced our knowledge of earlier medieval childhood, substantial progress on the archaeology of childhood especially of the later Middle Ages in England seems primarily to have occurred in the last decade, with groundbreaking studies by individuals including Mary Lewis, Heidi Dawson, Roberta Gilchrist and Sally Smith.[26] Dawson argued that the reason for this long neglect can be found in the prevalence of androcentrism in archaeology, a perspective which focused primarily on men and their concerns, to the neglect of the study of women and children.[27]

Conceptually women are associated with children, which explains not merely their neglect in various academic disciplines, but also why research has finally started to turn to Childhood.[28] However, despite great strides forward, research of childhood still seems to lag behind research on women and marginal groups. Accordingly, Dawson notes that while in archaeology gender studies have improved significantly, the study of childhood has still a long way to catch up.[29] This might in part reflect a view of children not just as inferior to adults, and adult men, but also to adult women. In this sense, the study of childhood suffered the double discrimination of not just being viewed as less important than the study of men and their pursuits, but also less important than research of women or indeed gender. Therefore one might well see the progress in the research of childhood as a direct reflection in the progress of women and gender studies.

The androcentrism which is largely to blame for the long-term neglect of childhood studies also has further, wider repercussions. In conceptualising childhood as dichotomous from (male) adulthood, a view of childhood is encouraged which focuses on precisely the development into adulthood—a full and 'important' human being with agency. As a result, the predominant view has been to see childhood as part of a developmental process—precisely towards adulthood. It is because of this conceptualisation of childhood as a clear, linear development—towards an adult human being—that the history of childhood in particular has encountered so many problems. Again, parallels can be seen here in a number of disciplines. In sociology, we can observe the problem most clearly in traditional socialisation theories, which perceives the development of a child from infancy to adulthood, in a plottable, linear fashion. It is, as Corsaro rightly argued, a very deterministic reading of childhood, where children are reduced to effectively passive recipients of knowledge and training from the adult world around them.[30] Again the approach is top-down, the perspective taken is from the adult, the child is virtually deprived of agency, but plotted and charted, in terms of physical as well as mental changes and 'developments' towards adulthood. The way such development has traditionally been represented is as transcending cultural differences, where the child is reduced to a universal being. Yet we know that even growth charts are influenced by cultural factors.[31] A society where breastfeeding is the norm will see babies developing in terms of size and weight in a different way to those where bottle—feeding is predominant. Similarly, in some cultural contexts, access to food can be gendered, leading to different growth patterns between boys and girls.[32]

Beyond the mere notions of the functionality of physical development, the theory of socialisation, is an inherently adult-centred perspective, as Alanen points out, the 'child remains negatively defined- defined only by what the child is not but is subsequently going to be'.[33] The child becomes a recipient of instruction under adult authority, rather than an active participant in learning, growing and changing. As such, Alanen concludes that socialisation frameworks are also an 'elitist perspective', as socialisation is considered important in maintaining and upkeeping a society's organs of governance, rule and social control.[34] Therefore socialisation is considered a necessary process whereby children learn social rules, laws, moral norms and codes, in order to develop into adults who are able to function as integrated law-abiding individuals in their societies.

For the historian concerned with the study of childhood in the past such conceptual frameworks matter, as they inform our own perceptions of childhood, firstly in defining childhood, and secondly in our interpretations of the experience of childhood. Children grow up within certain contexts, social, cultural, political and economic frameworks which influence and shape the child in varying ways. Yet if we see children primarily as passive recipients of adult input, we not only rob the child of agency, real, or potential, but we also reduce the child and young person to a status of almost perpetual, helpless potential victimhood, where the young person is conceptualised as existing entirely at the whim of adults. From this perspective medieval childhood reads like an endless horror story, punctuated by abusive relationships, exploitation, violence and neglect.[35]

Such perspectives can occasionally also be tinted by a rather dim or even hostile view of particularly working and peasant classes of the past.[36] Children are either seen as just tools of the household economy, or additional mouths to be fed.[37] Such narratives of medieval childhood also tend to whiggish perspectives, where the experience of childhood—and the perception of children—improves in a linear fashion presumably eventually leading to some contemporary period of total enlightenment.[38] The result is at best a distortion of the history of childhood. As E.P. Thompson rightly said, 'I am persuaded that we are different, as parents or as lovers, from those in the past; but I am not persuaded that we are much better, more companionate, more caring, than our forefathers and mothers'.[39] Accordingly, in order to provide a less distorted view of childhood in the past and the experiences of growing up, a different approach to the source material which we do have is required.

Corsaro suggests a more fruitful way forward would be to view children as active participants in their societies, whereby children are not merely viewed as passive recipients of an adult world.[40] This does not mean that we should never see children as vulnerable or under the authority of adults, but rather that we should appreciate a dialectical interplay between children and adults, or in Corsaro's words, 'the appreciation of the importance of collective, communal activity—how children negotiate, share, and create culture with adults and each other'.[41] Young people are thereby seen as actively influencing their world in a complex dance between their own desires, reactions and views and adult expectations, anxieties and desires, which are both centred on the individual and the community. In short, children do not merely receive society, but rather help shape it.

Dawson similarly argues that children 'can be active in social interactions and cultural learning'.[42] Ultimately therefore, the idea that children are helplessly under the power of adults is at least partly a result of the modern western notion of childhood as distinctly separate from adulthood. Perhaps it is particularly incumbent on historians to sidestep such a presentist trap, and appreciate that context means change. Anthropology is highly instructive in this context. Not all cultures exhibit such a 'clear distinction between adult and child' as we do in modern western Europe.[43] Dawson cites the example of Inuit culture which sees young children as both children and adults.[44] Ultimately the aims is a perspective which shifts into focus the agency of young people, it does not deny adult power as such, but acknowledges child influence within chronological and cultural context. Such a shift matters for historians. We know that medieval children participated in and helped shape medieval culture. For example, Orme has highlighted the importance of children's activities in the annual calendar, which were sometimes linked to the adult calendar and occasionally separate to it, such events included the famous role reversal of the election of the boy bishop, over to cock-fighting which was popular with boys during Lent.[45]

While Ariès can certainly be justifiably accused of looking at the wrong sources, misreading sources and ignoring others, he was also guilty of looking into the past and upon not seeing what he knew of his present age, declared the absence of childhood. Whereas, all he really highlighted—perhaps was an absence of the type of understanding of childhood he himself was familiar with.

Yet we also know that the concept of childhood cannot merely be reduced to socio-cultural constructions without reference to biology. Children's skeletons are different from adults, puberty means development—physically into potentially at least—sexually active adulthood with the potential to bear children. The lack of mental and physical maturity of the child is not merely down to social construction but also biological fact. What matters here, however is how the boundaries between adult and child, as well as the nature of mental and physical changes were contextualised, viewed and dealt with in any given society. We know that medieval commentators had various ideas about different stages in childhood development. Such ideas, as Shahar was one of the first to illustrate, centred usually around three stages, defined first by infancy, from birth to about the age of seven, followed by puerita, which lasted until the onset of adolescence, age 12 for girls and 14 for boys. This latter stage would last until adulthood.[46] Certain characteristics were also associated with these stages, thus children under 7 in particular were considered helpless and vulnerable, after that, a child was considered to be able to express themselves, but below the age of adolescence not all medieval authors agreed that children could be held accountable for crimes, and the law often dealt leniently with such young people, even in cases of murder. The final stage was considered to end at some point, but writers differed widely about the age of the actual onset of adulthood, ranging from the late teens into the thirties.[47] Such flexibility may seem confusing to us, accustomed as we are to fairly rigid age-related timelines of childhood development, but, as we shall see, medieval society viewed these demarcations very differently, and as a result they should be primarily understood to represent a framework of a general understanding of the maturing person, rather than a rigid developmental concept with clear and distinct chronologies.

The aim of this book in this context is therefore to recognise not merely the particular perception and ideas about childhood within their specific chronology and socio-economic context—the peasantry—but being sensitive to the way young people themselves shaped and operated within their societies. The way communities interacted with young people in later medieval villages is occasionally startling, rural societies showed little rigidity in dealing with their young people. Their views on reaching adulthood were certainly different from ours in many respects. The young peasants in this book might have been seen as vulnerable and open to exploitation by their own societies—as we will see, but they will also—it is hoped—emerge as participants in forging their own futures, often in negotiation with adults who offered guidance, but did not merely simply instruct, dominate and 'socialise'.

3 Sources: via Orphans and Underaged Heirs to Village Children

Fundamentally, it is always difficult to research the history of childhood, especially in the pre-modern world. Children very rarely wrote any letters or committed any thoughts about their lives to paper or parchment. Those who did came from the elite, and cannot be seen as representative of society more widely. The view we tend to be afforded of pre-modern childhood is therefore very much top-down. Sources were invariably composed by adults, whether this was in writing or pictorial evidence. We therefore gain views of children from the perspective of the adult world. The problem is in some respects compounded for medievalists.[48] Goldberg accordingly commented that 'As legal minors who held no land, paid no taxes, owed no services, and who brought no actions in court, children are comparatively invisible'.[49]

In general, it is true, sources on medieval family life are rare and those we do have are problematic and often difficult to interpret.[50] For example, neither Domesday Book nor the much later Poll Tax records recorded all members of individual families. Since the Poll Tax was only collected on individuals over the age of 14, younger children are, by definition, excluded. In addition, Poll Tax records are unreliable due to the extensive evasion of the tax. Domesday Book gives even less information, later medieval English custumals or Manorial Rentals, available in greater numbers from the thirteenth century onwards, are excellent sources allowing insights into the numbers of tenants at any given manor, but, of course, the tenant was only the head of the household, not always, but usually a man, and they exclude a lot of women and all children as well as landless residents in manorial communities. However, historians have demonstrated that we can catch important glimpses of the lives of children in Royal Statutes—legal codes as well as illuminations of manuscripts and important insights have been gained from the examination of hagiographies and other religious and didactic texts.[51]

The use of such sources is far from unproblematic. Religious sources always had certain didactic objectives, written from the perspectives of for the most part men who were for the most part childless. The voice of the child themselves thereby becomes almost impossible to ascertain. In recent years archaeologists have moved into the foreground with incredibly important insights into the culture of childhood in later medieval England. These covered topics as varied as toys, spaces in child socialisation, while advances isotopic analysis has offered important insights into childhood diets and ages of weaning, while the examination of child and adolescent skeletal remains revealed evidence of work-related stress and injuries.[52]

For researchers active in the field it seems to be the case that while unearthing the history of childhood is far from straightforward, sources are also far from absent. Sources, it was said similarly, on medieval women were scarce and hence difficult to research, we now know that this is not the case, it appears ditto with medieval children. Instead, the problem resides with the historian, we choose what we seek, we choose what we look at and we decide what we cannot see.[53] As historians, we have to use the available sources and decide how these can be used to tell us things which are perhaps only visible at times peripherally, or has our blinkered vision to certain topics moved them to the periphery? We might comment that medieval people did not concern themselves much with childhood and wrote little of this down. Yet is such an assertion not merely yet another contemporary androcentric perspective reflected into the past? We know that family and lineage was of utmost importance to the upper classes of medieval Europe, so how would it make sense to argue that children were of little importance to them? The Florentine Merchant Gregorio Dati kept detailed notes about the births and deaths and lives of his 20 plus children, of whom only a small handful survived.[54] Kings agonised over producing heirs, and couples worried about not being able to conceive, or indeed about limiting their fertility.[55] A society which placed so much emphasis and importance on the production of healthy offspring cannot have felt indifferent about them. On the one hand, sources were written for different purposes, survival of sources should not be interpreted as reflecting attitudes to women, children or anything else, but sources have to viewed in their own historic and cultural context. This is not merely a matter of working outsource bias and perspective, but to go beyond that and consider sources for what they are and not for what *we imagine* them they are not. Instead of working against sources by attempting to find material which medieval society rarely, if ever recorded, it is more important and productive to consider what it was that was produced and why and what this can tell us about the topic of our inquiry.

The historian who decides that they want to research the history of peasant children is thus confronted with the idea that not only do we supposedly lack sources on the peasantry, but also and especially so of children. Apart from Archaeologists, only a few historians have indeed ventured into this field. One of the first was Barbara Hanawalt, whose work on the exploration of the peasant family included one of the first discussions of medieval peasant childhood.[56] Hanawalt was not only arguing against Ariès in illustrating that children were perceived to follow certain developmental stages which were considered quite different from adults in medieval society, she also felt that in order to circumvent the problem of the scarcity of sources one could gain important insights into daily life of ordinary people—including children, by examining the documentary sources of the late medieval Coroner. To this day medieval Coroner's Rolls remain largely underexplored and underused. Hanawalt's important work on Coroner's Rolls was seminal, not just in highlighting their importance, but also in using them in an original and imaginative way to shed light on the lives of medieval children, including peasant children.[57] Coroner's Rolls contain essentially the investigations of medieval Coroners into suspicious deaths, which were deemed to be at least potentially not 'natural'. They are often exquisitely detailed in their descriptions of the circumstances and causes of individual deaths, and they contain invaluable information on living conditions, daily activities and evidence of numerous cultural expressions and work activities. They also regularly contain details of the deaths of children whose ages and often other familial relationships are provided. Coroner's Rolls thus show us children coming to accidents playing, or helping around the house and fields, being bitten by animals, perishing in devastating house-fires or falling into ditches and drowning. Hanawalt's study did however attempt to go further and extrapolate from the Coroner data gendered patterns of the accidental deaths of children alongside age-related patterns in relation to activities leading to a child's death which could be interpreted as evidence for children working.[58]

While a number of Hanawalt's findings have so far remained unchallenged, in recent years her interpretation of evidence of gendered socialisation of children has been questioned by another prominent historian of medieval gender and family life, Jeremy Goldberg.[59] In particular, Goldberg questioned Hanawalt's use of statistical evidence, which he felt was problematic and did not accord with his own analysis of the evidence contained in Coroner's Rolls.[60]

One fundamental problem with the evidence contained in Coroner's Rolls is that by definition they record what was not considered the norm. Not every death was investigated by the Coroner, but only those deemed, potentially at least, 'unnatural'. To what extent is it safe to extrapolate the norm from the unusual? Certainly incidental information which accompanies Coroner's inquests are safe enough, and is often also borne out in other evidence; children played in fields, housefires happened not infrequently, children played occasionally in dangerous ways, but if we find examples of young children drowning because they tried to fetch water, can this be read as a reflection of a common activity by young girls, which occasionally went wrong, or did it only end up as an accident so rarely precisely because most people did not send very young children out to wells and rivers to fetch water?

While it is certainly the case that archaeology is starting to add significantly to our knowledge of the lives of young people both in urban and rural contexts, we still seem to lack textual documentary evidence which can give us some insight into the lives of peasant children and adolescents from the perspectives of their contemporary adults and the children themselves.

The main written sources which have been used to examine the lives of medieval English peasants are manorial records. These were the sources generated through the administrative systems of the private jurisdiction bestowed upon manorial lords, both lay and ecclesiastical. The survival of such manorial records are locally patchy, but for some estates extant records are extremely voluminous and detailed, especially for larger ecclesiastical estates, as wealthy Abbeys and bishoprics in particular had the resources, both financial and in terms of trained clerks and administrators to manage estates on a large scale and keep relevant detailed records for long periods of time.[61]

There are several different types of manorial sources. On the one hand, we have records like rentals, which were conducted periodically in order to list all tenants—free and unfree-falling under the jurisdiction of an individual manor, usually listing their cash rent payments and occasionally also their other tenurial obligations. The latter are more commonly recorded in more detail in custumals, which also became more plentiful as well as detailed from the second half of the thirteenth century onwards, as manorialism was reaching its peak, and lords were successful in tightening their hold over their resident populations, not least by extending the number of unfree, or villein—tenants within their jurisdiction.[62] At the root of these developments was in part at least a growing population which drove up the value of land and also contributed to peasants accepting unfree tenements rather than sinking into smallholdership and landlessness.[63] As a result of the expansion of serfdom lords needed systems to record obligations, track the movements of unfree land, find tests of villein status, and a legal apparatus to enforce seigniorial power. The latter was the manorial court, held typically at least once every month, in some manors more frequently. Manorial courts yield for the historian manorial court rolls. These contain—depending on the individual extent of the jurisdiction granted to local lords—information ranging from land transfers between peasants, instances of lord–tenant conflict over servile obligations sizes of landholdings, cases of debt and credit, disputes over rent payments over to various detailed disputes and agreements between the peasants themselves, including broken contracts, disputes over boundaries, escaped animals, brawls at alehouses, marriages, and a myriad of other things which illuminate daily life in the medieval English countryside. The fruits of these administrative and legal systems offers the historian of later medieval rural England a veritable treasure trove of information about peasant communities, until the decline of the manorial system and the reduction in the importance of unfreedom from the beginning of the fifteenth century onwards.[64] In recent years, manorial court rolls have also been used to examine gendered relationships in peasant communities—despite earlier concerns by historians that manorial records only gave scarce information on women.[65] Historians have similarly turned to topics including the extent of credit and debt arrangements, in addition to patterns of inheritance and communal relationships.[66]

Manorial records are not unproblematic—no source is—fundamentally they are written from the lord's perspective, and the lord had no interest in recording what was not of immediate concern to him. At the core of the lord's interest was financial gain. Any cases which would yield a profit therefore tended to be recorded. So of course, where lords had Leet or equivalent jurisdiction over their tenantry they recorded brawls between peasants and raising of the hue and cry, not necessarily because he was interested in intra-peasant dispute, but because each such conflict yielded him a few pence revenue.[67] However, this does not mean that peasants merely appear in these sources as exploited puppets lacking agency. Peasants could and did use manorial courts and their resultant rolls to their advantage, including when they wanted to utilise the fact that the court roll offered indisputable fact regarding agreements made in front of witnesses—in writing.

Court rolls—alongside other manorial sources, like custumals, rentals and accounts—have only been used peripherally to explore aspects of childhood. Hanawalt thus suggested that manorial court rolls did not mention 'children with any consistency'.[68] Indeed, at first glance attempting to investigate medieval rural childhood using primarily manorial sources seems a hard task with scant hints in the sources. However, there are important exceptions, and these are the accounts in manor court rolls concerning child heirs.

The reason for this is simple. Lords were very concerned about tracking the status and maintenance of their landed and other tenurial assets, such as buildings, woods, arable and pastoral or meadow land. As such most lords attempted to ensure that any transfer of land was conducted through their manorial court. This included the transfer of land from parent to heir. Inheritance customs in peasant society were sacrosanct. While the precise inheritance customs varied both regionally as well as locally, from manor to manor, one of the effects of especially customary (unfree) tenure was that the unfree holding was heritable to the next generation. Some manors—especially those in areas with a substantial element of free tenure—thus practiced partible inheritance, or rather male partible inheritance whereby sons inherited equally, in other places male primogeniture, whereby the oldest son received the lion's share of a holding, prevailed. In the absence of sons daughters could, again, inherit either according to primogeniture, or partibly, where all daughters inherited equally.[69]

The recording of the transfers of unfree holdings in manorial records is thereby intertwined with the existence of unfree tenure, they start to appear along with manorial court rolls in the mid-to later thirteenth century, and decline in the later fourteenth century as serfdom waned and with it unfree tenures, which were increasingly being replaced by other forms of landholding, including leasehold tenures. These developments thereby provide us with a chronological window through which manorial, peasant holdings can be examined. It is an exciting chronology, which saw the rise and decline of serfdom, the end of the period of what has been termed 'high farming', the early fourteenth-century crisis, punctuated by the Great Famine, followed a few decades later by the first arrival of the devastating Black Death in 1348–1349. Through these periods of change, upheaval and at times severe trauma lived the children and young people of medieval rural England. Their traces in manorial records can be gleaned in particular though entries detailing the fates of underaged heirs and their holdings. Such underaged heirs were more common than one might think, and they were categorised as underaged by their communities, as they were not considered to be capable to run their own affairs, and instead, they and their land and other assets were handed over into the care of appointed guardians. It is true that such cases concerning child heirs are not as common as other entries dealing with adult affairs, but they are certainly plentiful enough to warrant a detailed enquiry.

While references to child heirs are common in some manors, in many court rolls references to underaged heirs are scant, and only a few contain significant enough data to warrant statistical analysis. This required the consideration therefore of a number of manors from across the country to facilitate a study of young people and children in medieval English rural society with sufficient and fairly representative data. The evidence has been gathered from published as well as unpublished manorial records. The manorial communities which are most frequently referred to in this study and which yielded the most plentiful and consistent data include the Yorkshire manor of Wakefield, The St. Albans manors of Norton in Hertfordshire and Winslow in Buckinghamshire, the manor of Walsham le Willows in Suffolk, the manor of Halesowen in Worcestershire and the Glastonbury Abbey manors of Longbridge Deverill, Monkton Deverioll and Badbury, which are located in

Wiltshire. The manor of Brandon, which was owned by the Bishopric of Ely was located in northern Suffolk and the manor of Heacham was located in Norfolk and held by the Priory and Convent of Lewes in Sussex. The manors are therefore a cross-section of later medieval rural society, representing a range of different types of social and economic structures. The East Anglian manors contained significant proportions of freeholders and provide some good evidence of partible inheritance structures, while the south-western manors were held by conservative lords and were dominated by unfree tenants. On some manors, we can detect a stronger market pull or market influences than at others, so Longbridge Deverill, for example contained a market. The Wiltshire manors in general were influenced by the cloth industry, while Halesowen had woodland and Heacham was influenced by the fishing industry, being a coastal manor.

Most of our most plentiful evidence comes from ecclesiastical manors, which were also known for their rather conservative style of landlordism. The main reason for this is that powerful ecclesiastical lords tended to keep full and detailed records, and this dominance explains the availability of sources.

The topic of fosterage and adoption has attracted some interest among medievalists. This includes some important studies of continental Europe, especially of medieval and early modern France and Italy.[70] Research into fostering and the care of, mainly urban, orphans extends into areas of apprenticeships and service, which has been explored by historians including Goldberg. He even considers it a possibility that 'servanthood constituted a structure for what were in effect fostering arrangements for fatherless or orphaned children' in England, in perhaps a similar fashion as has been observed in southern Europe.[71]

One of the first researchers who identified the value of analysing underaged heirs, many of whom would have been orphaned, in rural contexts in England—was Elaine Clark, who published a seminal, short study into these young heirs in 1985 in the journal of *Law and History Review*.[72] Clark then followed this study, which focused mainly on rural society with a similar study exploring orphans in urban contexts a few years later.[73] However, while, as we have seen, progress has been made in other areas of childhood studies including in archaeology, no other significant study on medieval village children followed and no wider analysis of underaged heirs or village orphans based on manor court records was undertaken.

However, cases of underaged heirs and village orphans can illuminate a whole range of areas, and—crucially—extent beyond our understanding of merely underaged heirs; but reflect on wider questions about village childhood. These include perceptions of children—as children, medieval views on growing child competences—including in running holdings and working, perceptions of rights and limitations on rights, views on child development, mentally, socially and physically. Additionally, it is possible to attempt an approach which considers the child and their experiences in their societies from the ground upwards.

This requires an approach which considers the interplay between lordship, community, and the position of the child within the dynamics governing these relationships, it also necessitates an attempt to look beyond what is immediately on the page and consider the wider socio-economic and cultural context within which young people found themselves in. As such the data on underaged heirs and orphans offers the wedge to help break open a much wider field on enquiry, in the hope that we can at least catch a glimpse of the voices of later medieval peasant children themselves, as well as the adults who accompanied them through life.

Notes

1. R. Louv, *Last Child in the Woods; Saving Our Children from Nature-Deficit Disorder* (London: Atlantic Books, 2010 edition).
2. The issue even made headlines with the BBC in December 2017. BBC News 'Thousands Petition Junior Dictionary Over Nature Words', https://www.bbc.com/news/uk-england-oxfordshire-42441025.
3. See for discussions of these issues for example: M. Müller, 'A Divided Class? Peasants and Peasant Communities in Later Medieval England', in: C. Dyer et al., eds., *Rodney Hilton's Middle Ages* (Past and Present Supplement 2 Oxford University Press, 2007), pp. 115–120; Z. Razi, 'The Toronto School's Reconstitution of Medieval Peasant Society: A Critical View', in: *Past and Present*, vol. 85 (1979), pp. 141–157.
4. Jean-Jacques Rousseau, *Emile or on Education* (Penguin Classics, 1991).
5. R.W. Southern, ed., *The Life of St. Anselm Archbishop of Canterbury by Eadmer* (Thomas Nelson and Sons Ltd., 1962), pp. 37–39.
6. M.A. Powell, N. Taylor, and A.B. Smith, 'Constructions of Rural Childhood: Challenging Dominant Perspectives', in: *Children's Geographies*, vol. 11, no. 1 (2013), pp. 117–119.
7. For a discussion of these issues see for example: C. Ward, *The Child in the Country* (Bedford Square Press, 1988), pp. 17–32.

8. C. Heywood, *A History of Childhood; Children and Childhood in the West from Medieval to Modern Times* (Polity Press, 2001), p. 10. See also his excellent discussion in 'Centuries of Childhood: An Anniversary—And an Epitaph?', in: *The Journal of the History of Childhood and Youth*, vol. 3, no. 3 (2010), pp. 346–348.
9. See for example some of the earliest and most important critics: S. Shahar, *Childhood in the Middle Ages* (London and New York: Routledge, 1992), esp. pp. 1–7; N. Orme, 'The Culture of Children in Medieval England', in: *Past and Present*, vol. 148, no. 1 (1995), pp. 48–88; N. Orme, *Medieval Children* (New Haven, London: Yale University Press, 2001); B.A. Hanawalt, *The Ties That Bound; Peasant Families in Medieval England* (Oxford University Press, 1986), pp. 171ff.
10. C. Heywood, 'Centuries of Childhood: An Anniversary—And an Epitaph?', p. 348.
11. See for example: S. Shahar, *Childhood in the Middle Ages* (London and New York: Routledge, 1992); S. Sheridan Walker, 'Widow and Ward: The Feudal Law of Child Custody in Medieval England', in: S. Mosher Stuard, ed., *Women in Medieval Society* (Philadelphia: University of Pennsylvania Press, 1976), pp. 159–172; N. Orme, 'The Culture of Children in Medieval England', in: *Past and Present*, vol. 148, no. 1 (1995), pp. 48–88; E. Clark, 'City Orphans and Custody Laws in Medieval England', in: *The American Journal of Legal History*, vol. 34, no. 2 (April 1990), pp. 168–187; N. Orme, *From Childhood to Chivalry: The Education of English Kings and Aristocracy 1066–1530* (London and New York: Methuen, 1984).
12. Two volumes are particularly good on these issues: S. Shahar, *Childhood in the Middle Ages*, pp. 21ff.; N. Orme, *Medieval Children* (New Haven, London: Yale University Press, 2001), esp. pp. 11ff.
13. The volume of publications on these topics is not insignificant. See for example: B.A. Hanawalt, *Growing Up in Medieval London: The Experience of Childhood in History* (Oxford and New York: Oxford University Press, 1993); P.J. Ryan, *Master–Servant Childhood: A History of the Idea of Childhood in Medieval English Culture* (Palgrave Macmillan, 2013); R. Goddard, 'Female Apprenticeships in the West Midlands in the Later Middle Ages', in: *Midlands History*, vol. 27 (2002), pp. 165–181; P.J.P. Goldberg, 'What Was a Servant?', in: A. Curry and E. Matthew, eds., *Concepts and Patterns of Service in the Later Middle Ages* (The Boydell Press, 2000), pp. 1–20; N. Orme, 'The Culture of Children in Medieval England', in: *Past and Present*, vol. 148, no. 1 (1995).
14. See for example for a discussion of these issues R.H. Hilton, 'Introduction', in: T.H. Aston and C.H.E. Philpin, eds., *The Brenner Debate; Agrarian Class Structure and Economic Development in Pre-industrial Europe* (Cambridge University Press, 1993 edition), pp. 5–7.

15. H. Montgomery, *An Introduction to Childhood Anthropological Perspectives on Children's Lives* (Oxford: Wiley-Blackwell, 2009), p. 54.
16. E. Clark, 'City Orphans and Custody Laws in Medieval England', in: *The American Journal of Legal History*, vol. 34, no. 2 (April 1990), pp. 168–187; B.A. Hanawalt, *Growing Up in Medieval London: The Experience of Childhood in History* (Oxford and New York: Oxford University Press, 1993).
17. See for example for an excellent, general discussion of life in towns: C. Dyer, *Making a Living in the Middle Ages: The People of Britain 850–1520* (New Haven and London: Yale University Press, 2002), esp. pp. 197–212. For concerns about fires see p. 200.
18. M. Müller, 'A Divided Class? Peasants and Peasant Communities in Later Medieval England', in: C. Dyer et al., eds., *Rodney Hilton's Middle Ages* (Past and Present Supplement 2 Oxford University Press, 2007), pp. 115–120.
19. C. Dyer, *Standards of Living in the Later Middle Ages; Social Change in England, c. 1200–1520* (Cambridge University Press, 1993), p. 23.
20. L. Alanen, 'Rethinking Childhood', in: *Acta Sociologica*, vol. 31, no. 1 (1988), p. 56.
21. L. Alanen, 'Rethinking Childhood', in: *Acta Sociologica*, vol. 31, no. 1 (1988), p. 56.
22. Alanen's excellent discussion on this can be found in her editorial 'Theorizing Childhood', in: *Childhood*, vol. 21, no. 1 (2014), p. 4.
23. W.A. Corsaro, *The Sociology of Childhood*, fourth edition (London, 2014), p. 6.
24. Alanen, 'Theorizing Childhood', pp. 3–4; Corsaro, *The Sociology of Childhood*, p. 6.
25. H. Dawson, *Unearthing Late Medieval Children, Health, Status and Burial Practice in Southern England* (BAR British Series 593, 2015), p. 4.
26. See for example: S. Crawford, *Childhood in Anglo-Saxon England* (Stroud: Sutton Publishing, 1999); M. Lewis, 'Work and the Adolescent in Medieval England ad 900–1550: The Osteological Evidence', in: *Medieval Archaeology*, vol. 60, no. 1 (2016), pp. 138–171; M.E. Lewis, *The Bioarchaeology of Children; Perspectives from Biological and Forensic Anthropology* (Cambridge University Press, 2007); R. Gilchrist, *Medieval Life Archaeology and the Life Course* (The Boydell Press, 2012); S.V. Smith, 'The Spaces of Late Medieval Peasant Childhood: Children and Social Reproduction', in: D.M. Hadley and K.A. Hemer, eds., *Medieval Childhood: Archaeological Approaches* (Oxbow Books, 2014), pp. 57–74. It should be noted that at the time of writing, the *Oxford Handbook of the Archaeology of Childhood*, edited by Sally Crawford, Dawn Hadley, and Gillian Shepherd, and due for publication in 2018; is being keenly awaited, although judging by the now available list of contents, medieval childhood does seem to be represented fairly slimly in the volume.

27. Dawson, *Unearthing Late Medieval Children*, p. 4.
28. Corsaro, *The Sociology of Childhood*, p. 6.
29. Dawson, *Unearthing Late Medieval Children*, pp. 4–5.
30. Corsaro, *The Sociology of Childhood*, pp. 7–8; M. Woodhead, 'The Child in Development', in: M. Woodhead and H. Montgomery, eds., *Understanding Childhood, an Interdisciplinary Approach* (Chichester: John Wiley & Sons Ltd/The Open University, 2003), pp. 106–113.
31. See also on this M. Woodhead, 'The Child in Development', p. 113.
32. The literature on this topic area is substantial. See for example: L.C. Chen, E. Huq, and S. D'Souza, 'Sex Bias in the Family Allocation of Food and Healthcare in Rural Bangladesh', in: *Population and Development Review*, vol. 7, no. 1 (March 1981), pp. 55–70; A. Oakley, *Sex, Gender and Society* (London: Maurice Temple Smith Ltd., 1972), p. 31
33. Alanen, 'Rethinking Childhood', p. 56.
34. Alanen, 'Rethinking Childhood', p. 58.
35. While some researchers reflect a rather dark view on medieval childhood, such as L. deMause, see for example his: 'The Evolution of Childhood', in: *History of Childhood Quarterly*, vol. 1, no. 4 (1973), pp. 503–575; but taking this perspective considerably further is the cheerfully entitled contribution by J. Atlas, 'The Terrible Rewards of Medieval Childhood: Abandonment, Abuse, Torture and Death or Traumatized Lives, Denial, Projection onto Others, Dysfunction and Violence', in: *The Journal of Psychohistory*, vol. 27, no. 3 (2000), pp. 276–301.
36. L. Stone, *The Family, Sex and Marriage in England 1500–1800* (New York, 1977).
37. E.P. Thompson, 'Happy Families', in: *Radical History Review*, vol. 20 (Spring/Summer 1979), pp. 43–45.
38. Again, one can draw parallels to the development of women's history here. See for example for a discussion of these issues: M. Müller, 'Peasant Women, Agency and Status in Mid Thirteenth to Late Fourteenth-Century England: Some Reconsiderations', in: C. Beattie and M.F. Stevens, eds., *Married Women and the Law in Premodern Northwest Europe* (Boydell Press, 2013), pp. 169–190
39. E.P. Thompson, 'Happy Families', p. 50.
40. W.A. Corsaro, *The Sociology of Childhood* (2015), p. 18.
41. W.A. Corsaro, *The Sociology of Childhood* (2015), p. 18.
42. H. Dawson, *Unearthing Late Medieval Children, Health, Status and Burial Practice in Southern England* (BAR British Series 593, 2014), p. 7.
43. H. Dawson, *Unearthing Late Medieval Children*, p. 7.
44. H. Dawson, *Unearthing Late Medieval Children*, p. 7.
45. N. Orme, 'The Culture of Children in Medieval England', in: *Past and Present*, vol. 148, no. 19, pp. 66–73.

46. S. Shahar, *Childhood in the Middle Ages* (London and New York: Routledge, 1992), p. 22. The issue is also discussed by H. Dawson, *Unearthing Late Medieval Children*, pp. 15–16.
47. S. Shahar, *Childhood in the Middle Ages*, pp. 23–28.
48. C. Heywood rightly commented on this in *A History of Childhood; Children and Childhood in the West from Medieval to Modern Times* (Polity Press, 2001), p. 6.
49. P.J.P. Goldberg, 'Childhood and Gender in Later Medieval England', in: *Viator*, vol. 39, no. 1 (2008), p. 249.
50. B.A. Hanawalt, *The Ties That Bound*, p. 90.
51. See for example the excellent work by S. Shahar, *Childhood in the Middle Ages* (Routledge, 1990); N. Orme, *Medieval Children* (New Haven, London: Yale University Press, 2001); See also more recent contributions including: Sari Katajala-Peltomaa and Ville Vuolanto, 'Children and Agency: Religion as Socialisation in Late Antiquity and the Late Medieval West', in: *Childhood in the Past*, vol. 4 (2011), pp. 79–99. For a useful discussion of some of the historiography see also B.A. Hanawalt, 'Medievalists and the Study of Childhood', in: *Speculum*, vol. 77, no. 2 (April 2002), pp. 440–460.
52. See for example: Mary E. Lewis, 'Children of the Golden Minster: St. Oswald's Priory and the Impact of Industrialisation on Child Health', in: *Journal of Anthropology*, vol. 2013 (2013), 11 pages; M. Lewis, 'Work and the Adolescent in Medieval England ad 900–1550: The Osteological Evidence', in: *Medieval Archaeology*, vol. 60, no. 1 (2016), pp. 138–171; P. Mahoney et al., 'Deciduous Enamel 3D Microwear Texture Analysis as an Indicator of Childhood Diet in Medieval Canterbury, England', in: *Journal of Archaeological Science*, vol. 66 (2016), pp. 128–136; N.M. Burt, 'Stable Isotope Ratio Analysis of Breastfeeding and Weaning Practices of Children from Medieval Fishergate House York, UK', in: *American Journal of Physical Anthropology*, vol. 152 (2013), pp. 407–416; C. Lewis, 'Children's Play in the Later Medieval English Countryside', in: *Childhood in the Past*, vol. 2 (2009), pp. 86–108; R. Gilchrist, *Medieval Life Archaeology and the Life Course* (The Boydell Press, 2012); H. Dawson, *Unearthing Late Medieval Children; Health, Status and Burial Practice in Southern England* (BAR British Series 593, 2014); N. Orme, 'The Culture of Children in Medieval England', in: *Past and Present*, vol. 148, no. 1 (1995), pp. 48–88; S.V. Smith, 'The Spaces of Late Medieval Peasant Childhood: Children and Social Reproduction'.
53. M. Müller, 'Peasant Women, Agency and Status in Mid Thirteenth to Late Fourteenth-Century England: Some Reconsiderations', in: C. Beattie and M.F. Stevens, eds., *Married Women and the Law in Premodern Northwest Europe* (Boydell Press, 2013), pp. 169–190.

54. G. Brucker, ed., and J. Martines, trans., *Two Memoirs of Renaissance Florence: The Diaries of Buonaccorso Pitti and Gregorio Dati* (New York and London: Harper & Row, 1967).
55. See for example: 'The English Trotula', dating from the fifteenth century, which includes recipes for couples wishing to conceive either a girl or a boy, extract can be found in: P.J.P. Goldberg, ed. and trans., *Women in England, c. 1275–1525 Documentary Sources* (Manchester University Press, 1995), p. 57.
56. B.A. Hanawalt, *The Ties That Bound; Peasant Families in Medieval England* (New York: Oxford University Press, 1986), esp. Chapter 11 'Childhood', pp. 171–187.
57. B.A. Hanawalt, 'Childrearing Among the Lower Classes of Late Medieval England', in: *The Journal of Interdisciplinary History*, vol. 8, no. 1 (1977), pp. 1–22.
58. B.A. Hanawalt, 'Childrearing Among the Lower Classes of Late Medieval England', pp. 1–22. Some such points were also picked up in her later publications, see for example: B.A. Hanawalt, 'Seeking the Flesh and Blood of Manorial Families', in: *Journal of Medieval History*, vol. 14 (1988), pp. 33–45; B.A. Hanawalt, 'The Child in the Middle Ages and the Renaissance', in: W. Koops and M. Zuckerman, eds., *Beyond the Century of the Child; Cultural History and Developmental Psychology* (University of Pennsylvania Press, 2003), pp. 21–42; B.A. Hanawalt, *The Ties That Bound; Peasant Families in Medieval England*, Chapter 11 'Childhood', pp. 171–187.
59. P.J.P. Goldberg, 'Childhood and Gender in Later Medieval England', in: *Viator*, vol. 39, no. 1 (2008), pp. 249–262.
60. P.J.P. Goldberg, 'Childhood and Gender in Later Medieval England'.
61. For discussions of these issues see in particular: M. Bailey, *The English Manor, c. 1200–c. 1500* (Manchester University Press, 2002), esp. pp. 18–21; Z. Razi and R.M. Smith, eds., *Medieval Society and the Manor Court* (Clarendon Press, 1996).
62. Such developments are well documented and discussed for example in: M. Bailey, *The English Manor, c. 1200–c. 1500*; M. Bailey, *The Decline of Serfdom in England; from Bondage to Freedom* (Boydell Press, 2014); C. Dyer, *Making a Living in the Middle Ages: The People of Britain 850–1520* (New Haven and London: Yale University Press, 2002), esp. pp. 137–145 and pp. 178–183.
63. See the discussion between Hilton and Hatcher on these matters: R.H. Hilton, 'Freedom and Villeinage in England', in: *Past and Present*, no. 31 (1965), pp. 3–19. And Hatcher's response: J. Hatcher, 'English Serfdom and Villeinage: Towards a Reassessment', in: *Past and Present*, no. 90 (1981), pp. 3–39.

64. For a good discussion of the Historiography of manorial records see Z. Razi and R.M. Smith, 'The Historiography of Manorial Court Rolls', in: Z. Razi and R.M. Smith, eds., *Medieval Society and the Manor Court*, pp. 1–12; see also the other contributions in this important volume.
65. See for example: B.A. Hanawalt, *The Ties That Bound*, p. 90.
66. See for example: J.M. Bennett, *Women in the Medieval English Countryside; Gender and Household in Brigstock Before the Plague* (Oxford University Press, 1987); M. Müller, 'Peasant Women, Agency and Status in Mid Thirteenth to Late Fourteenth-Century England: Some Reconsiderations', in: C. Beattie and M.F. Stevens, eds., *Married Women and the Law in Premodern Northwest Europe* (Boydell Press, 2013), pp. 169–190; C. Briggs, *Credit and Village Society in Fourteenth Century England* (Oxford University Press, 2009); P. Larson, *Conflict and Compromise in the Late Medieval Countryside; Lords and Peasants in Durham 1349–1400* (Routledge, 2006).
67. M. Bailey, *The English Manor, c. 1200–c. 1500*, pp. 178–184; M. Müller, 'A Divided Class? Peasants and Peasant Communities in Later Medieval England', in: C. Dyer et al., eds., *Rodney Hilton's Middle Ages* (Past and Present Supplement 2 Oxford University Press, 2007), pp. 115–120; M. Müller, 'Social Control and the Hue and Cry in Two Fourteenth Century Villages', in: *Journal of Medieval History*, vol. 31 (2005), pp. 29–53.
68. B.A. Hanawalt, *The Ties That Bound*, p. 90.
69. For discussions of the peasant land market and inheritance customs see J. Mullan and R. Britnell, *Land and Family; Trends and Local Variations in the Peasant Land Market on the Winchester Bishopric Estates, 1263–1415* (University of Hertfordshire Press, 2010), pp. 103–115; and contributions in: P.D.A. Harvey, ed., *The Peasant Land Market in Medieval England* (Oxford, 1984).
70. See for example the essays brought together in M. Corbier, ed., *Adoption et Fosterage*, De L'Archéologie à L'Histoire (Paris: De Boccard, 1999); especially A. Burguière, 'Un aussi long refus. Droit et pratique de l'adoption en France du XVe siècle au temps présent', pp. 123–137; K. Gager, 'Adoption Practices in Sixteenth- and Seventeenth-Century Paris', pp. 183–198; C. Klapisch-Zuber, 'L'adoption impossible dans l'Italie de la fin du Moyen Âge', pp. 321–337; A. Courtemanche, 'Lutter Contre La Solitude: Adoption et Affiliation a Manosque au XVe Siècle', in: *Médiéval*, no. 19, *Liens De Famille: Vivre et choisir sa parenté* (Automne 1990), pp. 37–42.
71. P.J.P. Goldberg, 'Orphans and Servants: The Socialisation of Young People Living Away from Home in the English Later Middle Ages', in: M. Corbier, ed., *Adoption et Fosterage*, De L'Archéologie à L'Histoire (Paris: De Boccard, 1999), p. 233.

72. E. Clark, 'The Custody of Children in English Manor Courts', in: *Law and History Review*, vol. 3, no. 2 (Autumn 1985), pp. 333–348.
73. E. Clark, 'City Orphans and Custody Laws in Medieval England', in: *The American Journal of Legal History*, vol. 34, no. 2 (April 1990), pp. 168–187.

Bibliography

Primary Sources

M. Bailey, *The English Manor, c. 1200–c. 1500* (Manchester and New York: Manchester University Press, 2002).

G. Brucker, ed., and J. Martines, trans., *Two Memoirs of Renaissance Florence: The Diaries of Buonaccorso Pitti and Gregorio Dati* (New York and London: Harper & Row, 1967).

P.J.P. Goldberg, ed. and trans., *Women in England, c. 1275–1525 Documentary Sources* (Manchester and New York: Manchester University Press, 1995).

R.W. Southern, ed., *The Life of St. Anselm Archbishop of Canterbury by Eadmer* (New York: Thomas Nelson and Sons Ltd., 1962).

Secondary Sources Books

M. Bailey, *The Decline of Serfdom in England: From Bondage to Freedom* (Woodbridge: Boydell Press, 2014).

J.M. Bennett, *Women in the Medieval English Countryside; Gender and Household in Brigstock Before the Plague* (Oxford: Oxford University Press, 1987).

C. Briggs, *Credit and Village Society in Fourteenth Century England* (Oxford: Oxford University Press, 2009).

M. Corbier, ed., *Adoption et Fosterage*, De L'Archéologie à L'Histoire (Paris: De Boccard, 1999).

W.A. Corsaro, *The Sociology of Childhood* (London: Sage Publications, fourth edition, 2014).

S. Crawford, *Childhood in Anglo-Saxon England* (Stroud: Sutton Publishing, 1999).

H. Dawson, *Unearthing Late Medieval Children; Health, Status and Burial Practice in Southern England* (BAR British Series 593, 2014).

C. Dyer, *Standards of Living in the Later Middle Ages; Social Change in England, c. 1200–1520* (Cambridge: Cambridge University Press, 1993).

C. Dyer, *Making a Living in the Middle Ages: The People of Britain 850–1520* (New Haven and London: Yale University Press, 2002).

R. Gilchrist, *Medieval Life Archaeology and the Life Course* (Woodbridge: The Boydell Press, 2012).

B.A. Hanawalt, *The Ties That Bound; Peasant Families in Medieval England* (New York: Oxford University Press, 1986).
B.A. Hanawalt, *Growing Up in Medieval London: The Experience of Childhood in History* (Oxford and New York: Oxford University Press, 1993).
P.D.A. Harvey, ed., *The Peasant Land Market in Medieval England* (Oxford: Oxford University Press, 1984).
C. Heywood, *A History of Childhood; Children and Childhood in the West from Medieval to Modern Times* (Cambridge: Polity Press, 2001).
P. Larson, *Conflict and Compromise in the Late Medieval Countryside; Lords and Peasants in Durham 1349–1400* (London: Routledge, 2006).
M.E. Lewis, *The Bioarchaeology of Children; Perspectives from Biological and Forensic Anthropology* (Cambridge: Cambridge University Press, 2007).
R. Louv, *Last Child in the Woods; Saving Our Children from Nature-Deficit Disorder* (London: Atlantic Books, 2010 edition).
H. Montgomery, *An Introduction to Childhood Anthropological Perspectives on Children's Lives* (Oxford: Wiley-Blackwell, 2009).
J. Mullan and R. Britnell, *Land and Family; Trends and Local Variations in the Peasant Land Market on the Winchester Bishopric Estates, 1263–1415* (Hatfield: University of Hertfordshire Press, 2010).
A. Oakley, *Sex, Gender and Society* (London: Maurice Temple Smith Ltd., 1972).
N. Orme, *From Childhood to Chivalry the Education of English Kings and Aristocracy 1066–1530* (London and New York: Methuen, 1984).
N. Orme, *Medieval Children* (New Haven, London: Yale University Press, 2001).
Jean-Jacques Rousseau, *Emile or on Education* (London: Penguin Classics, 1991).
P.J. Ryan, *Master–Servant Childhood: A History of the Idea of Childhood in Medieval English Culture* (Palgrave Macmillan, 2013).
S. Shahar, *Childhood in the Middle Ages* (London: Routledge, 1990).
C. Ward, *The Child in the Country* (London: Bedford Square Press, 1988).

Secondary Sources Chapters and Articles

L. Alanen, 'Rethinking Childhood', in: *Acta Sociologica*, vol. 31, no. 1 (1988), pp. 53–67.
L. Alanen, 'Theorizing Childhood', in: *Childhood*, vol. 21, no. 1 (2014), pp. 3–6.
J. Atlas, 'The Terrible Rewards of Medieval Childhood: Abandonment, Abuse, Torture and Death or Traumatized Lives, Denial, Projection onto Others, Dysfunction and Violence', in: *The Journal of Psychohistory*, vol. 27, no. 3 (2000), pp. 276–301.

A. Burguière, 'Un aussi long refus. Droit et pratique de l'adoption en France du XVe siècle au temps présent', in: M. Corbier, ed., *Adoption et Fosterage*, De L'Archéologie à L'Histoire (Paris: De Boccard, 1999), pp. 123–137.
N.M. Burt, 'Stable Isotope Ratio Analysis of Breastfeeding and Practices of Children from Medieval Fishergate House York, UK', in: *American Journal of Physical Anthropology*, vol. 152 (2013), pp. 407–416.
L.C. Chen, E. Huq, and S. D'Souza, 'Sex Bias in the Family Allocation of Food and Healthcare in Rural Bangladesh', in: *Population and Development Review*, vol. 7, no. 1 (March 1981), pp. 55–70.
E. Clark, 'The Custody of Children in English Manor Courts', in: *Law and History Review*, vol. 3, no. 2 (Autumn 1985), pp. 333–348.
E. Clark, 'City Orphans and Custody Laws in Medieval England', in: *The American Journal of Legal History*, vol. 34, no. 2 (April 1990), pp. 168–187.
A. Courtemanche, 'Lutter Contre La Solitude: Adoption et Affiliation a Manosque au XVe Siècle', in: *Médiéval*, no. 19, *Liens De Famille: Vivre et choisir sa parenté* (Automne 1990), pp. 37–42.
L. deMause, 'The Evolution of Childhood', in: *History of Childhood Quarterly*, vol. 1, no. 4 (1974), pp. 503–575.
K. Gager, 'Adoption Practices in Sixteenth- and Seventeenth-Century Paris', in: M. Corbier, ed., *Adoption et Fosterage*, De L'Archéologie à L'Histoire (Paris: De Boccard, 1999), pp. 183–198.
P.J.P. Goldberg, 'Orphans and Servants: The Socialisation of Young People Living Away from Home in the English Later Middle Ages', in: M. Corbier, ed., *Adoption et Fosterage*, De L'Archéologie à L'Histoire (Paris: De Boccard, 1999), pp. 231–246.
P.J.P. Goldberg, 'What Was a Servant?', in: A. Curry and E. Matthew, eds., *Concepts and Patterns of in the Later Middle Ages* (Woodbridge: The Boydell Press, 2000), pp. 1–20.
P.J.P. Goldberg, 'Childhood and Gender in Later Medieval England', in: *Viator*, vol. 39, no. 1 (2008), pp. 249–262.
B.A. Hanawalt, 'Childrearing Among the Lower Classes of Late Medieval England', in: *The Journal of Interdisciplinary History*, vol. 8, no. 1 (1977), pp. 1–22.
B.A. Hanawalt, 'Seeking the Flesh and Blood of Manorial Families', in: *Journal of Medieval History*, vol. 14 (1988), pp. 33–45.
B.A. Hanawalt, 'Medievalists and the Study of Childhood', in: *Speculum*, vol. 77, no. 2 (April 2002), pp. 440–460.
B.A. Hanawalt, 'The Child in the Middle Ages and the Renaissance', in: W. Koops and M. Zuckerman, eds., *Beyond the Century of the Child; Cultural History and Developmental Psychology* (Philadelphia: University of Pennsylvania Press, 2003), pp. 21–42.
J. Hatcher, 'English Serfdom and Villeinage: Towards a Reassessment', in: *Past and Present*, no. 90 (1981), pp. 3–39.

C. Heywood, 'Centuries of Childhood: An Anniversary—And an Epitaph?', in: *The Journal of the History of Childhood and Youth*, vol. 3, no. 3 (2010), pp. 346–348.

R.H. Hilton, 'Freedom and Villeinage in England', in: *Past and Present*, no. 31 (1965), pp. 3–19.

R.H. Hilton, 'Introduction', in: T.H. Aston and C.H.E. Philpin, eds., *The Brenner Debate; Agrarian Class Structure and Economic Development in Pre-industrial Europe* (Cambridge: Cambridge University Press, 1993 edition), pp. 1–9.

Sari Katajala-Peltomaa and Ville Vuolanto, 'Children and Agency: Religion as Socialisation in Late Antiquity and the Late Medieval West', in: *Childhood in the Past*, vol. 4 (2011), pp, 79–99.

C. Klapisch-Zuber, 'L'adoption impossible dans l'Italie de la fin du Moyen Âge', in: M. Corbier, ed., *Adoption et Fosterage*, De L'Archéologie à L'Histoire (Paris: De Boccard, 1999), pp. 321–337.

C. Lewis, 'Children's Play in the Later Medieval English Countryside', in: *Childhood in the Past*, vol. 2, no. 1 (2009), pp. 86–108.

M. Lewis, 'Work and the Adolescent in Medieval England ad 900–1550: The Osteological Evidence', in: *Medieval Archaeology*, vol. 60, no. 1 (2016), pp. 138–171.

Mary E. Lewis, 'Children of the Golden Minster: St. Oswald's Priory and the Impact of Industrialisation on Child Health', in: *Journal of Anthropology*, vol. 2013 (2013), 11 pages.

P. Mahoney, et al., 'Deciduous Enamel 3D Microwear Texture Analysis as an Indicator of Childhood Diet in Medieval Canterbury, England', in: *Journal of Archaeological Science*, vol. 66 (2016), pp. 128–136.

M. Müller, 'Social Control and the Hue and Cry in two Fourteenth Century Villages', in: *Journal of Medieval History*, vol. 31 (2005), pp. 29–53.

M. Müller, 'A Divided Class? Peasants and Peasant Communities in Later Medieval England', in: C. Dyer et al., eds., *Rodney Hilton's Middle Ages* (Past and Present Supplement 2 Oxford University Press, 2007), pp. 115–120.

M. Müller, 'Peasant Women, Agency and Status in Mid Thirteenth to Late Fourteenth-Century England: Some Reconsiderations', in: C. Beattie and M.F. Stevens, eds., *Married Women and the Law in Premodern Northwest Europe* (Woodbridge: Boydell Press, 2013), pp. 169–190.

N. Orme, 'The Culture of Children in Medieval England', in: *Past and Present*, vol. 148, no. 1 (1995), pp. 48–88.

M.A. Powell, N. Taylor, and A.B. Smith, 'Constructions of Rural Childhood: Challenging Dominant Perspectives', in: *Children's Geographies*, vol. 11, no. 1 (2013), pp. 117–131.

Z. Razi, 'The Toronto Reconstitution of Medieval Peasant Society: A Critical View', in: *Past and Present*, vol. 85 (1979), pp. 141–157.

Z. Razi and R.M. Smith, 'The Historiography of Manorial Court Rolls', in: Z. Razi and R.M. Smith, eds., *Medieval Society and the Manor Court* (Oxford: Clarendon Press, 1996), pp. 1–12.

S. Sheridan Walker, 'Widow and Ward: The Feudal Law of Child Custody in Medieval England', in: S. Mosher Stuard, ed., *Women in Medieval Society* (Philadelphia: University of Pennsylvania Press, 1976), pp. 159–172.

S.V. Smith, 'The Spaces of Late Medieval Peasant Childhood: Children and Social Reproduction', in: D.M. Hadley and K.A. Hemer, eds., *Medieval Childhood: Archaeological Approaches* (Oxford: Oxbow Books, 2014), pp. 57–74.

E.P. Thompson, 'Happy Families', in: *Radical History Review*, vol. 20 (Spring/Summer 1979), pp. 43–50.

M. Woodhead, 'The Child in Development', in: M. Woodhead and H. Montgomery, eds., *Understanding Childhood, an Interdisciplinary Approach* (Chichester: John Wiley & Sons Ltd/The Open University, 2003), pp. 106–113.

CHAPTER 2

Vulnerable Members of the Community

1 Communities and Lordship

Examining how villagers felt about orphans and underaged heirs gives us important insights into their attitudes to childhood in general. It also illuminates the dynamic relationship between the communities and the young people in their midst who strove towards gaining adult status and responsibilities. The process towards this goal was not uniform and linear. Communities operated within customs concerning the age of majority and other rituals which represented in some respects milestones to adulthood, and which were also partly gendered. Yet age—measured in years—was not everything. Individuals and their circumstances differed, and, as we shall see later, young people could also be considered to mature at different paces. Communities exercised a significant degree of discretion within the customary framework when it came to the nurturing of their young.

In general, from a purely practical point of view, once a young person was considered to be an underaged heir they represented a problem both for the community as well as for their lord. Entry into a holding and thereby becoming a full tenant carried with it a host of responsibilities as well as status. These were in relation to both other villagers and the lord.

As far as the lord was concerned, a tenant had to fulfil various obligations which came along with the landholding, this included obligations of rent payments in cash, kind, as well as various other dues, especially if the holding was unfree, or villein tenure.[1] As tenants of the lord were

M. Müller, *Childhood, Orphans and Underage Heirs in Medieval Rural England*, Palgrave Studies in the History of Childhood,
https://doi.org/10.1007/978-3-030-03602-7_2

also heads of the household they were held answerable to the lord for the fulfilment of the various requested and potential obligations which came with the acceptance of the tenement.[2] This included being answerable to the reeve and other manorial officials regarding labour services, which fell due on unfree holdings. Such might include, for example, weeding, ploughing, making hurdles for sheep pens, haymaking, harvest work, sheep shearing, carting goods to and from the manor, as well as for rent in kind which might be a portion of the harvest. In addition, tenants were required to attend the manorial court and play a full role in its workings, including sitting on and participating in court-ordered inquiries.

In relation to the village community, a tenant had to play a full part in the daily running of village affairs. These related to responsibilities of the individual holding as well as the community. In open field farming communities, this would also involve the participation in communal discussions of what grains were to be sown where and when, alongside the organisation of fields and the number and nature of crop rotations.[3] All communities held heads of households mutually responsible for policing a whole host of communal affairs. Mechanisms of social control linked individuals and their households to wider communal affairs.[4] These mechanisms operated both informally and formally. Informally through village regulation, communal activities which included by primary design or inadvertently the re-enforcement of norms and social control. Such mechanisms would have included gossip, communal disapproval of certain activities or views which might even be expressed through mechanisms like the Charivari.[5] Formal mechanisms which are mainly still visible to us are primarily associated with court systems of the secular and ecclesiastical areas of law. In the very secular, manorial court, this would have involved the lord or his representative at some level, alongside manorial officials, such as reeves or haywards, which were drawn from the local tenantry.[6] Such formal mechanisms are most directly visible to us as their workings have survived for us to be examined in extant manorial records, especially manorial court rolls, or at the St. Albans estates, manorial court books, which appear to have been extracted from the original court rolls, which do not survive for us and may have been destroyed in the 1381 rising.[7]

Diverted rivers, blocked ditches and ill-maintained highways or common pathways were a nuisance to all neighbours and the lord, and residents had a responsibility to maintain paths, roads and waterways.

Individuals who fell short of fulfilling their responsibilities in these regards could be brought to the manorial court and amerced for causing obstructions or a public nuisance. The fulfilment of such responsibilities was not just dependant on certain abilities and strengths, but also might involve a significant degree of skills of negotiation with other communal members, which in turn would have necessitated a degree of maturity as well as social, political and economic know how.

A responsible and mature tenant was therefore in the interest of the community, as the needs and interests of individual and community were interrelated and intrinsically linked. Survival itself in peasant societies was largely dependent on communal cooperation and resilience, and tenants who could not play a full part in communal affairs, including farming activities, jeopardised communal well-being and resilience. It therefore made sense for medieval villagers to plot out and negotiate the training and the developing independence of their offspring very carefully indeed. The evidence at hand indicates an understanding of mental and physical development from early childhood through adolescence into adulthood. At the same time, the notion that medieval villagers would have entertained little or no concept of childhood or adolescence as distinct from adulthood flies in the face of the economic, political and social realities these people had to face and overcome on a daily basis.[8] A conceptualisation of medieval rural society which perceives young children as fully socially and economically viable actors in their communities, betrays little understanding of either the social and political complexity of that society of the high level of skill, strength and dexterity required to fulfil daily tasks associated with late medieval agricultural management. Economically younger children can rather be understood to impact negatively on peasant households, potentially depressing productivity and circumscribing access to economic resources.[9] Yet, as I will show, village children were not without a voice and helpless in these matters. Children's views mattered and, it appears, were not simply overruled by adult tenants.

For the lord an unreliable tenant who could not meet their tenurial obligations or was reckless or unskilled represented a fundamental danger to seigniorial assets. Lords were concerned that their land and tenements were maintained and looked after to yield profit for both the tenant—who was then able to meet their financial obligations to the lord—as well as the lord, who also looked to the future safeguarding of his properties and assets.[10] Aside from such basic economic factors, other seigniorial concerns intersected with those of the community. The axis between seigniorial expectations, demands and communal expectations and demands also become visible in manorial documents, usually at the point when rules were broken or expectations of acceptable behaviour not met. In addition, tenants were expected to play a full role in various communal policing activities. Including in the shape of the tithing, where this was in force locally, to which all young boys were sworn into from the age of 12 to help enforce local order, apprehend miscreants, and even thieves, intervene in brawls and help in containing and resolving conflict.[11] Tenants were also often required to act as chief pledges and participate in formal, legal enquiries initiated by the manorial court. They were expected to know and maintain boundaries of their own fields and help safeguard the boundaries as well as the good conduct of others who might pass through the community or settle locally.[12] Such duties required a good knowledge and sense of the law, local custom as well as a good knowledge of the economics of agriculture, market values of goods, products and livestock alongside a working knowledge of local oral histories, which were often drawn upon to resolve long-standing disputes in the manorial court.

Aside from such communal concerns, a head of a household was held responsible for their livestock and daily farming activities. Entering a holding not only carried responsibilities of animal husbandry, heavy labour associated with farming and potentially hiring labourers in addition to meeting moral and ecclesiastical responsibilities associated with religious observance as well as paying tithe to the church.

As a result, it was in the interests of all members of manorial communities—both lords and peasants—to ensure that young children and the land they had inherited by right were watched over by responsible and trustworthy adults. This was the underlying concept of guardianship, it involved the acceptance of authority—and the concomitant responsibility—of looking after a young heir to a holding (and potentially, as we shall see, their siblings) alongside their lands until their determined full age, when they were deemed to be old and responsible enough to take charge of their inheritance.

Taking on the guardianship of a tenement was a significant commitment on the part of the guardian. In the case of customary holdings, such guardianships included the upkeep of the inheritance, but this included the rendering of rents and services associated with the holding. As obligations were attached to unfree, villein holdings, guardians were not only expected to render those which came with their own tenements, but also those associated with the holdings of their wards. Such obligations would have included cash rents as well as rent in labour and other services. Reminders to guardians that they were to hold their charges' tenements under agreements of customary tenure were frequently noted in guardianship agreements. At Winslow, one of the manors of the estates of the Abbey of St. Albans, Master Geoffrey King, the vicar of Greenburgh had agreed to act as guardian for 12-year-old Ralph and his inheritance of a virgate of land, and he was reminded to perform the 'services for them' for the entire duration of the guardianship.[13] This was by no means unusual, guardians were fully expected to render any customs which fell due on their temporary lands at each and every manor consulted. At Heacham, in Norfolk it was stipulated that guardians had to perform 'services due and accustomed', as was the case at the Yorkshire manor of Wakefield, where, for example, Thomas de Copgrave was told to 'do all customary services pertaining to the tenement', while he was the guardian of it in 1349, or at the Buckinghamshire manor of Newton Longville, where in 1408 a guardian was reminded to pay 'rent and services according to the custom of the manor'.[14]

Such demands for services could be substantial and especially in the case of larger holdings, which tended to carry the highest demand for services it was not an agreement entered lightly, no matter how much a relative or neighbour might care about an orphaned child. Therefore the agreement to look after an orphaned child was not merely down to an understanding that a child or young adolescent needed looking after, but these young people brought along with them occasionally significant economic burdens, which had to be added to the requirements of the guardian's existing holdings and hence workload and responsibilities. On the other hand, the temporary wardship over potentially highly productive and fertile land also came with its advantages. A family might well calculate that the addition of some acres for a set number of years without any long-term or permanent responsibility for the holding was at times desirable, such as in households where labour output was reaching its peak due to the presence of older, teenaged children who represented a full economic asset to the holding. Better off, larger peasant families with older children and labour capacity were therefore able to take advantage of the additional income from produce gained from the ward's lands. From a purely economic point of view at times of land hunger wardships were undoubtedly more attractive than at times of saturation, yet, as we will see, economic considerations were not always or solely at the forefront of people's minds when they accepted wardships. Wardships were also not always a simple choice offered in the manorial court. Many guardians of underaged heirs were their mothers and stepmothers, who might well desire to look after their own or their late partner's children, but who might not have been so keen on taking on the additional labour burden of a holding by themselves.

Any landholding required work to keep the land fruitful and productive, which included significant labour input, to which the child heir, depending upon their age, might not have been able to contribute much if at all. In addition, demands of the lord for labour services—for example, which might have fallen due on the child heir's lands also had to be satisfied, which in turn might have involved paying hired labour during busy agricultural periods to supplement any labour drawn from the household. Accordingly, harvest periods for guardians in charge of their own as well as an underaged heir's holding could be costly and extremely labour—intensive times. Such pressures were increased during any particular crisis period resulting in increased death tolls, including famines, but most dramatically in our period after the first arrival of the Black Death in 1348–1349.

In manors where lords placed communities under pressure to redistribute land left vacant after the death of the tenants, while trying to insist on the rendering of all traditional dues and rents one might anticipate a reluctance of survivors to take in orphans. Landholding reached saturation point for many households in the post-Black Death decades. The greater availability of land led to a general drop in demand for land in the post-Black Death decades.[15]

Whereas in times of land hunger families might be very willing to take on the responsibility of looking after underaged heirs and their holdings after the Black Death the reverse might well have been the case. A problem compounded by a rapidly growing number of orphans due to the sudden high mortality levels, this in turn would have led to an increase of younger people entering holdings in their own right, at ages, which their parents' and grandparents' generations might have considered far too tender. Confirmation of these economic forces can be found in some enticements to take on guardianships, which become more common after 1349. Guardians, upon agreeing to look after the land of the heir and the heir themselves normally had to pay a variable fine to the lord which was not unlike a traditional entry fine payable by heirs to the lord upon taking over a holding. In the case of guardianships the guardian paid a fine to have the custody over land and heir, and then upon coming of age, the heir paid the actual entry fine while swearing the oath of fealty.

However, after the first arrival of the Black Death some of these conventions changed as it became necessary to persuade more people to become guardians due to the combination of a growing number of orphans alongside an increasing number of tenements which lay unproductive in the hands of the lord. Enticements to accept wardships could take various forms. Earlier, in Halesowen in 1340 Phillip, who was granted custody of Thomas the 10-year-old heir of John and Margery, was promised that for his fine for the guardianship he was also to be 'quit of various offices, including woodward and reeve'.[16] However, most commonly we find waivers of fines for the guardianship. At Winslow, in October 1349 we find that several fees to take on guardianships were waived by the lord. This includes Richard Snowe, who took on the guardianship of one-year-old baby Alice, the heiress of Geoffrey Kybe, which included a cottage one acre of arable and some meadow for which Geoffrey was expected to perform services and customs, but Geoffrey's entry fee was excused 'due to poverty'.[17] Similarly John ate Welle, who took on the much more substantial holding of the three-year-old heir of William Houprest, which included a messuage and half a virgate of land, was noted to have his fine 'waived due to poverty'.[18]

At the manor of Winslow, no such wavers are recorded at all in the period of 1327 to 1348; after the first arrival of the Black Death, however, nine such waivers are recorded. In other manors, fine waivers upon taking on guardianships over lands and heirs are similarly practically unheard of before the Black Death, but become more in evidence after 1349.

At Walsham le Willows, William le Jay took over the guardianship for a total of 6 years, of the son of John Sket in June 1351 after the death of the boy's mother Agnes. While he pledged to maintain the tenement and two buildings associated with the holding, his fine for guardianship was waived.[19] If we take into account cases where no specific information was given regarding the payment of fines the change after the Black Death becomes even more apparent. At Winslow, only one case is recorded pre 1349 where no information regarding the payment of fees is given, however, between 1349 and 1400 a total of 14 such cases are recorded. This means that no money was collected for these properties taken into guardianship, even if no specific note was made regarding the reasoning behind such a financial shortfall. At the manor of Norton before the Black Death only one case is recorded of a guardian having paid no entry fee, but 5 after 1349. In addition two other cases hint at immediate post-Black Death poverty, When one couple took over the guardianship of a 15-year-old boy and his inheritance, and only 'give to the lord by agreement two small hens'.[20] At the St. Albans manors the collection of heriot payments, which were one off payments, and fell due upon the death of a tenant and head of the peasant household by the lord, the Abbot of St. Albans, occasionally speak tales of hardship on behalf of the tenantry after the first arrival of the plague epidemic. While heriot payments were meant to be the rendering of the best beast upon the death of the tenant, St Alban's tenants often appear to have had little left after heir upon heir to individual tenements perished in 1349. The Abbot thus started collected heriots including plates, pots or, as in the case after the death of Alice Swetekyn, who left her two-year-old daughter behind in April 1349 'no heriot, nothing else is known'.[21]

It is the case that there were some important local and regional variations in the death rates caused by the arrival of the plague in the mid-fourteenth century. At manors of the Abbot of Glastonbury death rates ranging from under 36 to over 70% have been observed.[22] Higher death rates would have had a greater impact on changes in the land: labour ratio, and thus exacerbated pressure also on tenants faced with vacant holdings, the lord wanted to have looked after and occupied. Razi argued that at the manor of Halesowen survivors were not saturated with excess land.[23] However, even here some changes in the way wardships were recorded can be observed. At Halesowen, every surviving recorded custody case before the arrival of the Black Death includes the note of the fine paid for the custody. After the Black Death however, three are recorded as excused, like the custody of John de Lappole over John the son and heir of Roger de Oveley, which explicitly stated that the 'fine is excused by the Cellarer', or they simply do not note a fine.[24]

The immediate impoverishing effect of the Black Death will account for some of these changes. This is reflected in a shortfall of cash and potentially livestock, as surviving tenants had to render heriots to their lords, entry fines—for their own holdings and any they might have accumulated from other close or more distant relatives upon their death, in addition to mortuary fees for the burial of the dead. However such shortfall in cash is not the sole explanation for the trend to waive payments for custody. With land becoming more abundantly available post-Black Death, the demand for land dropped significantly. This could have significant consequences for underaged heirs looking for guardians to help with maintaining their landholdings. Fundamentally it would have made it more difficult to find families willing to take on the additional burden of farming someone else's land, and it increased the risk of landholdings falling to waste and buildings into disrepair. For many peasant households, the post-Black Death decades represented a saturation point for the availability of landed resources. With available labour power inherent in the peasant household only a certain amount of arable was cultivable without having to resort to additional wage labour, the cost of which was rising in the second half of the fourteenth century. In other words, the attractiveness of looking after young heirs and their holdings was intimately linked to local availability of land, labour resources inherent in individual households as well as the price of agricultural produce, both livestock and arable, gained from such holdings.

Occasionally, lords or the community appear to have actively intervened in guardianship cases and in order to guarantee the protection of heirs and their properties distributed the responsibility of the heir and land to several people. An extreme and unusual case of this can be found in the same village of Horwood, under the manorial jurisdiction of Winslow, when in October 1349 one messuage, 1 virgate of land and 4 acres of land together with the young two-year-old heir of Geoffrey Terry were handed into the care and guardianship of 'all the villeins of Horwood', when the scribe noted in the Court Book that 'custody of the land and heir was entrusted to all the villeins of Horwood, to maintain the heir and perform services and customs' which would have fallen due on the villein holding.[25] Sometimes therefore medieval communities felt quite literally that the job of looking after a child took a village, and not just their close relatives by blood or marriage.

Very young people and children were not considered capable of meeting the complex requirements associated with holding a tenement. The perceived incapacity of the young went to the heart of medieval definition of a person considered to be underaged or a minor. The key concern was not just physical maturity, but also cognitive development which, however, could be a matter for debate in individual circumstances. The legal author known today as Bracton felt that minors had to be looked after by others, because 'they do not know how to govern themselves'.[26] The sentiment expressed here resides in both legal and economic realities, and in medieval society, legal and economic responsibilities went hand in hand. At the Worcestershire manor of Halesowen John Deepslough had accepted the guardianship over two young boys whose ages are not known in April 1295, promising that he will sustain the boys 'until they are able to sustain themselves'.[27] The implication is therefore that it was accepted that a certain degree of maturity was required to facilitate independent economic survival. By definition therefore, until such maturity could be guaranteed, survival needed to be safeguarded by others. As such, young people, especially those who were left orphaned were in very real terms a matter of communal concern, and their care therefore, as Hanawalt rightly indicated, was a communal undertaking.[28]

Full age was not merely judged to have been reached when economic independence was achieved. Maturity was also judged through cognitive capacity. At the coastal manor of Heacham in Norfolk, the court explained that a person who was considered not to be of full age was not able to 'consent to the surrender of land' or able to consent to selling or receiving money for land.[29] The aim was protection from exploitation by guardians and others, which will be explored further later. It was also the aim to protect young heirs from themselves. Young people could exercise certain agency over their assets, and ill-thought through actions on behalf of the minor had to be guarded against. As we shall see, this did not always stop young people from making some ill—advised choices at times, but mechanisms were in place to undo them if the minor desired to do so upon coming of age.

At the root for need of this protection was the conceptualisation of the underaged young person as an individual whose special vulnerability was judged to be due to their lack of maturity as reflected by the ability to make good and sound judgments. In this respect the sentiments expressed at the court of Heacham reflect Bracton's views of the inability of the immature to run their own affairs. Other medieval writers seemed to liken the limited understanding and inability of children to govern their own affairs to those with mental disabilities, who were similarly understood to need looking after and whose inheritances needed to be safeguarded by guardians.[30] The detailed care afforded to child heirs is therefore unsurprisingly also reflected in provisions for heirs with mental or learning disabilities.

We do not know how old Alice the daughter of Adam at the St. Albans manor of Norton was when her father died in the plague year of 1349, but the community felt that she needed a guardian for her entire life. She had inherited from her father a messuage and half a virgate of land. There was also livestock on the holding as the heriot to the lord was a cow valued at 3s. However, 'by reason of her foolishness wardship is committed of the land, and the tenement together with the body of the said Alice for the term of the life of the said Alice to John Loveleg'.[31] John was told that he had to provide for Alice for the remainder of her life, including 'food and clothing'. The community therefore determined that Alice would never make a competent tenant due to her inherent nature. Such cases were far from unknown, and medieval writers were aware of the concept of the legally incompetent.[32] It is notable though that Alice's condition did not disinherit her, and her rights over her holding remained paramount. John became, in essence, a proxy tenant, holding Alice's inheritance for her and in her name, being able to profit from it, but also having been given the responsibility to look after Alice and her needs to the rest of her life, in return for reaping the profits from her tenement.

Upon entering a holding a tenant was expected to do homage to the lord and swear an oath of fealty. Manorial customs made it clear that underaged heirs were not only considered to be unable to swear such an oath, but they could not even be asked to do so. At the manor of Tooting Beck in October 1413, 6-year-old orphan heiress Alice Crafte inherited 24 acres of land from her father Robert, but her swearing the oath of fealty to her lord was 'respited until her coming of age'.[33] While Orme argued that children were only considered able to swear a an oath 'when they reached years of discretion: twelve, fourteen or fifteen', in village communities swearing an oath of fealty was only expected from young people upon reaching the age of majority when they were considered capable of running a full holding.[34]

Only members of the community in possession of their full mental capacities could be asked to swear a legally binding oath. Neither the community nor the lord felt that a mere 6-year-old was capable of either understanding the implication of swearing such an oath nor were they able to be held to it. Instead in the case of under aged heirs and orphans it was their guardians who were required to swear fealty to the lord of the holding they were placed in charge of. Similarly, and importantly, the guardian could only be held answerable for their oath during the precise term of their guardianship. In Halesowen, Matilda the widow of Phillipp Faber was awarded custody over Phillipp's son and heir John and his holding, for which Matilda duly swore 'fealty for the term' of the custody.[35] The implication is that her fealty only extended during the period of her guardianship, after which the incoming heir would have to swear fealty himself, and Matilda was released from the tenurial obligations her oath had bound her to.

Medieval village communities felt that underaged heirs did require special protection and looking after. They were considered vulnerable, inexperienced and not ready to take on the responsibilities which came with holding a full tenement.[36] At the same time, communities let young people enter into adult responsibilities gradually, thereby recognising implicitly that young people went through various stages of physical and mental development. It was only at the age of 12 that young boys were sworn into tithings, thereby assuming responsibilities of local policing and peace keeping.[37] Indeed wilfully keeping a boy aged 12 or over from being sworn into the tithing system where this operated was an offence against manorial custom, and the guilty party could be amerced in the manorial Leet court. Guidelines on how to conduct a Leet court dating from 1340 were very explicit about the requirement by the court to investigate locally 'whether all those who are twelve years old and upwards be in a tithing'.[38] However, inclusion in communal policing roles did not imply the assumption of the full responsibilities associated with a tenant of full age.

The requirement to play an active role in local tithings implies an expectation that at this age young people had gained an acute understanding of right and wrong. This was essential if they were given the responsibility of having to raise the raising the hue and cry if an offence or a crime, real or threatened or even potential, was detected.[39] Conversely, it is implied that before the age of 12 young people could not be expected to either be in a position to intervene in matters involving peacekeeping responsibilities or know clearly enough right from wrong. Whether this can be equated to our understanding of criminal responsibility is a separate question. Orme suggests that certainly below the age of 12 children could not be held fully criminally responsible, thus below the age of 12 a young person could not be outlawed, 'since he was not in the law'.[40] Shahar, instead suggests that girls could be held responsible for their crimes at the age of 12 and boys at 14.[41] Citing Bracton, Shahar shows that courts often showed leniency towards the young, due to their tender age.[42]

That the young were not always held responsible for their actions is borne out by the evidence in manor court rolls. Accordingly, court rolls occasionally show how parents or guardians could be held answerable to the lord and the community for the misbehaviour of the children in their care. At the manor of Halesowen, for example, in 1277 Radulf Clan was placed in mercy 'for the transgression of his son'.[43] We do not know how old Radulf's son was when he committed the office, but in all likelihood he would have been under the age of 12. The tithing custom also placed responsibility on the young person to act in cases of fellow villagers being attacked or having a trespass committed against them, contributing actively to the policing of the behaviour of members of the community and potentially being held accountable for any judgements made in this regard. In addition, the expected participation in formal court proceedings was not just a step closer to full adult responsibilities, but also a deeper initiation into local village politics, adult concerns and disagreements, which could occasionally turn violent. Part of this initiation was also the assumption of powers to enforce moral norms as well as seigniorial jurisdiction. This could include raising the hue in cases of brawls or thefts from neighbours, or, in the case of seigniorial jurisdiction, thefts from the lord, poaching and rescuing animals which had been impounded by the lord.[44] This intersection of seigniorial and village authority, cemented in the tithing system, therefore aided to embed young males within the complexities of lord and village relationships. In this regard the activities of the tithing system are not very dissimilar to the activities of the Charivari, observed by Natalie Zemon-Davis in the sixteenth century France, whereby young, unmarried men and boys learned expected behaviour for adult men and women.[45] The key elements are entirely comparable, in representing an introduction to communal values, the enforcement of social norms, and active participation in certain aspects of adult responsibilities. This in turn meant that adolescent boys at least were accorded a significant element of active agency in communal affairs, and crucially, this happened before they were considered mature enough to enter their own holdings.

2 Growing Autonomy

Once young people entered the age of puberty, it was also recognised that their economic value began to rise, as adolescents often entered service, worked as wage labourers and became more actively involved on their parental holdings.[46] In urban areas young people can be found entering apprenticeships at this age.[47] Documentary evidence attesting this has also recently been significantly augmented by an important study of the osteological evidence of adolescent skeletons in rural and urban sites in Medieval England.[48] While noting an increase of young women entering urban places of work post Black Death, it is for our purposes interesting to note that—while far from absent in rural adolescent populations—signs of spine and joint stress due to work were lower in rural than in urban contexts.[49] This indicates that patterns of very physically strenuous work among young people were quite different in urban and rural areas. And indications are that backbreaking work was more rarely undertaken by rural than by urban young people.

At the manors of the Abbey of Glastonbury all landless males from the age of 12 onwards had to pay an annual tax to the lord which ceased only when they either died, left the manor or took up land. These adolescent males were recorded annually in the manorial court rolls of the Glastonbury manors at court proceedings held around Hocktide.[50] These lists represent an invaluable source offering important insights into patterns of work, responsibility and residence of adolescents from the age of 12 onwards, and allow the tracking of their activities until their names were removed from the annual list. Boys still residing at the parental home were exempt from payment of this annual head tax but they were included in these lists, usually alongside an additional note of 'with mother' or 'with father'. In part it was a way of the lords to keep track perhaps of landless labourers and subtenants as well as servants in the localities, but it is also a de facto recognition of economic realities which meant that from about the age of 12 young people did have a certain degree of earning potential.[51]

The system at Glastonbury manors acted very clearly as an entry into an array of formal proceedings of the manor court, which was also coupled with being sworn into the local tithing and thereby entry into formal community policing activities, but took on an economic dimension.

The boys and young men thus listed were compelled to pay usually quite small sums of cash, hovering typically around 2d. in most cases, with occasional payments of 6, being recorded, probably payments from older and more experienced landless workers.[52] In addition, most young men and boys listed had to provide pledges as surety for the payment of their fine. Often such pledges were the boys' fathers or their masters if they were in service. At the manor of Monkton Deverill in Wiltshire it is possible to track the development of some adolescent boys. In 1331 Robert Peter, makes his first appearance at the manor on the list of the landless.[53]

There is an extant list of the landless for the year 1329, when Robert is not mentioned. Therefore, upon his first listing he cannot have been older than 13 or younger than 12. He is noted to be residing with his father. He is listed in 1332 as well, but in May 1334, now in his mid-teens, Robert Peter is no longer noted as dependent upon his parents, but presumably earning wages of some sort as he was noted to be liable to pay a small fine.[54] At the Glastonbury manor of Longbridge Deverill meanwhile, a larger manor neighbouring Monkton Deverill in the Wye River valley, John Faber is listed for the first time as residing with his father in 1331.[55] Like his neighbour Robert Peter, John must have been either 12 or 13, as he is not listed in 1329. John continued to be listed as residing with his father in 1332; by 1333 however John was named independently and paying the lord 4d.[56] The implication is that by the age of either 14 or 15 John, while still landless, was nevertheless gaining sufficient economic independence to no longer be listed as fully dependent on his father, and having acquired sufficient autonomy to pay an annual levy to his lord.

At the Glastonbury Abbey manor of Badbury in Wiltshire similar patterns can be discerned. But due to the excellent and full series of the landless lists at this manor we can also detect certain changing patterns across the fourteenth century. Before the arrival of the Black Death in the village in 1348 the lists of the landless were very lengthy and detailed, containing the names of young resident boys, labourers, newcomers and young men waiting for land to become available. In 1307, six males were listed as living with their fathers, and three with their mothers, which means that their father had died and they were under their mother's guardianship. In total, 58 landless men and boys are recorded in that year.[57] This situation is indicative of a shortage of land, and at the same time a significant local demand for wage labourers to sustain a significant population of young men and teenage boys who were either too young to hold a tenement in their own right, or who were waiting for land to become available.[58]

In 1348, disaster struck when the bacterium yersinia pestis arrived in the village, and of the 47 named landless males no less than 34 were noted as having died in the Black Death, representing a staggering death rate of 72%.[59] Among the dead were 12-year-old Robert, the son of Walter Godefrey, and 14-year-old Walter, the son of John Cokkes. As far as reconstructions allow, at least two 12-year-old boys and three 14-year-old boys, all still living at home with either their mother or father were listed as having died.

Demographic calamity seems to have had two main effects at the village of Badbury. Teenage boys were able to move into landed properties more quickly and were able to pick up wage labour outside their parental home more readily. The progression from living at home to earning, to entering a holding was still in evidence, but the process was at least sometimes speeded up. In 1346, Robert the son of John Cockes was mentioned on the list of the landless for the very first time, when he must have been 12 years old.[60] In 1348 he was still living with his father aged 14, but two years later in 1350 when he cannot have been older than 16 or just turned 17, he was struck off the list as it was noted that 'he has land'.[61]

After the Black Death, the lists of the landless never recovered their pre-plague numbers. In 1352, for example, only 8 males were listed, of whom 2 had been noted as having died.[62] However, the shortage of labour probably meant that young people easily found paid employment at a younger age than previously. In 1367, Richard, the son of Phillipp ate Buctoks was named for the first time in the list of the landless and noted to be residing with his father. The existence of the list for the previous year makes it possible to determine with a fair degree of certainty that he must have been 12 years old.[63] In 1368, Richard was listed as no longer dependent on his father but paying the lord 1d. when he was just 13 years old.[64] This does not necessarily mean of course that he did not live at home anymore, but it does mean that he was no longer entirely economically dependent on his father.

When Richard was 15, he was considered to have gained in economic value as he now started to pay the lord 2d annually.[65] In 1375 the same Richard is listed still as paying 2d to the lord, then aged 18, but after a short gap in the records he had left the landless lists by 1379, which means that he either left the manor or picked up land between the age of 18 and 22.[66] The value of labour and hence the wages a worker was able to command were dependent on a number of factors, not least the level of demand for labour at any given time locally. Additionally the value of labour was dependent upon other hierarchical factors, which were related to age and gender. In general women have thus been observed to have earned lower wages than men, and adults higher wages than adolescents and children. Bardsley has accordingly argued that female wages were more on a par with young people than men in later medieval England.[67]

Rises in economic value in accordance with experience or age can also be tracked in other cases. In 1308 Simon Coleman was listed as residing with his mother, his elder brother John however was already paying the lord 4d, and hence economically productive. A few years later Simon also appears to have entered paid employment as he paid the lord 10d in 1313, attesting to his increased cash flow.[68]

The lists of these landless boys and men speak of a busy and thriving village community in the early fourteenth century which was then slumped into serious decline after the first arrival of the Black Death, but which nonetheless also offered opportunities for some. Using family reconstructions with the help of the garciones lists also allows important insights into how rural communities educated their young people about gaining economic independence and slowly moving outside of the parental home. The implications of the evidence gleaned from the lists of the landless is that the lord collected a head tax which was at least in some sense related to earning power of the adolescent (and also adult) males who were named on the list. One might certainly point to the element of seigniorial exploitation of these landless inhabitants in the collection of such head taxes. However, Fox's assertion that tenants were also guilty of exploiting these landless villagers, should be treated with caution. While we can gain little insights into their actual earnings, the importance in village societies to teach young people 'on the job' and paying them a wage for their efforts should probably be rather seen like a relationship defined by guardianship and training than merely exploitative.[69]

Such observations from the lists of the landless young men and boys echo the findings of Barbara Hanawalt, when she argued that Coroner's Roll evidence of the fourteenth century showed that many adolescents continued to live at home but were also starting to become economically more active.[70] The development to full adult responsibilities and economic independence was therefore a gradual process. It was punctuated by rituals, which are more directly visible for boys than for girls. The first such ritual was to be sworn into the tithing. The second was the assumption of more economic agency, by evidence of increased earning capacity, either by learning a trade, entering into service with either the lord or another tenant, or by working as a wage labourer. Linked to the responsibilities associated with keeping peace within the community through the tithing system, which also represented a direct and clear integration into the structures and workings of the manorial court were the military obligations placed on adolescent males from the age of 15 by the *Statute of Winchester* of 1285. The statute purports to have come into existence due to an increasing concern about criminality. All towns and villages were ordered to organise watches to apprehend strangers walking the streets at night, roads were to be widened to reduce the opportunities of robbers to waylay passers-by, and it was 'likewise commanded that every man have in his house arms for keeping the peace'. In practice this meant that 'every man between fifteen years and sixty be assessed and sworn to arms according to the amount of his lands and chattels'.[71] For young men of the peasantry, this would at the very least have involved bows and arrows, while those with less than forty shillings worth of land 'shall be sworn to have scythes, gisarmes, knives' and those with less than 'twenty marks in chattels, swords, knives and other small weapons'.[72] Being thus sworn to arms represented an important ritualistic step into adulthood, associated with responsibilities of keeping the peace, apprehending criminals and other miscreants and enforcing law and order.

Again, it can be observed that the process towards responsibilities in community policing was gradual, starting as it did with the swearing into the tithing, which came attached with responsibilities of raising the hue and cry, and enforcing local custom and social norms, while military involvement and the bearing of arms were considered to require greater skill and levels of responsibility which were beyond a twelve-year-old. The development towards adult responsibilities was therefore legal, economic and ultimately characterised by the mental capacity to bear the responsibilities of assuming the tenancy of a holding in the widest sense.

Evidence of the nature of the cultural integration of young people into village life comes to us also via a set of thirteenth century customs relating to the manors of Monkton and Longbridge Deverill in Wiltshire, which belonged to the Abbey of Glastonbury. Here it was noted that 'All men of Longbridge and Monkton' said that the lord permitted three Scotales to be held in Longbridge per annum, which were events only to be attended by resident members of the community, that is both free and unfree tenants, but not anyone else, such as itinerant labourers.[73] Scotales were traditionally charitable events, which involved communal drinking events for the collections of funds for charity.[74] At these events, in Longbridge and Monkton Deverill which were meant to be organised on three days after dinner, it was stipulated that on the first day, a Saturday, all wives and young people (juvenes) were to be allowed to come and drink, on the second day and third day, a Sunday and Monday, husbands and wives were meant to come, bringing a penny. However, young people were only to bring an obulus,a haypenny on the Sunday, while on Mondays young people should be allowed to attend and 'drink freely' without money, 'because they will not find seating on the benches'. If they were found to sit on the benches, they were to pay like the others.[75] At the manor of Sturminster Newton, another Glastonbury Abbey manor, the association of youth with service is further illustrated when a villein tenant's customs clearly state that he and his wife were able to drink at the lord's scotale, paying on Sundays 2d. and Mondays 1d, yet should he have a servant they should—again—only pay an obulus—a haypenny.[76] These texts illustrate not just the full integration and participation of young people in the celebratory and cultural socialising activities of adults, linked to charitable giving as well as entertainment, but it demonstrates that young people were not expected to have the same financial resources as their adult neighbours. They were also clearly not expected to want to sit on the benches next to their elders. At the same time the text also illustrates how young people were taught certain communal values, and the demarcation of the outsider. The text delineates the community member—a permanently locally resident individual, falling under the jurisdiction and customs of the manorial lord, and differentiates it from the 'other', who cannot participate in certain communal activities. Such others, 'who serve otherwise in the manor' as the text states, were not necessarily regarded in a hostile manner, but they were not considered to belong to the manorial community in the same way. Children were thereby taught that communal events like Scotales helped to reify the community itself in places like Longbridge Deverill, and that they, as young people, were an important and integral part in this process. In playing such defined parts in re-inforcing communal values and the very communal existence young people exercised agency in defining and delineating their own communities. Their role was recognised in written down custom, in negotiation with the lord. Their participation helped to define the event, and was part of local culture, so important to the community that they insisted this to be noted down in the manorial custom, lest their lord—or anyone else should ever desire to dispute their right to Scotales in the future.

While adolescents were expected to be able to contribute to household incomes, younger children were understood to be entirely dependent on their adult guardian for all their needs. In the case of underaged heirs this was often spelled out in some detail in the custody agreements noted down in the manorial court rolls. Reminders to provide the minor with food, clothing or both to adequate measure were written into no less than 20% of cases of guardianship at the manor of Halesowen between 1293 and 1401.

Guardians were frequently warned that they should 'provide necessary sustenance' for the children in their care. Such sustenance included food, but also adequate clothing. In Halesowen in 1297, Richard Jurdan was granted the guardianship over the then 14-year-old orphaned boy William, son of Phillipp Jurdan who had no surviving mother or father. Richard was granted the custody for 6 years and it was noted that 'each year he is to find William one new tunic and a pair of shoes at the feast of St Michael until the end of the said term'.[77] The feast of St. Michael, which took place on 29 September, would have been picked very deliberately. As the feast marked the end of the harvest season, when people were more likely to have some spare cash either from the sale of produce or from wage labour, and were therefore similarly able to purchase new items of clothing.

In 1352, Thomas Thedrich of the village of Oldbury in the manor of Halesowen had been granted the guardianship over Thomas son of Richard of Oldbury. Thomas was around 4 years old when he was left orphaned and Thedrich was told that he had to maintain the holding with all its buildings but also 'find for the said Thomas son of Richard sufficient food and clothes for the term' of his guardianship.[78] In 1330, at the manor of Winslow in Buckinghamshire Alice, the 5-year-old daughter of Ralph le Clakker, was orphaned and taken into the house Nicholas le Clakker, who was told that he had to 'provide appropriate sustenance for the said heir'.[79]

It seems logical that communities would have considered it needful to include reminders to adequately feed and clothe these children only because there were concerns that such heirs were vulnerable to exploitation and neglect. This concern seems to have been greater when a child was looked after by either a more distant relative or someone apparently unrelated to the child. At Halesowen exhortations to feed and clothe the minor adequately were only raised when the guardians were not the child's mother or step mother. The same pattern is repeated at the somewhat smaller manor of Norton, held by the Abbey of St. Albans. Here only two cases out of a total of 29 explicitly mention providing sustenance to the child, and these were concerned with guardians who were not closely related to the heir. It was clearly hoped that writing such clauses into custody arrangements made them contractually binding, especially as they would have been pronounced in front of plenty of witnesses. These witnesses would have constituted most of the local community who were obliged to attend the manorial court. This included all heads of households, who would have had the requirement to attend manorial courts written into their tenurial agreements, in addition to other interested parties and anybody else who was due to appear in the court, such as those accused of trespasses, involved in disputes with the lord or other tenants, or those who wanted to formalise a land transfer. In this sense, therefore, the arrangement of a guardianship was a public and performative affair. The underaged heir was at the centre of proceedings which involved the guardians, the lord and/or his representatives as well as the manorial community more broadly. The point which brought the heir into this protective framework of community and manor court was of course the inheritance, a cottage, a messuage or land made the heir valuable to the lord as well as the village or hamlet they resided in. As we shall see later, however, this does not mean that non—inheriting siblings were likely to fall through this communal security net, instead they appear to have often been taken in by the same guardians, as they were frequently recognised as heirs in waiting, or potential heirs, should the first heir not survive to full majority to enter their inheritance.

Looking after underaged heirs was a communal and cooperative effort as well, involving occasionally actively more than one guardian to satisfy the various needs of the minor as well as their holding. In the St. Albans manor of Norton in 1347 John Hasche and Richard Bates took on the guardianship of 7-year-old John son of John Ronge who had died. John was set to inherit a rather substantial holding of 36 acres of land, which probably explains why two guardians were appointed to look after John's inheritance. Again, they were told that 'they shall maintain between them the said boy in food and clothing'.[80] In a similar case in Halesowen, recorded in April 1279, William the son of John Steinwulf was around 14 years old when an agreement was reached whereby the boy himself was in the custody of his mother after his father's death, but his uncle William looked after half of the boy's lands. In return for being able to take the profits from this land he was to provide the boy annually with 6 measures of grain, 1 quarter of oats, as well as 'clothes and shoes and all necessaries'.[81]

It has to be stressed that unless specifically noted, guardianship agreements made with the lord included the full expectation that whosoever was the guardian of the underaged heir or orphan had to satisfy all customary seigniorial demands with pertained to the holding, including rents in cash, kind as well as labour services. There is no evidence at all that mothers or step mothers who took on the guardianship of their children or step—children were released from any part of such customary burdens. In other words, they were fully expected to perform the same dues for the holding as any other tenants. This was often spelled out explicitly, as in Halesowen in 1316, when Margery the mother of William son of William was granted the wardship over her then 2-year-old son and his inheritance, for which it was noted that she will do the services.[82] In such cases, especially where childcare of very young children was involved an agreement involving shared wardships would accordingly have been attractive.

Late medieval commentators were aware that the proper care for children did not merely involve their adequate feeding and clothing. Several late medieval texts on teaching children appropriate decorum have survived. They speak repeatedly of the importance of curtesy and good manners, 'curtesy comes from heaven' thus exclaims a text dating from 1480, while adult success was seen to reside in the teaching of good manners in childhood.[83] Such manners ranged from table manners to other aspects of behaviour and piety. That it was considered a parental duty to teach such social conventions is also reflected in the well-known text 'How the wise man taught his son', which does not only urge the importance of regular prayer, but stresses the importance of hard work, gives advise on how to deal with any future wife—don't marry for money, don't overburden her and do not call her bad names, be always 'soft and fair'—and gives some important advise on living in close knit communities and neighbourhoods—don't tell tales and never bear false witness.[84] Indeed, manor court rolls are littered with allegations of defamation, and this underlines the importance of the maintenance of good neighbourly relationships and a good reputation.[85]

While manorial records are generally fairly matter of fact about their recording of the expectations placed on guardians, focussing on the practicalities of daily life, occasionally entries do hint at these wider duties and responsibilities placed on parents in the care of their own offspring—and others in their care. One can even detect hints at a requirement to meet the emotional needs in the care of guardians. At the manor of Boxley in Kent in June 1349 Thomas of Eyxherst was noted as having come to the court seeking 'the nurture of Juliana and Sarah, the daughters and heirs of John de Hokynburi'.[86] The use of the word 'nutricura'—nurture in this context implies more than the mere guardianship of the heirs' lands, but the care and responsibility associated with looking after the two jointly inheriting young girls. In a similar case in Halesowen in 1279 two men, John Borri and William le Freman were granted joint guardianship over Henry the son of Thomas the Freman who had died. Henry was in his mid-teens when the court decided that Henry was to go into service with John and William who had to 'find him all necessaries until the end of the said term as if he was their own son'.[87] The manor court here made the role of John and William as standing in loco parentis very clear, and unusually explicit. The exhortation goes beyond mere maintenance and feeding, to looking after the boy as a son. That two men were being given joint wardship over an adolescent boy does deserve some further discussion. It is not clear what the relationship was between them, but the implication is that they resided in the same household. As William le Freman carried the same surname as the boy's father, Thomas the Freman, it is likely that he was related to the young heir Henry, and he might have been his uncle. It is unlikely that he was Henry's older brother, as it would be highly doubtful for the court to ask someone to look after their brother as if he were their son. The background of John Borri in relation to the Fremans is more difficult to ascertain. It is possible that John and William were a couple, which would also make sense in the context of the court's dealing with their relationship vis-à-vis Henry, but it is impossible to prove village tolerance of same sex couples. However, we can say with certainty that village society felt it was acceptable to place two men in charge of an underaged heir, and that furthermore it was felt that it was entirely appropriate to envisage these two men effectively acting as two fathers for the boy.

This case is also illustrative of the level of relative and growing agency accorded to adolescents. In keeping with the understanding of a young person's development towards economic autonomy, the court recognised that Henry was old enough to exercise some self-determination over his own life, and that his abode was Henry's own choice. Accordingly, it was decided that 'if the said Henry should not wish to stay with them, they owe to give him annually 3s. for clothes and shoes'.[88] In effect, this payment would have represented a rental payment for Henry's lands and tenement. In other words, the court recognised that Henry did not have the maturity to take on the full responsibility of taking over a holding as head of a household, but he was old enough to exert some autonomy over his choice of abode and economic activities. As recompense for being able to profit from Henry's holding John and William were expected to pay Henry. The note that this payment was meant for clothes and shoes has symbolic significance. Ultimately, if Henry did not live with his appointed guardians, a cash payment could have been used for anything, but as persons in loco parentis John and William would have been expected to look after Henry's physical needs, so the cash payment was expressly given in lieu of meeting these needs, rather than a mere and anonymous rent payment.

Reminders and exhortations to look after the physical needs of a young heir in providing adequate food and clothing were far from unusual. However, upon the appointment of guardians it was even more common to insert reminders of their responsibilities to look after the land of the heir into the wardship agreement. A particular concern was that guardians might let the heir's land and holding go to waste. Even mothers of the heir who took over their guardianship were told to look after the heir's inheritance. In 1328 at the manor of Walsham le Willows Matilda, the mother of William son of William Coppelowe who had died, was told that she could only have this custody over the boy and his inheritance of 7 acres of villein land, 'on condition that she maintains the house and messuage in as good a state as she received it'. In addition, she had to produce three pledges for this assurance, and another pledge, the reeve of the manor to guarantee for the lord the payment of 40 d for the custody.[89] The pledges would have been requested by the court—that is the village community as well as the lord, in order to safeguard both the debt to the lord and the inheritance of her son.

At the Yorkshire manor of Wakefield similarly custodians were told repeatedly not 'make any waste' within the heir's holdings. In 1316, Agnes who was appointed guardian over her son Adam's inheritance after the death of her husband Richard of Gaukthorp had to produce two pledges 'to see to the sufficient upkeep of the land and buildings' pertaining to the 26 acres, 3 roods and meadow he was due to gain in inheritance.[90] In 1350 Thomas de Birkenschagh likewise had to promise to make 'no waste or destruction' within the holdings which were the inheritance of Beatrix, the orphaned daughter of Adam Judson.[91] In 1352 Thomas Rogerson had to promise not make any waste within the tenement which Johanna daughter of Richard del Stevenrod was due to inherit.[92]

At the manor of Halesowen between 1293 and 1401, a total of 41 cases of underaged heirs are recorded who were given designated guardians. Just over 26% of these specifically included a clause to safeguard the inheritance by reminding the guardian that it was their responsibility to keep the land and buildings in good order and maintain them without causing waste or destruction. The wardship agreement itself was contractual, but also underpinned by trust offered by the community and the lord to the guardian to look after ward and land. In April 1349, nine-year-old heiress Juliana and her inherited smallholding were thus given into the guardianship of her mother, to whom 'custody was entrusted'.[93] The trust referred to here was implicitly not just the trust vested in her to look after the child's future interest, but the trust was also extended from the lord and the community via the manorial court. Such were not empty or meaningless words, they spoke of expectations and responsibilities by the guardian for the heir and the community in question.

The fear such clauses primarily expressed was, of course, mismanagement. Any inheritance was comprised of a set of assets for the incoming heir as well as for the lord. The lord therefore wanted assurances that his land was looked after andkept productive. This in turn would maintain the value of the holding, as to warrant the rents and dues levied on it. The heir's rights in this matter were also sacrosanct; to run down an inheritance by, for example, letting good arable land go to waste, diminished the value of the land and hence the value of the inheritance. Again, the double triangular interrelationship between tenant, land and lordship on the one hand and tenant, land and community on the other can be discerned with overlapping interests between the lord and the community, hinging on the axis of tenant and land (Diagram 1).

Just as in the case of exhortations to look after the physical needs of heirs, warnings against waste were not added to all wardship cases. This raises the possibility that the court decided to add the wording only in circumstances which may have caused the court at least potential concern in this regard. However, no particular pattern in the commenting on waste regarding the guardian in these cases can be discerned. There is no gender difference to indicate that more concerns were raised when a mother, step mother or other female head of a household was placed in charge of the guardianship over land instead of a male relative or other member of the community. However, while mothers and step mothers were rarely if ever warned to feed and clothe their wards adequately, they were considered to be as high a risk factor as anybody else when it came to maintaining assets and properties of heirs.

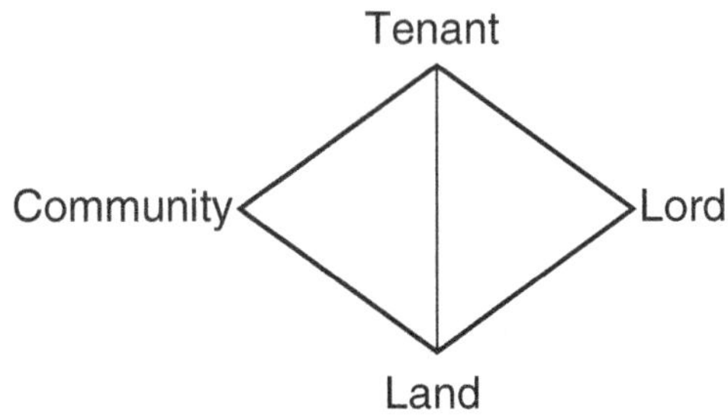

Diagram 1 Relationships between tenant, lord, land and communities

Occasionally, concern for the welfare of children was also expressed beyond their death. In Winslow in 1440, Robert the son of John ate Lane was noted to have inherited at the age of 14, a villein holding containing 10 acres of arable land. The guardianship was granted to Robert's mother Joan, John's widow. The custody agreement stipulated that Joan was to have the land until her death should Robert die before his mother. If this should happen, it was stated in a provision normally reserved to wills, that after her death all assets were to be sold 'and the money received for it disposed of for the souls of the said John, Joan and Robert'.[94]

While care and prayer for the souls of deceased children reflects parental concern for their spiritual wellbeing, occasionally peasant societies expressed hopes about the temporal wellbeing of their offspring. Children were also seen as the future of village societies, for whose futures it was worth risking conflict with the lord. When in 1348, the villagers of the Glastonbury Abbey Manor of Badbury in Wiltshire initiated a revolt through the courts against their lord by attempting to claim their freedom from villeinage, the manor court roll entry detailing the peasants' actions stated that the rebels felt that the profits from their actions were 'for their heirs in perpetuity'.[95]

3 The Age of Majority

Age mattered in medieval society, but not as much as it matters in our own. We have very specific age—defined rules, laws and rights in contemporary European society which link into our own conceptions of childhood as a fairly clear and plottable development, marked by regular age—related rituals and boundaries.[96] Furthermore, while much of our modern and concepts between adult and child intertwine notions of age and puberty, anthropology is illustrative in the importance of the concept of varying 'social maturity', which can become more important than physical biological factors.[97] When we consider medieval English rural society we are similarly faced with a concept of childhood and of transition into adulthood which is not purely fixed according to age in many respects, but uses ager almost as a guideline to judge other factors of social maturity against.

Some of these age-related concerns are reflected in medieval European culture and we can certainly discern attempts to regulate certain matter by referring to age.[98] Canon law stipulated that it was against ecclesiastical norms to marry a girl before the age of 12 and a boy before the age of 14. This rule alone caused much medieval ink to be spilled on parchment, especially in church courts where individuals tried to contest the validity of individual marriages.[99] Liability to pay the poll taxes also started at the age of 14, probably due to the presumed increasing economic activities with remuneration from this age onwards. However, medieval societies did not keep formal records of births, so, considering that so many ritualised life events hinged upon age, other methods had to be found to recall it. The main tool in this case, especially in cases of dispute, was the collective memory of the local community or interest group. It has been shown that this was by no means always accurate, and probably occasionally deliberately used to amend age to suit the purpose of the suiters.[100] However such collective memory regarding age could be called upon in courts as valid evidence. Moving testimony on reconstructing the age of a young woman whose age upon her marriage was disputed comes to us from the church courts of York in the 1360s. A number of the numerous witnesses who gave testimony to Alice's age were women, who specifically remembered Alice's age by referring to events relating to their own or their neighbour's children, in particular their births, their wet nursing or their premature deaths.[101] The event of childbirth thereby became an anchor point, allowing the mental reconstruction of timelines of events. The memories of local women can therefore be shown to have been key in communal oral histories, while childbirth, albeit a common enough event, had fundamentally such a significant impact on communities, to facilitate their use as such anchor points.[102]

In the cases of underaged heirs the age of the heir, when it was given, was sometimes provided with great precision. At Winslow, John, son of Richard Geffes, was noted to reach his sixth birthday on 29 of August.[103] John, son of John Smith was said to reach his 18th birthday 'next Michaelmas' in 1340.[104] The ages of very young children in particular were occasionally noted down in the number of individual weeks or days. At the manor of Eldersfield, Stephen, the orphaned son of Walter de Pobmer was noted as being 21 weeks old in the April court of 1316 at the manor.[105] Keeping track of the ages of the very young not only shows a concern and care for them but it also, again, can be seen as indicative of a concept of child development and change which was related at least partly to age. As we have seen, we know that medieval thinkers had views on the development from infancy to full adulthood, where the age of infancy was considered to have concluded around the age of 7, followed by the age of Puerita, followed by adolescence between about the ages of 12 and 20.[106] As such therefore natural, biological adulthood or physical maturity was considered to have been reached by about the age of 20.

Considering the deliberate and nurturing care communities took in guiding their young people to adulthood and preparing them to become responsible tenants in their own right, at which point was it considered to be the case that adulthood, or an age of majority had been reached in later medieval village society? The answer to the question is not straightforward. We are very used to particular numerical boundary markers in our society, demarcating rights and responsibilities, which typically increase with age, are enshrined in law. As Heather Montgomery has aptly pointed out, such modern, western demarcations are due to bureaucratic boundaries; at 'what age a child starts school, or when he or she has certain legal rights'.[107] However, such boundaries are also culturally and socially constructed, and therefore depend on context. To expect to find similarly recognisable age—related boundaries within a medieval context is therefore misguided. Anthropology can offer useful insights in this context, as there are many and varied definitions of childhood, and not in every culture are children perceived as incomplete adults or in some ways less competent than adults.[108] Accordingly different age restrictions apply in different countries and age-related boundaries are in a chronological flux, changing and adjusting with the changes in societal sensibilities on individual matters, from the right to vote, to marriage, to the consumption of alcohol and consensual sex.[109]

In general, medieval peasants seemed to feel that the age of majority could be a matter of debate as well as custom. There was not a single cut off point where after young men and women were considered to be adults. The age of majority was not a mere number of years which signified the initiation to adulthood. Instead the age of majority represented also the stepping stone to full adult responsibilities, including the assumption—potentially at least—of the role of the head of a household. In this sense, therefore, the distinct theories of medieval thinkers concerning the ages of childhood development are a somewhat simplistic rendering of medieval attitudes and concerns. Different stages of childhood and adolescence were recognised, but they were also elastic.[110] Anthropology is helpful in this context. As Montgomery shows, the idea that childhood can be understood as very distinct from adulthood is not universal. Instead she argues that in some places 'there are many stages of social immaturity that last well beyond puberty and even marriage'.[111] This accords with the view of some medieval thinkers who did not feel that adulthood was reached until the later twenties or the mid-thirties.[112] As a result some medieval commentators conceptualised further developmental stages after adolescentia, which appear rather to have been linked to an individual's social and economic status as well as competencies. The term 'juventus' was accordingly sometimes used to describe young men of the French upper classes, who, as Shahar shows, had 'completed his military training', but who had not yet 'acquired his own fief or took a wife'.[113] Dante similarly felt that adolescence only concluded at the age of 25, followed by a period of 'gioventute', which lasted until the age of 45.[114] Therefore, conceptually medieval commentators interlinked various different human developments into at times parallel stages, which were at least in part linked to notions of social and economic maturity. By definition, these could be a matter of debate according to individual circumstances and characteristics.

Fundamentally the age of majority was determined by a combination of factors, manorial—and hence local—customs, as well as communal judgement according to individual cases and circumstances, which can therefore be understood as a judgment on social maturity. What was important in this context was not a mere numerical attainment of years, although this was part of the consideration, but rather, among other factors, individual aptitude.[115]

At the Worcestershire manor of Halesowen the age of majority was set by custom at 20 from at least the later thirteenth century onwards.[116] In a court held in April 1293 this was spelled out when Juliana the widow of Phillipp de Hulle was awarded the guardianship over Phillipp's son John who was fourteen years old at the time, and it was noted that the tenement was granted to her until the boy reached the full age 'of 20 years'.[117] In the smaller Worcestershire manor of Eldersfield near Malvern the age of majority was slightly higher at 21 in the later fourteenth century.[118] At the manor of Norton in the early fourteenth century, the age of majority was 19. When Richard, the son and heir of William Bate was left an orphan in October 1336 his care and that of his inheritance was entrusted to his uncle Henry, for a period of 'six years or to the full age of the said heir'. Richard's birthday, it was noted, fell on St. Martin's day, the 11 November, when he was to turn 14. He actually entered his holding though not when he was 20, but rather when he about to turn 19, in October 1341, for as the court noted he was 'of full age' and formally entered his unfree holdings comprised of two messuages and two virgates of land.[119] It seems therefore that upon taking on the guardianship of Richard his uncle was granted an additional year's use of the tenement and guardianship, should this have been required. The implication is that the ultimate judgment on the final length of the guardianship was left to Richard and his uncle.

One might accordingly conclude that the typical age of majority was judged therefore to be at the very end of the teenage years into the early twenties. This would also accord with the age of majority recorded in Edward's I's reign in 1299–1300, when the Statute concerning Wards and Reliefs stipulated that a ward of 'of land that is holden in Knight's service' comes of age at 'One and twenty years'.[120] However, matters in rural societies were more complex and the age of majority could, depending on the locality, be pegged significantly lower. As Elaine Clark has shown, at the manors of Iselworth in Middlesex, Salle in Norfolk, and the manor of Wells in Norfolk the ages of majority were set by custom at fifteen.[121] At the manor of Hatfield Chase in Yorkshire it was similarly noted in 1336, that 'from time out of mind, ... when any boy reaches the age of fifteenth years, he can alienate [land] and his alienation is good', that is, such alienations of land would be upheld in court when challenged, and were therefore considered valid.[122] This test was crucial, majority implied full agency over the inheritance, while minority precluded it. As we shall see, land acquired from a transfer conducted by an underaged heir was risky, as minority meant that no informed decision over tenure could be made. Therefore, any such agreement made could not, in manorial custom, be considered binding. In this regard, manorial custom may well have been at odds with common law, as Poos and Bonfield pointed out. While common law might have considered the transfer of free land by an underaged heir not void automatically, but potentially if challenged, transfers of land held in customary or villein tenure appear indeed to have been considered invalid in at least some localities.[123] Accordingly, we have to conclude that at Hatfield Chase fifteen was considered the age of majority, unless local custom differentiated between a partial agency acquired at that age which included valid transfers of land.

The age of majority could also vary according to gender. At the manor of Winslow in 1332 an inquiery was conducted to explore the age of majority and it was considered that 'a boy when he completes the age of 20 years and a girl when she completes the age of 16 years can give and alienate their lands and holdings and not before that age'.[124] Two years later in 1334 it was similarly noted that 'a boy is of full age to hold his land from an inheritance when he is twenty and a girl when she is aged 16'.[125] For the legal author, known as 'Bracton', the test if a young woman was of full age was whether she was able to, and know 'how to arrange her house and those things which belong to the arrangement and management of her house'. 'Bracton' felt that 'she may know what pertains to 'cone and key' which cannot be before her fourteenth or fifteenth year, for this kind of age requires discretion and strength and sense'.[126] While Bracton may have been more concerned with household management and duties which are generally associated with domestic tasks, than with the management of land and agriculture, medieval villagers had other concerns. Absence of sons or a lack of surviving sons in many peasant families meant that about a quarter to a third of heirs to holdings in any given rural community were young women.[127] Seigniorial and communal expectations on them to fulfil all their tenurial duties—including labour services—as well as agricultural and other tasks associated with a tenancy, also meant the need for a wider knowledge, strength and skill base to complete these tasks.[128]

A connection between local customs concerning the age of majority and the nature of local inheritance practices does not appear to present itself either. Thus at three manors which recognised the age of majority at 15, three different inheritance customs were followed. At Iselworth, the predominant inheritance practice of unfree land was ultimogeniture, at Salle it was partible, at Well it was primogeniture.[129]

Occasionally, communities had to strike a balance between protecting the rights of an heir and pragmatic need. At the St. Albans manor of

Winslow it is possible to track a change in policy with regards to considerations of the age of majority due to the catastrophic effect of the Black Death, which arrived in the manor around late March 1349. The highest death toll at the manor was recorded in April 1349, when in a single court over one hundred tenants were recorded to have died.[130] While before the arrival of the Black Death the age of majority for boys was 20, at the start of the court held in April 1349 it is made clear that the age of majority at the manor was 17–18, as Ralph, the son and heir of William King was aged 12 when he was taken into guardianship for a total of five years, [making the age of majority at least 17 years, perhaps 18, as we cannot be certain of William's month of birth].[131] Indeed in the same court John Geffes was considered of full age when he entered his father's holding aged 18.[132] But after recording over seventy deaths in the same court thereafter, William son of William Ponteys entered his messuage and 1 virgate of land, and swore fealty to the lord, even though he had only just turned 16.[133] Similarly, John the son of William Sibily who had died in the plague, appears to have been allowed to enter his father's sole possession, a cottage when he was only 15 years old. The family was poor enough to own no livestock and the lord was instead given for death duty of his tenant, the heriot, of a chest which was merely valued at 4d.[134]

The manor was at crisis point. Overwhelmed with holdings, for which no surviving heir could be found, with the death toll due to the plague still rising and at the same time the lord exerting pressure to maintain his assets by securing tenants for his holdings, the community had little choice but to grant holdings to heirs in their mid-teens, especially in cases where the community felt that risks of mismanagement were low due to the social maturity of the heir or a relatively small size of the holding they inherited.

The age of majority was therefore partly dependent upon communal capacity to look after the land and persons of orphans. At the root of this were economic pressures and elements of negotiation between the community and the lord as well as communal and customary notions of what adulthood entailed. While some historians have argued that the end of childhood was considered to arrive with the 12th birthday, this should not be understood therefore to have been seen as the beginning of adulthood.[135] This would be entirely at odds with manorial evidence which posits the age of majority anywhere between 15 and 21. Rather, therefore, it may be more fruitful to think of the age of 12 as a stepping stone towards majority.

The apparent ability of medieval community to exercise considerable flexibility in their interpretation of the age of majority may seem strange to us, but they made their decisions advisedly and if veering from the customary norm, it seems on a considered case by case basis. It served their purposes, and simply confirms that medieval villagers did have not just a concept of adulthood in conceiving of adult abilities and responsibilities, but also, conversely therefore had concepts of childhood or adolescence which were merely different from ours.

Notes

1. Villein tenure is also referred to customary or unfree tenure. By the later thirteenth century the term had become synonymous with serfdom. Such unfree status was attached notionally to the land, but the person's status—who was the tenant of the land could become coloured by it, whereby the person was see and declared to be a villein 'by blood', and thus their children were unfree as well. Unfree status carried a number of disadvantages, such as higher rent payments and labour services, alongside personal dues, such as the obligation to pay a merchet—a marriage licence—and the requirement to have the lord's permission if the tenant wished to depart from the manor. However, on the other hand, villein tenure also benefited from the stability of tenure and protection from arbitrary rent increases by the lord. It has been argued that such benefits, including the heritability of villain holdings, made them very attractive to tenants. However, it was also possible, and indeed regionally common, for tenants to hold both free and unfree land. For discussions of these issues see: C. Dyer, *Standards of Living in the Later Middle Ages, Social Change in England c. 1200–1520* (Cambridge University Press, 1993), pp. 10–26; P.R. Schofield, *Peasant and Community in Medieval England 1200–1500* (Basingstoke: Palgrave Macmillan, 2003), pp. 11–17; M. Müller, 'A Divided Class? Peasants and Peasant Communities in Later Medieval England', in: C. Dyer et al., eds., *Rodney Hilton's Middle Ages* (Past and Present Supplement 2 Oxford University Press, 2007), pp. 115–120.
2. E. Clark, 'Social Welfare and Mutual Aid in the Medieval Countryside', in: *Journal of British Studies*, vol. 33, no. 4 (1994), see esp. p. 388.
3. For Open field farming see for example: W.O. Ault, *Open Field Farming in Medieval England: A Study in Village By-Laws* (London: Allen and Unwin, 1972).
4. See for example: C. Dyer, 'Power and Conflict in the Medieval English Village', in: C. Dyer, *Everyday Life in Medieval England* (London: Hambledon Press and London, 2000), pp. 3–6.

5. N. Zemon-Davis, 'The Reasons for Misrule: Youth Groups and Charivaris in Sixteenth-Century France', in: *Past & Present*, no. 50 (1971); C. Wickham, 'Gossip and Resistance Among Medieval Peasants', in: *Past and Present*, no. 160 (August 1998), pp. 3–24; See also: M.K. McInosh, *Controlling Misbehaviour in England, 1370–1600* (Cambridge University Press, 2009), esp. pp. 78ff. and 119ff.
6. For discussions of the manorial court see for example: Z. Razi and R.M. Smith, 'The Historiography of Manorial Court Rolls' in: Z. Razi and R.M. Smith, eds., *Medieval Society and the Manor Court*, pp. 1–12.
7. On the manor court books see A.E. Levett, 'The Courts and Court Rolls of St. Albans Abbey', in: *Transactions of the Royal Historical Society*, vol. 7 (1924), pp. 52–76; A.E. Levett, *Studies in Manorial History*, eds., H.M. Cam, M. Coate, and L.S. Sutherland (Oxford: Calrendon Press, 1938).
8. P. Ariés, *Centuries of Childhood* (New York: Alfred A. Knopf, 1962), p. 128.
9. A.V. Chayanov, *The Theory of Peasant Economy*, D. Thorner, B. Kerblay, and R.E.F. Smith, eds. (Homewood, IL: American Economic Association, R.D. Irwing, 1966), pp. 53–61.
10. For a discussion of the structure of medieval society see: C. Dyer, *Standards of Living*, pp. 10–26.
11. M. Müller, 'Social Control and the Hue and Cry in Two Fourteenth Century Villages', in: *Journal of Medieval History*, vol. 31 (2005), pp. 29–53.
12. See for example: M. Bailey, *The English Manor c. 1200–c. 1500* (Manchester University Press, 202) for a discussion of the regional tithing system and the Leet Court see esp. pp. 178–184.
13. D. Noy, ed. and trans., *Winslow Manor Court Books Part I 1327–1377*, p. 221.
14. NRO DA 1, 1286; H. Jewel, *The Court Rolls of the Manor of Wakefield from September 1348–September 1350*, p. 153; L.R. Poos and L. Bonfield, eds., *Select Cases in Manorial Courts 1250–1550, Property and Family Law*, p. 153.
15. For discussions of these developments see for example: C. Dyer, *Standards of Living in the Later Middle Ages* (Cambridge University Press, 1989), pp. 141–143; C. Dyer, *Making a Living in the Middle Ages The People of Britain 850–1520* (New Haven and London:: Yale University Press, 2002), pp. 346–362.
16. Halesowen Manor, Birmingham Archive, Wolfson Centre, MS 3279/346295.
17. D. Noy, ed. and trans., *Winslow Manor Court Books Part I 1327–1377*, p. 245.
18. D. Noy, ed. and trans., *Winslow Manor Court Books Part I 1327–1377*, p. 245.
19. R. Lock, *The Court Rolls of Walsham le Willows 1351–1399*, p. 29.
20. P. Foden, *Records of the Manor of Norton*, pp. 166–167.

21. Examples can be found here: P. Foden, *Records of the Manor of Norton*, p. 167, p. 192, p. 139; D. Noy, *Winslow Manor Court Books, Part I 1327–1377*, p. 249.
22. M. Eccleston, 'Mortality of Rural Landless Men Before the Black Death, The Glastonbury Head Tax Lists', in: *Local Population Studies*, vol. 63 (Autumn, 1999), p. 26.
23. Z. Razi, Life, *Marriage and Death in a Medieval Parish*, p. 113.
24. Halesowen Manor, Birmingham Archives, Wolfson Centre, MS 3279/346347.
25. D. Noy, ed., *Winslow Manor Court Book*, Part I, p. 248.
26. *Henrici de Bracton de Legibus et Consuetudinibus Angliae*, ed., T. Twiss, vol. 2 (London, 1879), p. 3.
27. J. Amphlett ed., *Court Rolls of the Manor of Halesowen 1270–1307* (Oxford, Printed for the Worcestershire Historical Society by James Parker, 1912), p. 330.
28. B.A. Hanawalt, 'Narratives of a Nurturing Culture: Parents and Neighbours in Medieval England', in: B.A. Hanawalt, *Of Good and Ill Repute, Gender and Social Control in Medieval England* (New York, Oxford: Oxford University Press, 1989), p. 167.
29. Norfolk Record Office MF/RO 206 DA 1, June 1278.
30. W.J. Turner, *Care and Custody of the Mentally Ill, Incompetent, and Disabled in Medieval England* (Brepols, 2013), pp. 37–38 and p. 50.
31. P. Foden, *Records of the Manor of Norton in the Liberty of St. Albans, 1244–1539* (Hertfordshire Record Society, 2013), p. 142.
32. E. Clark, 'Social Welfare and Mutual Aid', pp. 389–390; A. Musson, *Medieval Law in Context: The Growth of Legal Consciousness from Magna Carta to the Peasants' Revolt* (Manchester University Press, 2001), p. 86.
33. *Court Rolls of the Manor of Tooting Beck, Volume 1, 1394–1422*, London County Council (London, 1909), p. 163.
34. N. Orme, *Medieval Children* (New Haven, London: Yale University Press, 2001), p. 216.
35. J. Amphlett ed., *Court Rolls of the Manor of Halesowen 1270–1307* (Oxford, Printed for the Worcestershire Historical Society by James Parker, 1912), p. 276.
36. See also E. Clark, 'The Custody of Children in English Manor Courts', in: *Law and History Review*, vol. 3, no. 2 (Autumn, 1985), p. 341.
37. M. Müller, 'Social Control and the Hue and Cry in Two Fourteenth-Century Villages', in: *Journal of Medieval History*, vol. 31, no. 1 (2005), pp. 29–53.
38. M. Bailey, *The English Manor c. 1200–c. 1500* (Manchester University Press, 2002), p. 223.
39. See also on this N. Orme, *Medieval Children*, p. 322; Müller, 'Social Control and the Hue and Cry', p. 39.

40. N. Orme, *Medieval Children* (New Haven, London: Yale University Press, 2001), p. 322.
41. S. Shahar, *Childhood in the Middle Ages* (London and New York: Routledge, 1992), p. 25.
42. S. Shahar, *Childhood in the Middle Ages*, p. 25.
43. J. Amphlett, *Court Rolls of the Manor of Hales 1272–1307*, Part I (Oxford: Worcestershire Record Society, 1910), p. 80.
44. Livestock was usually impounded by lords to exert pressure on tenants to force them to comply with a variety of seigniorial demands, from rent payments to damages done to the lord to be made good. See for a discussion of this for example: M. Müller, 'Conflict and Revolt: The Bishop of Ely and His Peasants at the Manor of Brandon in Suffolk ca. 1300–1381', in: *Rural History*, vol. 23, no. 1 (April 2012), pp. 1–19.
45. N. Zemon-Davis, 'The Reasons for Misrule: Youth Groups and Charivaris in Sixteenth-Century France', in: *Past & Present*, no. 50 (1971), p. 54.
46. For servants and apprentices see for example: R. Goddard, 'Female Apprenticeships in the West Midlands in the Later Middle Ages', in: *Midlands History*, vol. 27 (2002), pp. 165–181; P.J.P. Goldberg, 'Masters and Men in Later Medieval England', in: D.M. Hadley, ed., *Masculinity in Medieval Europe* (London and New York, 1999), pp. 56–70; P.J.P. Goldberg, 'What Was a Servant?', in: A. Curry and E. Matthew, eds., *Concepts and Patterns of Service in the Later Middle Ages* (The Boydell Press, 2000), pp. 1–20; B.A. Hanawalt, *Growing Up in Medieval London The Experience of Childhood in History* (Oxford and New York: Oxford University Press, 1993); B.A. Hanawalt, *The Ties That Bound, Peasant Families in Medieval England* (New York, Oxford: Oxford University Press, 1986), esp. pp. 156–168; L.R. Poos, *A Rural Society After the Black Death Essex 1350–1525* (Cambridge University Press, 1991), esp. pp. 192–206.
47. See for example on this: S. Shahar, *Childhood in the Middle Ages*, pp. 227ff.; R. Goddard, 'Female Apprenticeships in the West Midlands', pp. 165–181; P.J.P. Goldberg, 'Masters and Men in Later Medieval England', pp. 56–70; P.J.P. Goldberg, 'What Was a Servant?', pp. 1–20.
48. M. Lewis, 'Work and the Adolescent in Medieval England ad 900–1550: The Osteological Evidence', in: *Medieval Archaeology*, vol. 60, no. 1 (2016), pp. 138–171.
49. M. Lewis, 'Work and the Adolescent in Medieval England ad 900–1550: The Osteological Evidence', pp. 158–163.
50. These garciones lists were first discussed in a seminal paper by Harold Fox: H. Fox, 'The Exploitation of the Landless by Lords and Tenants in Early Medieval England', in: Z. Razi and R.M. Smith, eds., *Medieval Society and the Manor Court* (1996), pp. 518–568.
51. Harold Fox: H. Fox, 'The Exploitation of the Landless by Lords and Tenants in Early Medieval England', pp. 518–568.

52. Examples about garciones in the manor court rolls are recorded at the spring Hocktide at Glastonbury Abbey manors. See for example at the manors of Longbridge Deverill and Monkton Deverill Glastonbury Abbey Records held at Longleat House, sourced from microfilm. MS 9633; MS 9633 skin no. 7v; MS 9629 no. 2v; MS 8085 skin no. 7; MS 8085 skin no. 7v; MS 6366 skin no. 5v; MS 6367 skin no. 7.
53. Glastonbury Abbey Records, MS 6367 no. 7.
54. Glastonbury Abbey Records MS 11237 no. 4v; MS 6368 no. 5v; MS 6369 no. 6v.
55. Glastonbury Abbey Records MS 6367 no. 7v.
56. Glastonbury Abbey Records MS 11237 no. 4; MS 6368 no. 5v.
57. Glastonbury Abbey Records MS 11252 no. 4v.
58. There is significant evidence that this was indeed the case at the manor. The Abbot of Glastonbury was hostile to sublets and a large number of local holdings contained significant acreages being comprised of half a virgate (20 acres) or more. See.
59. Glastonbury Abbey Records MS 11179 no. 30. This death rate is significantly higher than traditional death rate estimates of one third or half of the population, see M. Eccleston, 'Mortality of Rural Landless Men Before the Black Death, The Glastonbury Head Tax Lists', in: *Local Population Studies*, vol. 63 (Autumn, 1999), pp. 6–29.
60. Glastonbury Abbey Records MS 11251 no. 49.
61. Glastonbury Abbey Records MS 11179 no. 30; MS 11222 no. 14v.
62. Glastonbury Abbey Records MS 11223 no. 37.
63. Glastonbury Abbey Records MS 11181 no. 47.
64. Glastonbury Abbey Records MS 10636 no. 51.
65. Glastonbury Abbey Records MS 11182 no. 44.
66. Glastonbury Abbey Records MS 10644 no. 42; MS 112221 no. 40; MS 10658 no. 41.
67. S. Bardsley, 'Women's Work Reconsidered; Gender and Wage Differentiation in Late Medieval England', in: *Past and Present*, vol. 165 (November 1999), pp. 3–29.
68. Glastonbury Abbey Records MS.
69. H. Fox, 'The Exploitation of the Landless by Lords and Tenants in Early Medieval England', pp. 518–568.
70. B.A. Hanawalt, 'Childrearing Among the Lower Classes of Late Medieval England', in: *The Journal of Interdisciplinary History*, vol. 8, no. 1 (Summer, 1977), pp. 18–19.
71. Statute of Winchester (13 Edw. 1) Michaelmas 1285, in: H. Rothwell, ed., *English Historical Documents 1189–1327* (London: Eyre & Spottiswoode, 1975), pp. 461–462.
72. Statute of Winchester (13 Edw. 1), p. 462.

73. *Rentalia et Customaria Michaeilis de Ambresbury 1235–1252 et Rogeri Ford 1252–1261 Abbatum Beatae Mariae Glastoniae* (Somerset Record Society, 1891), p. 143.
74. See for a discussion of Scot ales: J.M. Bennett, 'Conviviality and Charity in Medieval and Early Modern England', in: *Past and Present*, no. 134 (1992), pp. 20–35.
75. *Rentalia et Customaria Michaeilis de Ambresbury 1235–1252*, p. 143.
76. *Rentalia et Customaria Michaeilis de Ambresbury 1235–1252*, p. 82.
77. J. Amphlett, ed., *Court Rolls of the Manor of Halesowen 1270–1307* (Oxford, Printed for the Worcestershire Historical Society by James Parker, 1912), p. 368.
78. Manor of Halesowen MS Birmingham Archives Wolfson Centre MS 3279/346328.
79. D. Noy, ed. and trans., *Winslow Manor Court Books Part I 1327–1377*, Buchkinghamshire Record Society, no. 35 (2011), p. 24.
80. P. Foden, ed. and trans., *Records of the Manor of Norton in the Liberty of St. Albans, 1244–1539*, vol. 29 (Caxton Hill, Hertford: Hertfordshire Record Publications, 2014), pp. 135–136.
81. J. Amphlett, ed., *Court Rolls of the Manor of Halesowen 1270–1307*, p. 52.
82. Manor of Halesowen MS Birmingham Archives/Wolfson Centre, September 1316.
83. 'The Lytylle Childrenes Lytil Boke', and 'The Young Childrens Book', in: F.J. Furnivall, ed., *The Babees Book, The Bokes of Nurture* (London: Early English Text Society, 1868), p. 16 and p. 17.
84. F.J. Furnivall, ed., *The Babees Book*, pp. 48–52.
85. See for example on this topic: T. Fenster and D.L. Smail, 'Introduction', in: T. Fenster and D.L. Smail, eds., *Fama: The Politics of Talk and Reputation in Medieval Europe* (London: Conell University Press, 2003), pp. 1–14; S. Bardsley, 'Sin, Speech and Scolding in Late Medieval England', in: T. Fenster and D.L. Smail, eds., *Fama: The Politics of Talk and Reputation in Medieval Europe*, pp. 145–165.
86. The phrase used is: 'Thomas de Eyxherst venit and petit nutricturam', in: L.R. Poos and L. Bonfield, eds., *Select Cases in Manorial Courts 1250–1550, Property and Family Law*, Selden Society, vol. CXIV (London, 1998), p. 150.
87. J. Amphlett, ed., *Court Rolls of the Manor of Halesowen 1270–1307*, pp. 53–54.
88. J. Amphlett, ed., *Court Rolls of the Manor of Halesowen 1270–1307*, pp. 53–54.
89. R. Lock, ed., *The Court Rolls of Walsham le Willows, 1303–1350* (Woodbridge: Boydell & Brewer and Suffolk Record Society, vol. xli, 1998), p. 109.
90. J. Lister, ed., *Court Rolls of the Manor of Wakefield, 1315–1317* (Yorkshire Archaeological Society, vol. IV, 1930), p. 114.

91. H. Jewel, *The Court Rolls of the Manor of Wakefield from September 1348–September 1350*, Yorkshire Archaeological Society, Second Series, vol. II, p. 189.
92. H. Jewel, *The Court Rolls of the Manor of Wakefield from September 1348–September 1350*, p. 80.
93. D. Noy, ed. and trans., *Winslow Manor Court Books, vol. I 1327–1377*, p. 229.
94. D. Noy, ed. and trans., *Winslow Manor Court Books, Part II 1423–1460*, Buckinghamshire Record Society, no. 36 (2011), p. 606.
95. Glastonbury Abbey Records at Longleat, MS 11179 no. 31. For a detailed discussion of the case and the event of the revolt see: M. Müller, 'The Aims and Organisation of an Early Fourteenth Century Revolt in Wiltshire', in *Rural History*, ...
96. See for example: H. Montgomery, *An Introduction to Childhood: Anthropological Perspectives on Children's Lives* (Oxford: Wiley-Blackwell, 2009), p. 53.
97. H. Montgomery, *An Introduction to Childhood*, p. 214.
98. S. Shahar, *Childhood in the Middle Ages*, p. 22.
99. See for example: P.J.P. Goldberg, *Women in England c. 1275–1525* (Manchester University Press, 1995), p. 10. For contested marriages, including due to age of at least one of the parties, see for example: P.J.P. Goldberg, *Women in England*, pp; S. McSheffrey, ed., Love and Marriage in Late Medieval London (Kalamazoo, MI: Published for TEAMS the Consortium for the Teaching of the Middle Ages; Medieval Institute Publications, 1995).
100. M. Holford, 'Testimony (to Some Extent Fictitious)': Proofs of Age in the First Half of the Fifteenth Century', in: *Historical Research*, vol. 82, no. 218 (November 2009), pp. 635–654.
101. P.J.P. Goldberg, ed., *Women in England, c. 1275–125,* pp. 58–81.
102. For discussions on communal memory see especially J. Fentress and C. Wickham, *Social Memory, New Perspectives on the Past* (Blackwell Publishers, Oxford, 1992), esp. pp. 26ff.
103. D. Noy, ed. and trans., *Winslow Court Books Part I 1327–1377*, p. 75.
104. D. Noy, ed. and trans., *Winslow Court Books Part I 1327–1377*, p. 97.
105. Court Rolls of the Manor of Eldersfield, Worcester Archives, BA 1531/69.
106. S. Shahar, *Childhood in the Middle Ages*, pp. ADD, and a more recent discussion of these issues can be found in: H. Dawson, *Unearthing Late Medieval Children, Health, Status and Burial Practice in Southern England* (BAR British Series 593, 2014), pp. 15–16. See also for a discussion of the evidence B.A. Hanawalt, 'The Child in the Middle Ages and the Renaissance', in: W. Koops and M. Zuckerman, eds., *Beyond the Century of the Child; Cultural History and Developmental Psychology* (University of Pennsylvania Press, 2003), pp. 24–33.

107. H. Montgomery, *An Introduction to Childhood: Anthropological Perspectives on Children's Lives* (Oxford: Wiley-Blackwell, 2009), p. 53.
108. H. Montgomery, *An Introduction to Childhood*, pp. 56–61.
109. Such perceptions are intertwined with the idea of childhood as a stage of development and growth. See for example: M. Woodhead and H. Montgomery, eds., *Understanding Childhood an Interdisciplinary Approach* (Chichester: John Wiley & Sons Ltd/The Open University, 2003), esp. Chapters 3 and 4; see also W.A. Corsaro, *The Sociology of Childhood*, Fourth Edition (London, Los Angeles, New Delhi, Singapore, Washington, DC, 2014), pp. 6–10.
110. See also on this E. Clark's discussion in her 'The Custody of Children in English Manor Courts', in: *Law and History Review*, vol. 3, no. 2 (Autumn, 1985), p. 341.
111. H. Montgomery, *An Introduction to Childhood*, p. 54.
112. See for a discussion of this: S. Shahar, *Childhood in the Middle Ages*, p. 28.
113. S. Shahar, *Childhood in the Middle Ages*, p. 28.
114. S. Shahar, *Childhood in the Middle Ages*, p. 28.
115. Again, anthropology can be instructive here. See for example the discussion concerning Initiation and ritual in H. Montgomery, *An Introduction to Childhood*, pp. 214ff.
116. Z. Razi, *Life, Marriage and Death in a Medieval Parish Economy, Society and Demography in Halesowen 1270–1400* (Cambridge: Cambridge University Press, 1980), p. 61.
117. J. Amphlett, ed., *Court Rolls of the Manor of Halesowen 1270–1307*, p. 226.
118. Worcester Archives, BA 1531/69 B.
119. D. Noy, ed. and trans., *Winslow Manor Court Books Part I 1327–1377*, pp. 111–112 and p. 121.
120. *Statutes of the Realm*, volume I (London, 1810), p. 228.
121. E. Clark, 'The Custody of Children in English Manor Courts', p. 347.
122. L.R. Poos and L. Bonfield, eds., *Select Cases in Manorial Courts 1250–1550, Property and Family Law*, Selden Society, vol. CXIV (London, 1998), pp. 148–149.
123. L.R. Poos and L. Bonfield, eds., *Select Cases in Manorial Courts 1250–1550*, 'Introduction', p. cxxxiv.
124. D. Noy, ed. and trans., *Winslow Manor Court Books Part I 1327–1377*, p. 37.
125. D. Noy, ed. and trans., *Winslow Manor Court Books Part I 1327–1377*, p. 48.
126. *Henrici de Bracton de Legibus et Consuetudinibus Angliae*, ed., Travers Twiss, vol. 2 (London, 1879), p. 5.

127. R.M. Smith, Müller, see also for a fuller discussion of these issues part III.
128. M. Müller, 'Peasant Women, Agency and Status in Mid—Thirteenth to Late—Fourteenth Century England: Some Reconsiderations', in: C. Beattie and M. F. Stevens, eds., *Married Women and the Law in Premodern Northwest Europe* (Boydell Press, 2013), pp. 91–114.
129. E. Clark, 'The Custody of Children in English Manor Courts', p. 347.
130. D. Noy, ed. and trans., *Winslow Manor Court Books Part I 1327–1377*, pp. 221–240.
131. D. Noy, ed. and trans., *Winslow Manor Court Books Part I 1327–1377*, p. 221.
132. D. Noy, ed. and trans., *Winslow Manor Court Books Part I 1327–1377*, p. 226.
133. D. Noy, ed. and trans., *Winslow Manor Court Books Part I 1327–1377*, p. 235.
134. D. Noy, ed. and trans., *Winslow Manor Court Books Part I 1327–1377*, p. 234.
135. See for example: C. Lewis, 'Children's Play in the Later Medieval English Countryside', in: *Childhood in the Past*, 2 (2009), p. 88; and B.A. Hanawalt, B.A. Hanawalt, 'Childrearing Among the Lower Classes of Late Medieval England', in: *The Journal of Interdisciplinary History*, vol. 8, no. 1 (1977), pp. 18–19.

Bibliography

Primary Sources

Records of the Manor of Elderfield: The Hive, Worcester Archives, BA 1531/69 (A and B).

Glastonbury Abbey Records held at Longleat House, sourced from microfilm, held by the University of Birmingham.

Halesowen Manor Court Rolls, Birmingham Library and Archive, Wolfson Centre.

Heacham Manor Court Rolls, sourced from microfilm held at the Norfolk Record Office, Le Strange Collection, MS DA1.

J. Amphlett, *Court Rolls of the Manor of Hales 1272–1307*, Part I (Worcestershire Record Society, Oxford, 1910).

P. Foden, ed. and trans., *Records of the Manor of Norton in the Liberty of St. Albans, 1244–1539*, vol. 29 (Caxton Hill, Hertford: Hertfordshire Record Publications, 2014).

F.J. Furnivall, ed., *The Babees Book, the Bokes of Nurture* (London: Early English Text Society, 1868).

P.J.P. Goldberg, *Women in England c. 1275–1525* (Manchester: Manchester University Press, 1995).
H. Jewel, *The Court Rolls of the Manor of Wakefield from September 1348–September 1350* (Yorkshire Archaeological Society, Second Series, vol. II, 1981).
J. Lister, ed., *Court Rolls of the Manor of Wakefield, 1315–1317*, vol. IV (Yorkshire Archaeological Society, 1930).
R. Lock, ed., *The Court Rolls of Walsham le Willows, 1303–1350* (Woodbridge: Boydell & Brewer and Suffolk Record Society, vol. xli, 1998).
R. Lock, *The Court Rolls of Walsham le Willows 1351–1399* (Woodbridge: Boydell Press and Suffolk Record Society, vol. xlv, 2002).
D. Noy, ed. and trans., *Winslow Manor Court Books Part I 1327–1377*, Buckinghamshire Record Society, no. 35 (2011).
Rentalia et Customaria Michaeilis de Ambresbury 1235–1252 et Rogeri Ford 1252–1261 Abbatum Beatae Mariae Glastoniae (Somerset Record Society, 1891).
Henrici de Bracton de Legibus et Consuetudinibus Angliae, ed., Travers Twiss (London, vol. 2, 1879).
L.R. Poos and L. Bonfield, eds., *Select Cases in Manorial Courts 1250–1550, Property and Family Law*, Selden Society (London: Selden Society, vol. CXIV, 1998).
H. Rothwell, ed., *English Historical Documents 1189–1327* (London: Eyre & Spottiswoode, 1975).

Secondary Sources Books

P. Ariés, *Centuries of Childhood* (New York: Alfred A. Knopf, 1962).
W.O. Ault, *Open Field Farming in Medieval England: A Study in Village By-Laws* (London: Allen and Unwin, 1972).
M. Bailey, *The English Manor c. 1200–c. 1500* (Manchester: Manchester University Press, 2002).
A.V. Chayanov, *The Theory of Peasant Economy*, eds., D. Thorner, B. Kerblay, R.E.F. Smith (Homewood, IL: American Economic Association, R.D. Irwing, 1966).
W.A. Corsaro, *The Sociology of Childhood*, Fourth Edition (London, Los Angeles, New Delhi, Singapore, Washington, DC: Sage, 2014).
H. Dawson, *Unearthing Late Medieval Children, Health, Status and Burial Practice in Southern England* (BAR British Series 593, 2014).
C. Dyer, *Standards of Living in the Later Middle Ages, Social Change in England c. 1200–1520* (Cambridge: Cambridge University Press, 1989).
C. Dyer, *Making a Living in the Middle Ages the People of Britain 850–1520* (New Haven and London: Yale University Press, 2002).
J. Fentress and C. Wickham, *Social Memory, New Perspectives on the Past* (Oxford: Blackwell Publishers, 1992).

B.A. Hanawalt, *The Ties That Bound, Peasant Families in Medieval England* (New York, Oxford: Oxford University Press, 1986).
B.A. Hanawalt, *Growing Up in Medieval London The Experience of Childhood in History* (Oxford and New York: Oxford University Press, 1993).
A.E. Levett, *Studies in Manorial History*, eds., H.M. Cam, M. Coate, and L.S. Sutherland (Oxford: Clarendon Press, 1938).
M.K. McInosh, *Controlling Misbehaviour in England, 1370–1600* (Cambridge: Cambridge University Press, 2009).
S. McSheffrey, ed., *Love and Marriage in Late Medieval London* (Kalamazoo, MI: Published for TEAMS the Consortium for the Teaching of the Middle Ages; Medieval Institute Publications, 1995).
H. Montgomery, *An Introduction to Childhood: Anthropological Perspectives on Children's Lives* (Oxford: Wiley-Blackwell, 2009).
N. Orme, *Medieval Children* (New Haven, London: Yale University Press, 2001).
L.R. Poos, *A Rural Society After the Black Death Essex 1350–1525* (Cambridge: Cambridge University Press, 1991).
Z. Razi, *Life, Marriage and Death in a Medieval Parish Economy, Society and Demography in Halesowen 1270–1400* (Cambridge: Cambridge University Press, 1980).
P.R. Schofield, *Peasant and Community in Medieval England 1200–1500* (Basingstoke: Palgrave Macmillan, 2003).
S. Shahar, *Childhood in the Middle Ages* (London and New York: Routledge, 1992).
M. Woodhead and H. Montgomery, eds., *Understanding Childhood an Interdisciplinary Approach* (Chichester: John Wiley and Sons and the Open University, 2003).

Secondary Sources Articles and Chapters

S. Bardsley, 'Women's Work Reconsidered; Gender and Wage Differentiation in Late Medieval England', in: *Past and Present*, vol. 165 (November 1999), pp. 3–29.
S. Bardsley, 'Sin, Speech and Scolding in Late Medieval England', in: T. Fenster and D.L. Smail, eds., *Fama: The Politics of Talk and Reputation in Medieval Europe* (London: Conell University Press, 2003), pp. 145–165.
J.M. Bennett, 'Conviviality and Charity in Medieval and Early Modern England', in: *Past and Present*, vol. 134 (1992), pp. 19–41.
E. Clark, 'The Custody of Children in English Manor Courts', in: *Law and History Review*, vol. 3, no. 2 (Autumn, 1985), pp. 333–348.
E. Clark, 'Social Welfare and Mutual Aid in the Medieval Countryside', in: *Journal of British Studies*, vol. 33, no. 4 (1994), pp. 381–406.
C. Dyer, 'Power and Conflict in the Medieval English Village', in: C. Dyer, ed., *Everyday Life in Medieval England* (London: Hambledon Press and London, 2000), pp. 1–13.

M. Eccleston, 'Mortality of Rural Landless Men Before the Black Death: The Glastonbury Head Tax Lists', in: *Local Population Studies*, vol. 63 (Autumn, 1999), pp. 6–29.

T. Fenster and D.L. Smail, 'Introduction', in: T. Fenster and D.L. Smail, eds., *Fama: The Politics of Talk and Reputation in Medieval Europe* (London: Conell University Press, 2003), pp. 1–14.

H. Fox, 'The Exploitation of the Landless by Lords and Tenants in Early Medieval England', in: Z. Razi and R.M. Smith, eds., *Medieval Society and the Manor Court* (1996), pp. 518–568.

R. Goddard, 'Female Apprenticeships in the West Midlands in the Later Middle Ages', in: *Midlands History*, vol. 27, no. 1 (2002), pp. 165–181.

P.J.P. Goldberg, 'Masters and Men in Later Medieval England', in: D. M. Hadley, ed., *Masculinity in Medieval Europe* (London and New York: Routledge, 1999), pp. 56–70.

P.J.P. Goldberg, 'What Was a Servant?', in: A. Curry and E. Matthew, eds., *Concepts and Patterns of Service in the Later Middle Ages* (Woodbridge: The Boydell Press, 2000), pp. 1–20.

B.A. Hanawalt, 'Childrearing Among the Lower Classes of Late Medieval England', in: *The Journal of Interdisciplinary History*, vol. 8, no. 1 (Summer, 1977), pp. 1–22.

B.A. Hanawalt, 'The Child in the Middle Ages and the Renaissance', in: W. Koops and M. Zuckerman, eds., *Beyond the Century of the Child: Cultural History and Developmental Psychology* (Philadelphia: University of Pennsylvania Press, 2003), pp. 21–42.

M. Holford, 'Testimony (to Some Extent Fictitious)': Proofs of Age in the First Half of the Fifteenth Century', in: *Historical Research*, vol. 82, no. 218 (November 2009), pp. 635–654.

A.E. Levett, 'The Courts and Court Rolls of St. Albans Abbey', in: *Transactions of the Royal Historical Society*, vol. 7 (1924), pp. 52–76.

C. Lewis, 'Children's Play in the Later Medieval English Countryside' in: *Childhood in the Past*, vol. 2, no. 1 (2009), pp. 86–108.

M. Lewis, 'Work and the Adolescent in Medieval England ad 900–1550: The Osteological Evidence', in: *Medieval Archaeology*, vol. 60, no. 1 (2016), pp. 138–171.

M. Müller, 'A Divided Class? Peasants and Peasant Communities in Later Medieval England', in: C. Dyer et al., eds., *Rodney Hilton's Middle Ages* (*Past and Present Supplement* 2. Oxford: Oxford University Press, 2007), pp. 115–120.

M. Müller, 'Conflict and Revolt: The Bishop of Ely and His Peasants at the Manor of Brandon in Suffolk ca. 1300–1381', in: *Rural History*, vol. 23, no. 1 (April 2012). pp. 1–19.

M. Müller, 'Peasant Women, Agency and Status in Mid-Thirteenth to Late-Fourteenth Century England: Some Reconsiderations', in: C. Beattie

and M.F. Stevens, eds., *Married Women and the Law in Premodern Northwest Europe* (Woodbridge: Boydell Press, 2013), pp. 91–114.
M. Müller, 'The Aims and Organisation of an Early Fourteenth Century Revolt in Wiltshire', in: *Rural History*, vol. 14, no. 1 (2002), pp. 1–20.
M. Müller, 'Social Control and the Hue and Cry in Two Fourteenth Century Villages', in: *Journal of Medieval History*, vol. 31, no. 1 (2005), pp. 29–53.
Z. Razi and R.M. Smith, 'The Historiography of Manorial Court Rolls', in: Z. Razi and R.M. Smith, eds., *Medieval Society and the Manor Court* (Oxford: Oxford University Press, 1996), pp. 1–12.
C. Wickham, 'Gossip and Resistance Among Medieval Peasants', in: *Past and Present*, vol. 160, no. 1 (August 1998), pp. 3–24.
N. Zemon-Davis, 'The Reasons for Misrule: Youth Groups and Charivaris in Sixteenth-Century France', in: *Past & Present*, vol. 50, no. 1 (1971), pp. 41–75.

CHAPTER 3

Inheritance, Rights and Goods

1 Heirs, Rights and Communities

In April 1349 the Black Death was still taking its toll at the Buckinghamshire manor of Winslow, when William Harry lying on his deathbed surrendered half a virgate of land into the hands of the lord to be granted to his son John, who was merely 8 years old. The child was to hold the land at the will of the lord, 'by the rod'—indicating the obscure ritual whereby land was transferred symbolically by the lord to the tenant, with each side holding one end of a rod, in villeinage. However, as John was underage the payment of the fine was respited until he was to reach maturity. Until then custody was granted to Ralph Harry 'by reason of the said John being underage'.[1] The property transfer pre-mortem of William was important, as the next entry in the Court Book of Winslow makes it clear that both William and his wife Alice died, and their villein holding of 1 virgate of land and a messuage was automatically inherited by their eldest son Richard, who was of full age, paid a heriot of two valuable oxen, swore fealty and entered the holding.

The simple entry in the manor court, so factual and devoid of emotion actually illustrates a very common fourteenth-century human tragedy. With the plague ravaging his village, William must have realised that both he and his wife were going to die, and therefore it is highly likely that they were already suffering symptoms of the plague. In order to safeguard the future of their younger son John, they conducted the

M. Müller, *Childhood, Orphans and Underage Heirs in Medieval Rural England*, Palgrave Studies in the History of Childhood,
https://doi.org/10.1007/978-3-030-03602-7_3

land transfer and probably also arranged the guardianship to Harry. The lion's share of the inheritance still went to their firstborn son Richard, but without their parents' intervention John, according to the custom of male primogeniture, would have been left with nothing.

The adoption of such partible inheritance strategies where male primogeniture was the norm has been observed in several medieval English rural communities.[2] Fundamentally it demonstrates concern by parents to provide for non-inheriting siblings, and would have softened the blow of a harsh custom which would have otherwise left non-inheriting siblings landless and potentially poverty-stricken. In order for such strategies to be effective, portions of parental land had to be transmitted to non-inheriting siblings in pre-mortem transfers, either on the deathbed or before, in order to have validity. It is rarely seen in such dramatic circumstances though involving transfer of land to a very young child. Recorded transfers of land as deathbed surrenders, while not unheard of before, become more common from the later fourteenth century onwards.[3]

A similar case is recorded in Winslow, though considerably later in 1423, when John Taylor 'lying on his deathbed' surrendered via the hands of the lord a messuage and a virgate of land for Robert, John's son. The boy was a minor and the wardship of both child and land were granted to Geoffrey Taylor until the coming of age of Robert.[4] Again the choice of guardian was not left to chance or the decision of the community in this case, as the dying father made arrangements for his young child on his deathbed. Such surrenders were considered inalienable and binding. As they were conducted in front of witnesses, their performative aspect safeguarded the future well-being and care of the child and their inheritance in question. The guardian had entered clear contractual obligations in front of the dying and witnesses.

23 years later the same family with the same holding re-appeared in similar circumstances in the Court Book. Robert Taylor, now a man between about the age of 27 and 31 was on his own deathbed and surrendered his holding of one virgate to his oldest son John, who was 6 years old, and was presumably named after Robert's father, John Taylor. He also employed a partible strategy, by handing a smallholding of five and a half acres to his younger son Thomas who was only 4 years old. Guardianship was granted to Joan, Robert's widow, but, it was also noted that if Thomas was to die before coming of age, the land was to revert to his older brother John, and similarly if John should die, the virgate should go to his younger brother Thomas.[5]

Such pre-mortem arrangements are often moving, especially when they were conducted under such desperate circumstances as the Black Death. Such entries also often allow insights into the worries and concerns of the villagers of later medieval England. Children were seen to represent the future, and their parents' hopes for the future. While they might not have been viewed as carriers of lineage in the same way as offspring were in aristocratic households, the survival of family and inheritance was still considered important. Yet rarely do we see as clear an indication of such sentiments as we do in a case recorded at Winslow in 1450. John Pycot surrendered on his deathbed a shop in the butcher's market of Wynslow together with a small plot of land to Joan, his widow and their daughter Agnes and Agnes' heirs. Various possibilities of what the future might hold were weighed up, and it was noted that just in case Agnes were to die without legitimate heirs herself, the shop and plot were to revert to John's collateral heirs. Yet, the hopes and fears of John and Joan for the future of their daughter Agnes were summed up in the simple note that 'may it not happen'.[6]

Child mortality in medieval communities was high, especially among poorer families, who tended to have fewer surviving children than better off families in rural communities, especially before the arrival of the Black Death.[7] Accordingly Razi found that at the manor of Halesowen substantial tenants holding a virgate or more tended to have larger families and 53% more children than their poorer neighbours who were smallholders.[8] As such families often felt the need to plan ahead for the eventuality that their heirs might not survive, and further lines of inheritance needed to be established for the court. In April 1349 in Winslow Ralph, the 12-year-old heir of William King and his inheritance of one messuage and a virgate of land were handed over to the vicar of Greneburgh. The uncertainty of that year speaks through the court records, as it is noted that should Ralph die within the next 5 years, the holding was to go to his next younger brother Walter, and should he die as well it should then pass to his sister Agnes, 'to hold for themselves or either of them who survives'.[9] The line of inheritance thus established, with the children lined up according to custom, and the hope expressed was survival of at least one of them.

Similar considerations can be seen at work in Halesowen, where in January 1338 Roger de Walloceshale, a villein of the lord died, leaving behind his widow Christina and four daughters, aged 10, 8, 5 and 2. The spacing of the children between 2 and 3 years apart is remarkable and may indeed be a reflection of the use of contraceptive methods. This may have included the natural contraceptive effect of breastfeeding children beyond one year until their second year.[10] Cessation of breastfeeding of infants between one and two years of age has also been suggested following isotopic analysis of skeletal remains at Wharram Percy, the consistency of which also indicates local cultural conventions in transitioning infants to a diet of purely solid foods by the age of two.[11] A recent 'stable isotope ratio analysis of rib fragments' based on skeletal remains of 51 children at the urban site of Fishergate House Cemetary in York similarly found that breastfeeding continued there 'until around the age of 1.5 years of age', with a 'fully weaned state at around 2 years of age'.[12] This may indicate that weaning at the age of 2 was not a custom which was particular to rural society. Such weaning patterns were furthermore confirmed in a more recent study which examined the wear on the tooth enamel of the skeletal remains of children.[13]

In the case of Roger de Walloceshale's inheritance, the guardianship over the land and the girls was granted to Christina, who paid the lord 10s., in order to have custody over the land and her daughters 'until the full age of whoever of them shall attain full age..'[14] While it may have been hoped that all of the girls should survive to adulthood, it was clearly expected that some of them might not.

Much earlier in a similar case in 1279, the widow of Thomas de Monte, Clementia paid the lord 20s to be granted the guardianship over Thomas' son and heir Richard 'until his full age or to the full age of his brother, Thomas, should Richard die before coming of age'.[15] The concern of the community and the lord's representative was to establish in front of the witnesses attending the manor court once again, the correct line of inheritance, and for this to be noted down in the manorial court roll, which might be relied upon in an inheritance dispute in years to come. In this case, it was established that Richard was the eldest son and according to male primogeniture the holding was his by right and in the case of premature mortality the inheritance should go to his younger brother.

Any heir's rights to their inheritance were protected and safeguarded as a matter of communal concern. This also included the rights of potential heirs, as the examples above show. In this sense, therefore, younger siblings were far from regarded as unimportant. Legally speaking they were potential heirs, whose rights to the lands and holdings which in the first instance were to go to an older brother or sister, but who were just as safeguarded and protected as those of the first born, principal heir.

Therefore it would not be accurate to assume that manorial courts only cared about the principal heir. They might have been first in line, but in a society where premature death was a common reality of life, communities needed practical solutions for the eventuality of the first heir's demise.

The unusually detailed inventory of goods left behind upon the death of William Lene of Walsham le Willows in 1329, provides further important evidence for the care accorded to non-inheriting children. William Lene was a substantial and clearly prosperous tenant. Upon his death he held a messuage, a cottage, 37 acres of arable land in addition to an acre and 2 roods of meadow, one acre as well as 2 roods of woodland.[16] His principal heirs were his young sons William and Robert, aged 10 and 6, yet his will made on his deathbed also stipulates that his daughters Olivia and Catherine should be given no less than the rather substantial sum of £4 in cash. His 'bastard son' William was to be given a mare and three ewes.[17] Not even his illegitimate son was therefore to go without, who was also fully acknowledged as, indeed, his son.

The lengths communities occasionally went through to protect the rights of children demonstrate the firm rights and ultimately the agency heirs held when it came not just to their holdings, but also the position of their holdings with all the rights, obligations and interests this entailed within wider village affairs. As such, considerations could extend over decisions the village community had to make which may not even have directly impacted on the lands of the heir. In the early fifteenth century at the St. Albans manor of Winslow an inquiry took place in the village of Greneburgh with custodians representing the interests of Ralph Elyot's underaged son and heir John Elyot. John Elyot had been taken under the guardianship of Nicholas Hamond and his wife Joan. The inquiry concerned the fate of 1.5 acres of land which merely abutted to the holding of the heir, but were not actually part of John's inheritance.[18]

The matter deliberated upon concerned two related aspects, Firstly, whether this small plot of land could be enclosed or should remain in common. Secondly, the inquiry sought to ascertain whether a certain road should be in this location or not. The inquiry concluded that the land should remain in common and the road stays where it was to protect the heir's interests and rights. The road, it was stated, had been used in times of fallow 'for animals and carts of tenants', because it 'is a droveway into the fields and had been there since time out of mind'. It was therefore not just the current interests of the heir the communities sought to protect but also potential future ones. The recognition of such potential interest meant that underaged heirs were effectively afforded significant degrees of agency by the community through the mediation of tehri guardian.

The heir's interests were not overridden by the views of the guardian, but rather the guardian's role was the maintenance and the preservation of the inheritance in its entirety, that is not just in land and chattels, and buildings, but also in its associated rights and obligations. In this sense the guardian should not really be seen as acting as the heir's voice; instead their role was one of protection and management. It should also be considered in this context that any actions taken by a guardian regarding the lands and chattels of an underaged heir were reversible upon the young heir's coming of age. Any transfer of goods and services purportedly conducted in the name of the heir could be rescinded.[19] Underaged heirs, whether orphans or not had choices and strong rights. Young heirs were above all given the power to change their minds about almost any decision which they took during their minority over their possessions, although, as we shall see later, this was not without its complications at times. As Elaine Clark, pointed out, it was one of the signs of acquired maturity to be able to make appropriate and rational decisions regarding the inheritance, and to display 'sound judgment'.[20] The ability to make such decisions was occasionally written into the wardship arrangements, as in 1347 in Winslow where the court determined that it was the heir's decision whether to receive from his guardian his inherited chattels in goods or their financial value.[21] Far from being victims of circumstance without rights, in cases such as this we see the potential strength of the position of young heirs, able to influence communal decisions even while being a minor.

The guardians were put in place to look after the heir's inheritance and his or her bodily well-being, but such concerns were also enshrined within the wider umbrella of communal safeguards which acted to stop incursions into any heir's interests or rights by individuals or groups, including, potentially at least the guardians themselves. As such the child heir's interests are accordingly taken into consideration in questions over the communal management of resources—such as concerns over access and communal use of resources, and effectively seen as part of the interests of the whole community. That the heirs themselves were not asked, and could not, for as we have seen underaged heirs were not considered competent to handle their own affairs, therefore did not really disempower him. While John may have been silent in court, the halimot spoke on his behalf.

A similar case can be found at the manor of Methley in 1355. Here a dispute over land between three parties involved young William son of Hugh William, who was underage. The case was 'respited', that is postponed, by the court until such time when William might be deemed to be of full age, because 'it is not found among the customs of the tenants... that an heir below age ought to answer concerning his inheritance, not ought an inquest be taken therein, until such an heir reaches his full age'.[22] While therefore the underaged heir cannot answer, and is thus silenced, their interests are given voice by the community by proxy, through issuing a halt in all proceedings until the heir was to come of age. The heir's agency is therefore mediated and in fact protected, but not undermined. In some respects, one might even suggest that underaged heirs enjoyed greater agency and protection of rights than other children and young people. The particular circumstances of underaged heirs meant that their protected status was the maintenance of the status quo. Children with living parent tenants were potentially more vulnerable to actions of their parents which could lead to their possible disinheritance. Parent tenants could sell and alienate their lands and assets within the confines of manorial custom as they wished. However, guardians were prevented from doing so, or at the very least, communities tried to put safeguards in place to stop guardians impoverishing their wards.

While a fuller discussion of the perils of dealing with underaged heirs and their inheritance will follow, it suffices to say at this stage that young heirs only needed to seek verification of their minority in the case of disputes over parts of their inheritance which they might have alienated during their minority, to regain control over such assets.[23] In the case of land transfers it was up to the recipient of the land to ensure that the person transferring the land was of full age. Child heirs could claim properties back which they had alienated during their minority, while the recipient of such lands could be faced with an amercement payable to the lord for having entered into a land transaction with a minor.

The rights of heirs were accordingly threefold. Firstly, if their parents held customary, villein holdings and the heir him or herself was legitimate, then the heir was considered to have the absolute individual right to the holding, with all the rights and obligations to the lord and the community this entailed. Secondly, this basic right of inheritance bestowed upon the heir an important political and economic role and therefore agency within the village community itself, including, for example, rights to participate—or be represented—in discussions about access roads and common land. This right of communal agency was suspended during the minority, but was inalienable, and non-transferrable, that is, guardians were not in a position to answer for the heir in such cases. Thirdly, the heir had the effective right to be protected from their own ill-advised and 'foolish' or 'incompetent' decisions, due to their lack of experience, by not being considered valid if called into question. Transfers of land and chattels from minors were perilous, as courts would have considered any such transactions de facto null and void when questioned.

While the sum of these factors leaves underaged heirs in medieval villages in rather strongly protected positions, it also raises the questions of what happened to such protective measures upon the decline of customary tenure and feudal relationships within village communities. For, as we have seen, such rights and protections are intrinsically intertwined with the structures of customary tenure, and as such both the concerns of the community as well as lordship. Before considering the implications of long-term socio-economic change in the English countryside from the second half of the fourteenth century onwards, we need to consider the material inheritances which were recorded for child heirs.

2 Chattels, Buildings and Material Culture

Entries in manorial courts which detail the inheritance and duties of incoming underaged heirs and their guardians can give us important insights not only into the rights—protected by custom and in communal safeguarding of child heirs, but also the structures of rural settlements and the material culture of later medieval peasant families. Most entries regarding inheritances are quite formulaic and repetitive. They note the name of the tenant who died, their holding, usually the size of his holding, and the name of the heir to the holding. Not infrequently the age of the heir is given alongside various provisos and warnings to guardians to perform services and dues falling upon the tenement. The heriot, or death duty, collected from the family by the lord also often recorded, alongside the payment collected by the lord from the guardian in order to have the term of the guardianship.

From the perspective of the guardian therefore, the wardship contract involved looking after the heir or heirs to the holding alongside a temporary addition to their own lands for a period of years, which could span from a few months to the best part of 20 years in length, depending on when the heir or heirs were to reach the age of majority.

The responsibilities involved were therefore serious, often substantial and occasionally long term.

The details gleaned about the inheritances recorded range from the very general and non-descript 'a holding', to detailed expositions of how many acres are held in which field, buildings and even, in rare cases, inventories of chattels and other goods the heir would be eventually entitled to. While information has been drawn from all manors in this study, as the court rolls of Walsham le Willows, Winslow, Halesowen and Norton are the most complete, consecutively across the longest time span, they have been predominantly relied upon in the compilation of statistical evidence, which allows for long-term comparison.

As we can see from Table 1, significant numbers of custody arrangements mentioned specific aspects of individual holdings. While one might assume that a general description of an inheritance as 'a holding' would have contained arable land and a house within a messuage, it is interesting that such elements were often picked out as especially noteworthy.[24] The term messuage carried topographical, structural as well as jurisdictional meanings. It would have referred to that plot of land which contained both the domestic dwelling, any other structures or buildings built upon it as well as any smaller plots used as gardens, orchards waste

Table 1 Details of inheritance proportionally mentioned in custody agreements from 1270 to, and including 1348

	Walsham le Willows (%)	*Halesowen (%)*	*Winslow (%)*	*Norton (%)*
Messuage	66.7	6.9	55	33.4
Arable	66.7	10.3	37.9	40
Pasture	–	–	–	–
Meadow	19	–	10.3	–
Buildings	–	20.7	3.4	33.4
Woodland	4.8	3.4	–	–
Chattels (nondescript)	–	3.4	–	–
Cottage	14.3	6.9	6.9	4.8
'Other things'	–	3.4	–	20
Croft	–	–	–	–
Toft	–	–	–	–
Forge			3.4	–
Lead vessel in cottage	–	–	3.4	–
Walls	–	–	–	4.8

heaps or pits.[25] Entries concerning wardships almost always drew a clear distinction between 'houses and buildings', implying different uses of the house (domus) as a residential dwelling and other buildings (edificia) for various agricultural uses, housing of livestock and storage for example. These are often referred to in the same context as other specificities, as part of exhortations to the guardian to look after them appropriately, while effectively acting as an aide memoire for the community that for future reference the holding in question did contain various buildings and other elements which would have seen to add to the value of a tenement.

So Rosaya, the widow of William Everard, who took on the guardianship of William's son William was told to 'maintain the building and other things'. Of the tenement at the manor of Norton in 1273, while in 1275 Joan, the widow of Stephen was told to 'maintain the houses and buildings, nor make waste' for Stephen's heir Agnes.[26] While the guardianship arrangements can therefore give us some insights into the buildings and their probable uses typically found on peasant holdings, specific types of buildings, such as barns, byres, cow sheds or pig sties for example, and their uses are very rarely mentioned, apart from cottages, which almost always also indicated smallholdings.

An exception can be found in Walsham le Willows, where in June 1351 William le Jay was noted to have taken on the guardianship of John the underaged heir of Agnes Sket who had died. William was told to 'maintain the building called the Insethouse, and the new house by the gate, with roofing in as good a condition as he received them or better'.[27] The term 'Insethouse' has been shown to designate a living space for people, also sometimes referred to the 'hall', or chief house, which could sometimes be positioned between two other buildings, and was occasionally constructed of two bays or more.[28]

In Winslow William the son of Richard Chaunesson was set to inherit a fairly substantial holding containing a messuage and half a virgate of land. Perhaps in accordance with a larger holding the buildings found within it included a hall, again the main accommodation for the tenant family, as well as a grange.[29]

Woodland was very rarely mentioned, presumably because some access to woodland was regulated through commons, but where woods played an important part in the local economy, as it clearly did in Winslow and Halesowen, references to woodland occasionally occur. Simon le Smith of Winslow left his son John a smallholding which included a forge, indicating that his surname was a descriptor of his occupation and probably the presumption that in due time his son might follow into his footsteps.[30] When Matthew Miller died in 1330 and his older daughter Agnes took on the guardianship of her younger brother John, the custody arrangement very explicitly noted that she was to be held accountable 'for a lead vessel which is fixed in the ground of the cottage'.[31] Such vessels are most likely to have been used either in brewing or wool or cloth dyeing as dye baths, and not only marked the holdings in which they were contained as special or different, but also increased their value to the heir in question.

If we consider Table 2, we find that from the arrival of the Black Death onwards the level of detail contained in custody arrangements is starting to decline in some places. At Halesowen nearly 21% of entries used to contain details of buildings other than cottages before the Black Death, yet only 9% did so thereafter. At Walsham le Willows there was a 26% decline in the number of messuages mentioned, while no cottages and no woodland were noted at all anymore. A different picture emerges however from the two manors held by the very conservative lord, the Abbot of St. Albans. At Winslow the proportionate number of entries mentioning messuages and arable land rose post-Black Death,

Table 2 Details of inheritance mentioned in post-Black Death custody arrangements

	Walsham le Willows (%)	*Halesowen (%)*	*Winslow (%)*	*Norton (%)*
Messuage	40	9	68.6	60
Arable	60	9	47.1	26.7
Pasture	10	9	–	–
Meadow	10	9	9.8	–
Buildings	10	9	–	–
Woodland	–	–	–	–
Chattels (nondescript)	–	–	–	–
Cottage	–	9	37.3	20
'Other things'	–	–	–	–
Croft	–	–	–	27
Toft	10	9	–	13.4
Walls	–	–	–	–
Forge	–	–	–	–

and at Norton both the number of messuages and cottages mentioned increased quite significantly.

One important aspect in these developments is that the Abbot of St. Albans was keen to maintain pre-Black Death tenurial structures, which were essentially unfree, customary holdings across his estates, which caused a significant amount of friction with his tenantry.[32] In many other manors tenurial changes, especially shifts from unfree, customary tenure to leaseholds, often as a direct result of tenant pressure to move away from traditional villein—customary—forms of tenure, resulted in a decline of the importance of customary tenures.[33] Fundamentally, leaseholds did not automatically include a right of inheritance; they were often, especially in the later fourteenth century fairly short agreements spanning only a few years or the lifespan of the current leaseholder.[34] Significantly they fall outside of the remit of the traditional arrangements of customary (unfree) tenure, which involved a right to inherit and also the careful monitoring of all transfers of the land between tenants via the hands of the lord, arranged through the manorial court. These developments in changing relationships and terms of tenure, therefore indicate a decline in the concomitant custody arrangements in the case of child heirs. This does not mean that there were fewer child heirs or that no guardians were found for them. It does however mean that such matters did not concern the lord directly anymore in most cases and hence made few appearances in the manorial court as leasehold tenures gained ground.

The type of 'other things' mentioned in some custody cases remains obscure and nondescript in most cases. However, such items were sometimes listed in inventories, akin to wills, and give some important insights into the types of goods which might have been typically found in rural household of the fourteenth century, and considered valuable or important enough to be mentioned as left to heirs. Again, a fundamental reason for such lists was for the family and the community to ensure that the heir or heirs would eventually receive all the items to which they were entitled as heirs to the holdings. Listing various goods, chattels, alongside building and occasionally livestock represented therefore the cementing of a contractual understanding and agreement of all that was owed to the heir upon their reaching the age of majority. In many cases the value of items and livestock was also recorded, presumably to allow the like for like recompense of such possessions if these were no longer available when the heir was old enough to enter their holding. This was occasionally spelled out. In 1446 Robert Taylour on his deathbed stipulated that his widow Joan was to have the guardianship over his two young sons, of whom John at age 6 was the eldest son. He also requested that 'Joan is to deliver to the aforementioned John when he comes of age the principle items written below. ...'[35] Clearly such inventories were therefore a safety measure, with peasants insisting that they should be set down in writing in the manorial court roll. Such detailed lists are rare to say the least. In total only 8 such lists of goods have survived from the manors of this study pertaining to underaged heirs, of which only two dates from the early fourteenth century, the remainder date to the late fourteenth or even the early fifteenth century.

Nonetheless, the lists do allow some important insights into the material culture of medieval villagers and the value attached to certain goods.

Peasant Inventories have attracted some scholarly attention. In Worcestershire R.K. Field has examined lists of principalia, which contained goods, which incoming tenants took over after the death of the previous head of the household. As such, he argued, these principalia reflected not so much the goods directly owned by the tenants, but rather items which were considered to have belonged to the lord.[36] Therefore such goods were merely in the hands of tenants in de facto ownership. Furthermore, because these represented seigniorial possessions attached to holdings, they would, by definition, have excluded large numbers of chattels and possessions, such as agricultural produce and items, which tenants had purchased or otherwise acquired themselves, including ceramics or earthenware pots, linens, and such like.[37]

Other types of inventories, as studied recently by Briggs and Dyer, contain a much fuller, or even complete lists of peasant possessions and assets.[38] The lists of items to be inherited in this study however, raise some interesting problems. They differ from the principalia lists of peasant goods, but also from the inventories listing all possessions, in that they list only items which seem to have been personal possessions of the deceased head of the household. Seigniorial items which can be identified as clear assets of lords, which were seen by lords as being part of the peasant holdings—namely houses and other buildings—are listed separately and are most commonly the only items listed as pertaining to the incoming heir. These also do not provide very much information of the structure of buildings, chambers, or indeed the number of buildings within a holding.

However, occasionally one can glean a sense of the list of goods being ordered according to location or use alongside the wealth or social standing of individual families. When Robert Taylor of Winslow died in 1446 he held a significant holding containing a virgate of land, he left his eldest son John a list of possessions, starting with a cow valued at 8s. The list of items which followed seem to meander around the holding, including a brass pot, a brass dish, a saw, a chair, a stool, pitchforks, before leading into sleeping quarters, where a 'coverlet and a pair of linen sheets', valued at 2s. 1d, as well as a mattress worth 12d. are mentioned.[39] There is however still little, if any, sense of a separation of different spaces with differing uses, such as sleeping, eating, working, cooking etc. The nature in which such inheritances are recorded therefore confirms that before the fifteenth-century clear separation of work spaces and more private spaces were rare in peasant households.[40] Overall therefore children would have grown up understanding that the entire holding was economically functional, unless they happened to be born in families which were wealthy enough to construct special spatial arrangements with such specifically different uses. The tools of work, trade and agriculture were part of the buildings, including the domestic building, and probably kept in the same spaces which were used for sleeping and eating.[41]

An exception to this general rule can be found in the most elaborate and extensive inventory in our sample of underaged heirs, which comes from the possessions of William Lene of Walsham le Willows, who died in 1329, and whose heirs were William aged 10 and Robert aged 6, who were placed under the custody of William Lene's widow, Hilary.[42] Ray Lock speculates that the reason for the existence of William's inventory was the nature of his death, which may well have been judged as due to unnatural causes; all the same, the context of the inventory rather indicates that it was presumably undertaken as part of a list of possessions to be left to his heirs.[43] That said, there are certainly indications that Lene may have died due to unusual circumstances. The value of a cow trapped in a blaze is noted in the inventory, and very detailed depositions of money and goods to be bestowed to their various children in addition to stipulations regarding alms to be given to the poor on the day of his burial and the expenses of visiting a shrine, probably indicate that William Lene arranged these pre-mortem on his deathbed, perhaps indeed as Locke suggests, following a catastrophic fire which also killed his cow.[44]

Lene's inventory is one of the few indicating chattels in different spaces around his holding. In his Granary are thus listed quantities of wheat, rye, barley, peas and beans alongside oats and malt. In his 'principal house' are listed brass pots containing 7.5 gallons, brass pans, a posnet, a basin and ewer, one board with trestles as well as a chair.[45] Lene, however, was wealthy, and from a child's perspective wealthier neighbours were probably seen as graced with more buildings, different areas of specific uses and a clearer separation between work and private spaces.

In general, most goods left to heirs which were listed in inventories were items which could be classed as household goods, as seen in Table 3. Most commonly recorded were various types of pots, of which brass pots were considered the most valuable, followed by plates and storage items like, coffers, chests, probably for clothing, linens and bedding, or a barrel or basket.[46] Some other items clearly had practical applications, such as a measure or a spinning wheel. Seating is comparatively rarely mentioned; only two chairs and one stool are recorded in our sample, and no table, despite the presence of a table cloth. It is possible that this may in part be a reflection of benches or stools to be considered of such low value that they were not recorded, or that seats, like chairs, were indeed uncommon and status symbols utilised primarily by the head of the household.[47]

Ceramic and earthenware goods are similarly rarely noted, according with findings by Briggs and Field, however, archaeology does suggest that such items were ubiquitous in peasant society, and their relative absence from lists including inventories, may well be indicative of their low value.[48] Similarly, while numerous spindle whorls and loom weights have been found in village sites, these are conspicuous for their absence from such inventories.[49] Conversely, the more valuable equivalent, the spinning wheel, which in this period would have still been a treadle free great wheel, where the wheel had to be turned by hand to twist the yarn and pull it unto the spindle, was indeed listed.

References to any games or toys are absent too, one obscure reference to a 'trinket', perhaps being an exception. However, we know that source survival can deceive us. The households children grew up in would not have been quite so bare and devoid of items used for pleasure and past-time. While a lot of medieval archaeological finds which have been interpreted as toys, and very probably children's toys, have been associated with the upper classes, they are by no means absent from lower status sites.[50] It has been pointed out that the survival chances of cheaply home-made toys, such as rag dolls or items made from wood, precisely the type of items one would imagine village children would have had access

Table 3 Household goods recorded in inventories of underaged heirs across all manors

Item recorded	*Number recorded across court rolls*
Horn	1
Knife	1
Dagger	1
Plate	2
Barrel	4
Coffer	1
Basket	1
Tub	1
Trivet	1
Brass pot	7
Brass pans	2
Bowls	3
Metal pot	1
Pot	1
Brass dish	1
Posnet	1
Basin and ewer	1
Chest	1
Trough	3
Spinning wheel	1
Chair	2
Board with trestles	1
Forms?	3
Stall	1
Stool	1
Measure	1
Coverlet and linen sheet	5
Matrass	1
Supertunic	1
I robe(or shroud?)	1
Table cloths	2
Towels	2
Pestle and mortar	1
12 pound wool	1
Trinket	1
Pieces of pewter	2
Vat	4
Tub	2
Russet cloth 10 yards	1
Griddle	1
Tripod	1

(continued)

Table 3 (continued)

Item recorded	*Number recorded across court rolls*
Iron pan	1
Iron bound bucket	1
Straw baskets	2

to, would be very low, as the material they were made from were highly perishable.[51] Nonetheless, archaeological finds of smaller items, such as flutes and whistles made from bone have also been found in village sites, which young people may well have used.[52] It is also likely that children made use of items which were not directly intended to be used as toys, but would still have offered significant entertainment to them, such as buzzers, which made a noise when swung through the air, especially at high speed, and have been found in village sites, as at Wharram Percy, where some examples were found fashioned from pig bones.[53] Other items more clearly intended for use as toys were found to have been crafted from pewter, including rattles, puppets, and pewter miniature toys as well as miniatures, such as cooking and table wares. While such finds are predominantly associated with urban contexts, some have also been found in rural sites.[54] Dawson refers to a study in Bergen for example, which has identified over 2000 artifacts which were probably used by children, these included toys such as balls, dolls, rattles and small weapons. Medieval toys have also been identified in London, including 'miniaturised household objects.'[55]

The next most common items recorded in the inventories for underaged heirs were tools and items used for agricultural uses. It is perhaps unsurprising that most of the common items recorded in this section were carts, ploughs, or elements of ploughs, namely a coulter and a ploughshare (Table 4).

Animals were only very rarely recorded, and as with any other items, it has to be assumed that if the heir were to outlive the animal inherited they were to be recompensed through the replacement of the animal or paid according to their perceived value. What is not clear, however, is why it was so comparatively uncommon for such livestock to be listed, considering the frequency of tenants and guardians handing over livestock in heriot payments for the same heirs (see Sect. 3). The infrequency of such recorded livestock does therefore not indicate low levels of livestock husbandry (Table 5).

Table 4 Tools recorded in inventories of underaged heirs across all manors

Item recorded	*Number recorded*
Cart	4
Plough	3
Plough bound with iron incl. coulter and share	1
Unshod plough	1
Cart without iron on wheels	1
Ploughshare	1
Coulter	1
Shovel	1
Saw	1
Auger	1
Pitchfork	1
Seedcot	3
Saddle	1
Hane	1
Ladder	3
Traces	1
Harrow	1
Threshing sledge	1
Axe	1
Mattock	1

Table 5 Livestock recorded in inventories of underaged heirs across all manors

Animal recorded	*Number*
Horse	3
Oxen	3
Cow	12
Bullock	2
Calf	3
Stot	2
Filly	1
Sheep	1
Sow	1
Piglets	8
Castrated swine	1
Geese	4
Gander	2
Cockrel	1
Hens	6

Occasionally other items were also listed. Timber and no less than 25 timber rafters, which were part of an inventory of good which eventually were to be handed over to the heir of Geoffrey ate Green of the manor of Winslow were valuable and considered to be worth 3s. (Table 6).[56]

The scarcity of sources detailing such particular inherited goods makes a systematic gender analysis impossible, but it was the case that some tenants left specific items to either their sons or daughters. Towards the end of our period in June 1427, John Mayho distributed his various meagre household goods to his three surviving children. His eldest son was to have his land, alongside 'a very big brass pot', his daughter Joan was to be given two bowls and his daughter Agnes a metal pot, another pot as well as a bowl.[57] Such brass pots could be valuable, in 1446 Robert Taylour of Winslow left a brass pot to his heir which was valued at no less than 3s., while at Norton John the son of William ate Church was set to inherit a brass pot and plate which were valued together 5s., worth more than the entire plough 'with all the apparatus' he was also due to inherit and which was valued at 4s. 4d.[58]

The nature of the surviving inventories is not inclined to tell us much directly about the material culture of children as children. The heirs' material possessions as would pertain to them as adults was a different matter, if considered valuable enough, in monetary or perhaps other terms, such might be listed in inventories. We have therefore plenty—and with the growing body of research, increasing knowledge about the

Table 6 Other items recorded in inventories of underaged heirs across all manors

Items recorded
6 Blocks of timber
25 Timber rafters
1 Bushel of malt
8 Bushels of rye
14 Quarters of oats
1 Bow
24 Arrows
50 Bushels
5 quarters wheat
4 quarters of barley
1 quarter 4 bushels beans and peas
1 quarter 4 bushels of malt
4 Bushels maslin

material cultural environment village children would have grown up in. Much of the material culture of village children was defined by functionality and agricultural production. This does not mean however that children would not have experienced items for joy or entertainment. Yet most children's things bore no directly measurable value to the adult world, and thus slip beneath the radar.

3 Heriots and Livestock

While inventories can give us valuable insights into material goods bequeathed to children and their value, heriots extracted by lords upon the death of the tenants can give us an indication of relative wealth as well as livestock ownership in the families of underaged heirs. Heriots fell due to the manorial lord on unfree holdings when the head of the household, the tenant, died. Precise customs varied according to individual lordship and locality. In most manors the heriot thus taken was the best beast of the household, and on some manors, including the manor of Walsham le Willows, no heriots were collected from households who did not have livestock, even if in theory they would have been liable to pay the due. That this was a customary way of doing things at Walsham was stated in 1318, when William Goche, who was a villein of the lord died and left his holdings to his two young sons John and Peter. No heriot was noted, as 'William had no beasts, therefore he gives no heriot'.[59]

While an absence of a heriot payment at Walsham can therefore be taken as confirmation that the tenant in question had no livestock, or at any rate, any livestock the lord might have been interested in, in other manors different heriot customs prevailed. At Wakefield the lord accepted cash sums in lieu of the heriot payment of an animal. In the famine year of 1316, for example, Richard of Gaukthorp died, leaving his young son Adam over 26 acres of land to inherit upon him reaching majority. The heriot was comprised of a cash payment of 20s. This was the same sum given in heriot payment upon the death of William of the Bothes, in the same year, who left his underaged son 18 acres of land with meadows and buildings to inherit.[60]

The absence of heriot payments in livestock should therefore not automatically be interpreted as a sign of poverty. However, occasionally lower heriot payments were explained in court rolls by poverty of the heir. In 1339 at Wakefield upon the death of William son of Robert, his young son and heir to a messuage and over 18 acres of land only gave a heriot of 5s, 'and no more because he is poor'.[61] Cash flow problems, the absence of chattels and poverty could also be cited as reasons for non-payment of heriots. When John Wyot of Winslow died in the plague year of 1349, and left his single cottage to his 8-year-old daughter Juliana, it was noted that 'his heriot is nothing because poor', and even any other fine normally associated with taken on a custody arrangement was waived in this case.[62]

The Abbots of St. Albans were not particularly picky, but grasping and exploitative when it came to heriot payments, and while livestock payments might have been preferred, other chattels and goods were also accepted, including brass pots, plates and a vat in one case. It is particularly noticeable (see Table 8) that such items tended to be collected in the post-Black Death period, and as such they can be read as a sign of impoverishment immediately following the first arrival of the plague, when, due to very high death rates, and some holdings changing hands repeatedly from heir to heir in a single year, several heriots were collected from single households or families. In April 1349 ten-year-old John Elyot became the heir to his father's holding of a virgate of land. Accordingly a heriot of an ox was rendered to the lord, Isabella Elyot, who was a smallholder also died, John became her heir to three and a half acres of land and a heriot of a cow was given to the lord, Walter Elyot also died, leaving young John Elyot a mere acre of land for which a heriot of a bullock was collected.[63]

While we have seen that items such as brass pots could be valuable, and as valuable as livestock, this was not always the case, and often such items were taken from households which were not wealthy, like the heriot of a brass pot, which was valued at 40d. at the manor of Norton and was given in payment upon the death of John Colyn in 1361 who left his 4-year-old daughter Cecily nothing but a cottage to her name.[64] Similarly no monetary value was even attached to the two plates the Abbot of St. Albans collected in heriot payment when Thomas Olyve died in the same year, leaving his son Thomas a smallholding containing less than 6 acres of land (Tables 7 and 8).[65]

Heriots can nonetheless be a good indicator of the type of animals kept by tenants, and as such also the proportion of young heirs who were wealthy enough to have livestock, and there is significant variation in this across the manors and chronology. At the manor of Winslow before the Black Death no less than 71% of tenants handed over livestock to

Table 7 Types of heriots given at Winslow in per cent

	1327–1348 (%)	*1349–1377 (%)*
Nothing	29	5.9
Cattle	58	66.7
Horses	4	5.8
Pigs	3	2
Sheep	3	9.8
Draught animal	3	2
Chattels	–	7.8

Table 8 Types of heriots given by underaged heirs at the manor of Norton in per cent

	1266–1348 (%)	*1349–1400 (%)*
Money	5.9	11.8
Nothing	58.8	11.8
Cow	5.9	17.6
Oxen	–	–
Bullock	–	5.9
Horses	17.6	23.4
Filly	5.9	–
Draught animal	5.9	–
Sheep	–	5.9
Plates	–	11.8
Brass pots	–	11.8

the lord in heriot payments, after the Black Death this proportion rose to 86.3%. This means that the vast majority of underaged heirs were wealthy enough to own livestock, and most of those would have counted cattle as their most valuable animals. Of all animals given in heriots at Winslow before the Black Death 81.8% were cattle, making up 58% of all heriots given, after the Black Death it was 67%. Cows and Oxen topped the list (see Table 9) across the period, with cows highly valued for dairy production and oxen as a valuable draught animal.

The sentiment that cattle were very highly valued, especially cows and oxen, is reflected in the monetary value which was often attached to heriot payments. (see Table 10) While it is impossible, due to comparatively small sample of heriots across the period, to extract more detailed information of movement of values and prices of livestock, it is notable that the value of all livestock associated with underaged heirs appears to have declined in Winslow in the second half of the fourteenth century.[66]

Table 9 Cattle heriots by underaged heirs at Winslow

	1327–1348 (%)	*1349–1377 (%)*
Cows	44	35
Oxen	33	53
Bullock	17	3
Heiffer	6	3
Calf	–	6

Table 10 Average values of livestock and other possessions given in heriot payments at the manor of Winslow by underaged heirs

	1327–1348	*1349–1377*
Cow	8s. 6d.	4s. 5d.
Oxen	7s.	5s. 8d.
Bullock	4s. 5d.	1s.
Horse	10s.	4s. 2d.
Calf	–	4d obulus
Heifer	10s.	8s.
Sheep	10d.	4d quarter
Pigs/ piglets	2s.	8d.
Vat	–	6d.
Brass pots	–	1s. 10d.

However, this was not the pattern repeated across all manors. Dyer has previously noted that prices of livestock tended to hold up much more steadily across the later fourteenth and into the fifteenth century, than cereal crops.[67] Certainly at the manor of Norton livestock prices do not seem to have declined.

Surviving data at the manor or Norton is not as plentiful as it is for Winslow, and here heirs were less likely to hand over livestock in heriots. Before the Black Death 35% of heriots at the manor were comprised of livestock, with horses more important than cattle (see Table 7) before 1349, and about equally important after the arrival of the Black Death. However, as at Winslow, post-Black Death livestock ownership appears to have risen at the manor when 50% of heriots were comprised of livestock. One might expect increasing numbers of livestock given in heriots from the second half of the fourteenth century onwards due to the now well-established expansion in pastoral agriculture post-Black Death. This was stimulated both by a reflection of increasing labour costs, especially associated with arable agriculture, and rising consumer demand of meat and dairy products in the period (Table 11).[68]

Table 11 Average and individual values of livestock and other goods given in heriot payment by underaged heirs at the manor of Norton

	1266–1348	*1349–1400*
Horse	6s. 1d.	14s.
Cow	5s.	6s. 8d.
Filly	2s.	–
Draught animal	40d.	–
Brass pots	–	2s. 2d.

Table 12 Average value (where more than one animal was given) of livestock given in heriot payments at Halesowen, note that in the later period only 3 animal heriots were recorded at the manor

	1266–1348	*1349–1401*
Cow	2s. 6d.	–
Cow with calf	6s. 6d.	9s.
Pigs	1s.1d	1s.
Horse	3s.	–
Colt	20d.	–

However, this was not universally the case. At the manor of Halesowen and at Walsham le Willows post-Black Death heriot payments in animals were comparatively low. Overall at Halesowen livestock heriots accounted for 38% of all heriots, 25% of which were pigs, indicating perhaps the importance of a local woodland economy. In fact, the majority of tenements of underaged heirs at Halesowen did not hand over any heriot payments to the lord (61.9% before the Black Death and 75% after 1348) (Tables 12 and 13).

At Walsham le Willows similar but more acute developments can be observed. Animal heriots all but disappeared at this manor after the Black Death. Once again one can suspect that one reason for this development is at least in part due to changes in tenure. One can observe a local increase in leasehold tenure, while this manor also contained an important number of freeholders, which further contributed to the decline in customary tenure. As heriots only fell due on unfree, customary tenements, fewer would be collected with the advance of leasehold tenures (Tables 14 and 15).

Table 13 Livestock heriots given by underaged heirs at Halesowen in per cent

	1266–1348 (%)	*1349–1401 (%)*
Nothing	61.9	75
Cattle	21.4	8.3
Horses	4.8	–
Pigs	9.5	16.7
Sheep	–	–
Draught animal	2.4	–

Table 14 Average value of livestock given as heriots by underaged heirs at Walsham le Willows

	1303–1348	*1349–1399*
Cows	10s. 6d.	–
Mares	3s. 4d.	–
Oxen	11s. 7d.	–
Calf	12d.	–
Sheep	–	2d.

Table 15 Heriot given by underaged heirs at Walsham le Willows

	1303–1348 (%)	*1349–1399 (%)*
Nothing	59.2	55.6
Money	4.5	22.2
Cattle	27.3	11.1
Horses	4.5	–
Pigs	–	–
Sheep	4.5	11.1

The complexity concerning the analysis of heriot payments across the entire period arises from the difficulties posed by post-Black Death developments in tenure. In manorial communities which witnessed a significant shift to leasehold tenures, as can be found, for example, in Halesowen in the second half of the fourteenth century, we would concomitantly expect to see a shift away from heriot payments, as well as a decline in the overall reported number of underaged heirs. At Halesowen not a single underaged heir is recorded in the period from January 1385 and the end of 1401, yet a number of leases of land and holdings for lifetimes are recorded at the manor. The shift to leaseholding eroded and diminished the importance of inheritance customs, which were an integral part of traditional customary tenures and unfree status and yet continued to play important roles in the manors of very conservative lords like the Abbot of St. Albans, lord of Winslow and Norton. The development of leasing cut out an avenue for seigniorial profits from custody arrangements, while at the same time diminishing the incentive for courts to record underaged heirs as their parents had effectively surrendered their hold over customary holdings in favour perhaps of greater personal freedom, yet insecure or more temporary tenures.[69] In other words, cases recording custody arrangements were a by-product of customary tenure, a phenomenon in archival detail which waxes and wanes with the rise and decline of serfdom on the one hand and seigniorial ties of lordship to free tenants. Therefore, heriot payments are a good indicator for the proportion of tenants including of underaged heirs owning livestock as well as the value of livestock while customary tenure was of high importance, in our cases certainly before the arrival of the pestilence. However, from the second half of the fourteenth century onwards they are better understood as providing an insight into the declining importance of customary tenure in many places, and the continued efforts—and relative success—of some lords to hold unto the old ways of villein tenure in other communities.

4 The Tenement

A crucially important aspect in our consideration of the types of inheritances and associated wealth and standards of living of child heirs is the size of the holdings they were set to inherit upon coming of full age. For some manors, due to the availability of significantly voluminous extant data it is possible to make a comparison of pre-to post-Black Death land holding data, as well as a comparison to general tenurial structures. Overall tenurial structures can be arrived at by analysing all deaths which occurred during the year of the pestilence. If all sections of rural communities were equally affected by Yersinia Pestis, and indications are that they were, then the information provided in the relevant manorial courts recording such deaths should provide a usable cross section of land holding structures at the communities at that time (Table 16).

The manor of Winslow provides us with a excellent example of very rich sources on child heirs. Here during the year of the pestilence no less than 25% of all recorded deaths at the manor left an underaged heir behind.

Table 16 Landholdings of underaged heirs compared to general landholding at Winslow

Size of holding	*Overall land holding at the manor in 1349 (%)*	*Child heirs plague year 1349 (%)*	*Child heirs pre-Black Death (%)*	*Child heirs post-Black Death including 1349 (%)*
Under 5 acres	48.5	33	23.4	31
5–10 acres	7.9	9.5	6.7	7.3
11–20 acres	9.1	9.5	16.7	25.5
½ virgate	9.1	16.7		
1 virgate or more	19.4	26		
20+ acres	3	–		
Unknown	3	4.7	40	5.5

It becomes quickly apparent that the general landholding picture at the manor is not quite reflected in the types of holdings which were more likely to be left to child heirs. While over 48% of tenants who died during the plague at Winslow were smallholders with less than 5 acres to their name, only 33% of them left a child heir, but half virgaters and virgaters were much more likely to leave their holdings to child heirs. This may well be a reflection of higher infant mortality alongside decreased fertility among smallholding tenants, some of whom would have been living in poverty. Indeed in his study of families in Halesowen Razi has shown that families with larger holdings tended to have more surviving children. The differences between the number of surviving children of smallholders or cottagers and virgaters were significant, before the Black Death rich tenants had '65% more children than poor peasants'.[70] If smallholders had fewer surviving children one might indeed suspect them to have fewer child heirs. In the post-plague decades we can also observe a shift to slightly more substantial holdings inherited by child heirs.

The data at Walsham le Willows is more difficult to interpret due to the rather substantial number of custody arrangements which merely stated that a minor had inherited a holding without providing details regarding the size of the holding. However, we can still discern a landholding community which is dominated by smallholding peasants with a small minority holding more than 20 acres of land at the time of the Black Death. Here again we can observe a decline of smallholding child heirs in the post-Black Death period alongside a slight increase in

Table 17 Landholding and inheritance at Walsham le Willows

	Overall landholding at the manor in 1349 (%)	*Child heirs pre-Black Death (%)*	*Child heirs post-and including Black Death (%)*
0–5 acres	51.3	50	36.5
6–10 acres	7.1	30	36.5
11–20 acres	9.7	5	18
21–30 acres	1.9	5	–
30+ acres	1	5	–
Unknown	29.2	5	9

middling sized holdings, indicating once again a growth in holding sizes for some sections of rural society who were able to take advantage of the increasing land availability coupled with lower prices per acre in the decades following the first arrival of the Black Death (Table 17).

Unfortunately at Halesowen the details regarding the size of holdings cannot be established in 84% of cases prior to the arrival of the Black Death. While after the Black Death only one tenement is identified at the manor to be of a certain size, a smallholding containing less than 5 acres of land. Thereby constituting statistically irrelevant small samples.

The most dramatic death rates across all manors can be found in the year of the first arrival of the plague. However, the arrival of the Black Death was not the first time a serious crisis hit the fourteenth century. Hardship during the most acute famine years from ca 1316 to 1319 was widespread. At some manors death rates also rose during these early fourteenth-century famine years. At the same time manorial court rolls record rising numbers of thefts, especially of food stuffs from other villagers and from the lord.[71] Studies have shown that child mortality, in this period in particular, was locally at least, high.[72] The children at the manor of Wakefield would also witnessed concomitant rising social tensions between 1316 and 1317 in the communities of the manor. Poverty and desperation fuelled crime in the manor, with thefts, several burglaries, followed by executions by hanging and one by decapitation in 1317 being recorded there.[73]

The cause of the famine was poor weather with heavy rainfall causing crops to rot in the fields. Peasant households had to make important and fairly complex calculations regarding their required resources across a year. A peasant household had to produce enough in terms of crops as well as other goods—eggs, meat, wool etc. to feed everybody in the household. In addition, enough needed to be produced to be sold and converted into coins, which were on the one hand required as rent payments and other dues which the household was liable to hand over to the lord. On the other hand, coins were also required to acquire goods and services for the household itself which the household could not provide through their own labour or other forms of barter with their neighbours. Typical examples would be iron wear and goods required for tools, or horse and ox shoes, as well as leatherwear. On top of these resource requirements rural households had to set aside harvested grain for sowing in the coming year. Such seed grain resources were a crucial insurance for adequate harvests in the future. Of course, such requirements of resources changed considerably across life cycles of individuals as well as the life cycle of a peasant household. The requirement of a young family being rather different from those with older or grown-up children. The balancing acts involved were considerable, and sudden unexpected costs could drive households into debt. Smallholding peasants and labourers were clearly in a much more precarious position whatever the ages of their offspring, and many poorer households may have spent a lot of their lives on the edge of an economic precipice. The risk aversion common in peasant societies meant, however, that rural communities made sure, wherever possible, to put aside enough resources to weather a poor harvest. Nonetheless, households could face serious hardship when repeated poor harvests depleted such resources. Such crises could be disastrous and poorer peasant households would have been forced to eat into their seed grain, or were forced to buy grain a very high price. The consumption of seed grain due to hunger almost guaranteed severe economic pressures in the following year as well; with less seed grain leading to diminished harvests and undoubtedly for many families who were able to bargain for credit from their lord or neighbours, a lot of debt. While all grains were affected by repeated poor harvests in the early fourteenth-century famine, the price of wheat in particular skyrocketed.[74]

At Walsham seven child heirs are recorded in 1317, six of whom came from poorer smallholding households, three holding less than 5 acres and 3 between five and ten acres of land. The size of the seventh holding is unknown. In 1318 a further two tenants died leaving their child heirs holdings of between 5 and 10 acres in size. At the tail-end of the crisis years in 1320 another child heir was left a holding smaller than 5 acres.

It is highly likely that hardship contributed to the deaths of these smallholders. Only one of the ten smallholders who died in 1317–1320 had an animal heriot to give to the lord, further indication of their poverty.

Other manors also experienced a spike in recorded child heirs during the famine years. At the manor of Eldersfield two child heirs were recorded in 1316 and two in 1317.[75] At the manor of Halesowen two child heirs were recorded in 1316, two in 1317 and three in 1318. However, we can establish the size of the tenements in only two of these cases, which were cottagers and hence smallholders.[76] Overall over 60% of underaged heirs in the famine years only inherited holdings containing 10 acres or less. The true proportion may well have been higher due to the significant number of young heirs, amounting to 38%, whose precise holding size was not known. While reported deaths during the famine years are spread fairly evenly across the seasons, the winter months of January and February appear to have witnessed a spike, with 36% of deaths recorded in the months most associated with harsh climatic conditions, illnesses such as in influenza, as well as higher food prices. The overall effect was a perfect storm for the poorer children in rural England. Children and adults weakened by hunger or poor nutrition had few physical resources to fight off infections and were more likely to succumb to illnesses their better-off neighbours were able to survive. At the same time repeated harvest failures cumulatively added to hardship.

If landholding is an indicator of wealth and available family resources, then we can conclude that the two crises which hit peasant families in the fourteenth century affected death rates of families differently. The Black Death claimed victims less discriminately than the famine, which appears to have affected poorer households most severely. Poorer families were more likely to leave child heirs in the famine years than wealthier households. In the Black Death wealthier families are likely to leave child heirs, but they are more numerously represented as poorer families simply because poorer families had fewer children, or fewer surviving children.

The tenements of child heirs allow important insights into the economic structures and changes to these in their rural communities. They show the practical planning on the part of parents even when faced with imminent death in their attempt to safeguard the well-being of their offspring. We can see the fortunes of rural societies shift to increasing pastoral agriculture and a decline in customary tenure. And we can see the effect of poverty and famine on individual families.

Notes

1. D. Noy, *Winslow Manor Court Books Part I 1327–1377*, Buckinghamshire Record Society, no. 35, 2011, p. 230.
2. One of the first studies into this phenomenon was conducted by Z. Razi, *Life, Marriage and Death in a Medieval Parish Economy, Society and Demography in Halesowen 1270–1400* (Cambridge: Cambridge University Press, 1980), pp. 50–57; C. Dyer, *Making a Living in the Middle Ages The People of Britain 850–1520* (New Haven and London: Yale University Press, 2002), pp.158–159.
3. For the nature and development of deathbed surrenders see for example: L. Bonfield and L.R. Poos, 'The Development on Deathbed Transfers in Medieval English Manor Courts', in: Z. Razi and R.M. Smith, eds., *Medieval Society and the Manor Court* (1996), pp. 117–142.
4. D. Noy, *Winslow Manor Court Book, Part II 1423–1460*, Buckinghamshire Record Society, no. 36, 2011, p. 476.
5. D. Noy, *Winslow Manor Court Book, Part II 1423–1460*, p. 629.
6. D. Noy, *Winslow Manor Court Book, Part II 1423–1460*, p. 649.
7. Z. Razi, *Life, Marriage and Death in a Medieval Parish*, pp. 83–85. Infant mortality—that is death of infants under one year of age has been estimated to have been comparatively low at between 11–15% at the village of Wharram Percy, indicating widespread and prolonged breastfeeding. S. Mays, 'The Human Remains', in: S. May, C. Harding, and C. Heighway, eds., *Wharram, a Study of Settlement on the Yorkshire Wolds, XI, The Churchyard* (York University Archaeological Publications 13, 2007), p. 94. See also C. Klapisch—Zuber on differentials in child mortality due to economic familial background in: C. Klapisch—Zuber, *Women, Family and Ritual in Renaissance Italy* (Chicago: University of Chicago Press, 1985) see also: B.A. Hanawalt, 'The Child in the Middle Ages and the Renaissance', in: W. Koops and M. Zuckerman, eds., *Beyond the Century of the Child: Cultural History and Developmental Psychology* (University of Pennsylvania Press, 2003), p. 34.
8. Z. Razi, *Life, Marriage and Death*, pp. 143–144.
9. D. Noy, *Winslow Manor Court Book, Part I, 1327–1377*, p. 221.
10. For discussions on the length of nursing in medieval society see for example: S. Shahar, *Childhood in the Middle Ages* (London and New York: Routledge, 1992), pp. 78–80.
11. S. Mays, 'The Human Remains', p. 93.
12. N.M. Burt, 'Stable Isotope Ratio Analysis of Breastfeeding and Weaning Practices of Children from Medieval Fishergate House York, UK', in: *American Journal of Physical Anthropology*, vol. 152 (2013), p. 407 and p. 413.

13. P. Mahoney, et al., 'Deciduous Enamel 3D Microwear Texture Analysis as an Indicator of Childhood Diet in Medieval Canterbury, England', in: *Journal of Archaeological Science*, vol. 66 (1016), p. 129.
14. Manor of Halesowen, Birmingham Archives, Wolfson Center, MS 3279/346279.
15. J. Amphlett, ed., *Court Rolls of the Manor of Halesowen 1270–1307* (Oxford, Printed for the Worcestershire Historical Society by James Parker, 1912), p. 377.
16. R. Lock, ed., *The Court Rolls of Walsham le Willows, 1303–50* (Woodbridge: Boydell & Brewer and Suffolk Record Society, vol. xli, 1998), p. 132.
17. R. Lock, ed., *The Court Rolls of Walsham le Willows 1303–1350*, p. 135.
18. D. Noy, ed. and trans., *Winslow Manor Court Books Part II 1423–1460*, Buckinghamshire Record Society, no. 36, 2011, p. 476.
19. See also for a discussion of this A. Musson, *Medieval Law in Context, the Growth of Legal Consciousness from Magna Carta to the Peasants' Revolt* (Manchester University Press, 2001), p. 86.
20. E. Clark, 'The Custody of Children in English Manor Courts', in: *Law and History Review*, vol. 3, no. 2 (Autumn 1985), p. 341.
21. The case is mentioned by E. Clark, 'The Custody of Children in English Manor Courts', p. 341.
22. L.R. Poos and L. Bonfield, eds., *Select Cases in Manorial Courts 1250–1550 Property and Family Law* (Seldon Society, 1998), p. 152.
23. See Part IV.
24. For typical tenement structures see for example: C. Dyer, *Standards of Living in the Later Middle Ages, Social Change in England c. 1200–1520* (Cambridge University Press, 1989), pp. 22–24. P. Schofield, *Peasant Community*, pp. 11–33.
25. An excellent recent examination of these details can be found in: C. Dyer, 'Documentary Evidence', in: N. Alcock and D. Miles, eds., *The Medieval Peasant House in Midland England* (Oxford and Oakville: Oxbow Books, 2013), p. 108. For the position of rubbish pits within holdings, close to buildings, see also: M. Aston and C. Gerrard, *Interpreting the Medieval Village; Landscape and Community in Shapwick, Somerset* (Oxford: Oxbow Books, 2013), p. 202.
26. P. Foden, ed. and trans., *Records of the Manor of Norton in the Liberty of St. Albans, 1244–1539* (Caxton Hill, Hertford: Hertfordshire Record Publications, vol. 29, 2014), p. 19 and p. 20.
27. R. Lock, ed. and trans., *The Court Rolls of Walsham le Willows 1351–1399* (Woodbridge: Boydell Press and Suffolk Record Society, vol. xlv, 2002), p. 29.
28. C. Dyer, 'Living in Peasant Houses in Late Medieval England', p. 20; N.W. Alcock, 'The Meaning of Insethouse', *Vernacular Architecture*, vol. 27, no. 1 (1996), pp. 8–9.

29. D. Noy, *Winslow Manor Court Book*, Part I, p. 453.
30. D. Noy, *Winslow Manor Court Book*, Part I, p. 34.
31. D. Noy, *Winslow Manor Court Book*, Part I, p. 19.
32. M. Müller, 'Arson, Communities, and Social Conflict in Later Medieval England', in: *Viator, Medieval and Renaissance Studies*, vol. 43, no. 2 (2012), pp. 193–208; R. Faith, 'The Class Struggle in Fourteenth Century England', in: R. Samuel, ed., People's History and Socialist Theory (London, 1981), pp. 50–60.
33. The bibliography on this topic is substantial and not uncontroversial. See for example: C. Dyer, *Making a Living in the Middle Ages The People of Britain 850–1520* (New Haven and London: Yale University Press, 2002), pp. 346–349; J. Mullan and R. Britnell, *Land and Family; Trends and Local Variations in the Peasant Land Market on the Winchester Bishopric Estates, 1263–1415* (University of Hertfordshire Press, 2010), esp. pp. 58–68; M. Müller, 'Peasants, Lords and Developments in Leasing in Later Medieval England', in: B. van Bavel and P. Schofield, eds., *The Development of Leasehold in Northwestern Europe, c. 1200–1600* (CORN Series, vol. 10, Brepols, December 2008), pp. 155–178; M. Müller, 'Seigniorial Control and the Peasant Land-Market in the 14th Century: A Comparative Approach', in: L. Feller and C. Wickham, eds., *Le Marché de la Terre au Moyen Âge* (Collection de L'École Française De Rome -350, 2005), pp. 297–313; For an excellent recent discussion of the issues see: M. Bailey, *The Decline of Serfdom in England; From Bondage to Freedom* (Boydell Press, 2014), esp. pp. 20ff..
34. See on this for example: M. Bailey, *The Decline of Serfdom in England*, esp. pp. 20ff.; M. Müller, 'Seigniorial Control and the Peasant Land-Market', pp. 297–313.
35. D. Noy, ed., *Winslow Manor Court Boos, Part II 1423–1460*, p. 629.
36. R.K. Field, 'Worcestershire Peasant Buildings, Household Goods and Farming Equipment in the Later Middle Ages', in: *Medieval Archaeology*, vol. 9 (1965), pp. 121–122.
37. R.K. Field, 'Worcestershire Peasant Buildings, Household Goods and Farming Equipment in the Later Middle Ages', p. 122.
38. C. Dyer, 'Living in Peasant Houses in Late Medieval England', in *Vernacular Architecture*, vol. 44 (2013), pp. 19–27; C. Briggs, 'Manorial Court Roll Inventories as Evidence of English Peasant Consumption and Living Standards, c. 1270–c. 1420', in: A. Furio and F. Garcia-Oliver, eds., *Pantas de Consumo y niveles de vida en el mundo rural medieval* (Valencia, forthcoming).
39. D. Noy, *Winslow Manor Court Book, Part II 1423–1460*, Buckinghamshire Record Society, no. 36 (2011), p. 629.
40. See for example on this issue: S. Wrathmell, *Domestic Settlement 2: Medieval Peasant Farmsteads; Wharram, a Study of Settlement on the Yorkshire Wolds, VI* (York University Archaeological Publications 8, 1989), p. 13.

41. For a discussion of the peasant household as functional see also C. Dyer, 'Documentary Evidence', in N. Alcock and D. Miles, eds., *The Medieval Peasant House in Midland England*, pp. 108–109. Such evidence also indicates how problematic a concept of separate work and 'domestic' spheres according to gender is in peasant societies. Sere also: M. Müller, 'Le genre en théorie et en pratique: le statut des femmes, la question des espaces genrés, publics et privés dans le village anglais médiéval', *Cahiers électroniques d'histoire textuelledu LaMOP*, vol. 8 (Paris, 2015).
42. R. Lock, ed., *The Court Rolls of Walsham le Willows 1303–1350*, p. 132.
43. R. Lock, ed., *The Court Rolls of Walsham le Willows 1303–1350*, p. 19.
44. R. Lock, ed., *The Court Rolls of Walsham le Willows 1303–1350*, p. 19 and p. 135.
45. R. Lock, ed., *The Court Rolls of Walsham le Willows 1303–1350*, pp. 133–134.
46. See also on the use and locations of such items C. Dyer, 'Living in Peasant Houses in Late Medieval England', in: *Vernacular Architecture*, vol. 44, no. 1 (2013), p. 22.
47. C. Dyer, 'Living in Peasant Houses in Late Medieval England', p. 24.
48. C. Briggs, 'Manorial Court Roll Inventories as Evidence of English Peasant Consumption and Living Standards', p. 9; D.A. Hinton, 'Deserted Medieval Villages and the Objects from Them', in: C. Dyer and R. Jones, eds., *Deserted Villages Revisited* (University of Hertfordshire Press, 2010), esp. pp. 101–104; M. Aston and C. Gerrard, *Interpreting the Medieval Village*; for pottery in particular, found in large quantities, both across medieval fields, when it was mixed in with manure and spread as well as in rubbish pits, pp. 163–165 and pp. 202–203.
49. For loom-weights and spindle whorls see for example: E.A. Clark, G.D. Gaunt, with milling stones by S. Watts, 'Stone Objects', in: S. Mays, C. Harding and C. Heighway, eds., *The Churchyard, Wharram, a Study of Settlement on the Yorkshire Wolds*, XI (York University Archaeological Publications 13, 2007), pp. 294–299.
50. N. Orme, 'The Culture of Children in Medieval England', in: *Past and Present*, vol. 148, no. 1 (1995), pp 52–56; C. Lewis, 'Children's Play in the Later Medieval English Countryside', in: *Childhood in the Past*, vol. 2 (2009).
51. C. Lewis, 'Children's Play in the Later Medieval English Countryside', in: *Childhood in the Past*, 2 (2009), pp. 86–108; see also R. Gilchrist, *Medieval Life; Archaeology and the Life Course* (The Boydell Press, 2012), p. 149.
52. A.G. MacGregor, 'Bone and Antler Objects' with a note on wooden objects by E.A. Clark in: P.A. Stamper and R.A. Croft, *The South Manor Area, Wharram, a Study of Settlement on the Yorkshire Wolds, VIII* (York University Archaeological Publications 10, 2000), p. 153; for play and toys see also: C. Lewis, 'Children's Play in the Later Medieval English

Countryside', pp. 86–108; N. Orme, 'The Culture of Children in Medieval England', in: *Past and Present*, vol. 148, no. 1 (1995), pp. 51–65.

53. G. MacGregor, 'Bone and Antler Objects' with a note on wooden objects by E.A. Clark, p. 153.
54. R. Gilchrist, Medieval Life; *Archaeology and the Life Course* (The Boydell Press, 2012), p. 150.
55. H. Dawson, *Unearthing Late Medieval Children, Health, Status and Burial Practice in Southern England* (BAR British Series 593, 2014), p. 25.
56. D. Noy, *Winslow Manor Court Book*, Part I, p. 14. On the value of timber for peasant houses see for example: C. Dyer, *Standards of Living*, p. 167.
57. D. Noy, *Winslow Manor Court Book*, Part II, p. 501.
58. D. Noy, *Winslow Manor Court Book*, Part II, p. 629; P. Foden, ed. and trans., *Records of the Manor of Norton*, pp. 194–195.
59. R. Lock, ed., *The Court Rolls of Walsham le Willows, 1303–50*, p. 63.
60. J. Lister ed., *Court Rolls of the Manor of Wakefield, vol. iv, 1315–1317* (Yorkshire Archaeological Society, 1930), p. 114 and p. 131.
61. K.M. Troup, ed., *Court Rolls of the Manor of Wakefield October 1338 to September 1340* (Yorkshire Archaeological Society, 1999), p. 71.
62. D. Noy, ed., *Winslow Manor Court Books Part I*, p. 243.
63. D. Noy, ed., *Winslow Manor Court Books Part I*, p. 137.
64. P. Foden, ed., *Records of the Manor of Norton*, p. 167.
65. P. Foden, ed., *Records of the Manor of Norton*, p. 167.
66. For the prices of livestock see for example: D.L. Farmer, 'Some livestock Price Movements in Thirteenth Century England', in: *Economic History Review*, 2nd series, 22 (1969).
67. C. Dyer, *Standards of Living in the later Middle Ages*, pp. 144–145.
68. See for example on these developments: C. Dyer, *Making a Living in the Middle Ages*, pp. 293–297; C. Dyer, *Standards of Living*, pp. 158–160; M. Müller, 'Food, Hierarchy and Class Conflict', in: R. Goddard, J. Langdon, and M. Müller, eds., *Survival and Discord in Medieval Society Essays in Honour of Christopher Dyer* (Brepols, 2010), pp. 231–248.
69. Miriam Müller, 'Peasants, Lords and Developments in Leasing in Later Medieval England', in: B. van Bavel and P. Schofield, eds., *Emergence and Early Development of Lease Holding in the European Countryside During the Middle Ages* (CORN Series, vol. 10, Brepols, December 2008).
70. Z. Razi, *Life, Marriage and Death in a Medieval Parish*, pp. 143–144.
71. For a study looking at the link between the economy and crime in this period see: B.A. Hanawalt, 'Economic Influences on the Pattern of Crime in England 1300–1348', in: *American Journal of Legal History*, vol. 18 (1974), pp. 281–297.
72. H. Dawson, *Unearthing Late Medieval Children, Health, Status and Burial Practice in Southern England* (BAR British Series 593, 2014), p. 29.

73. J. Lister, ed., *Court Rolls of the Manor of Wakefield, vol. iv, 1315–1317* (Yorkshire Archaeological Society, 1930), The decapitation can be found on p. 177. For an in-depth discussion on the relationship between crime and grain prices see B.A. Hanawalt, 'Economic Influences on the Pattern of Crime in England 1300–1348', in: *American Journal of Legal History*, vol. 18 (1974), pp. 281–297.
74. C. Dyer, *Making a Living in the Middle Ages*, p. 230; I. Kershaw, 'The Great Famine and Agrarian Crisis in England, 1315–1322', in: R.H. Hilton (ed.), *Peasants, Knights and Heretics* (Cambridge, 1976); P. Slavin, 'The Great Bovine Pestilence and Its Economic and Environmental Consequences in England and Wales 1318–50', in: *Economic History Review*, vol. 65, no. 4 (2012), pp. 1239–1240.
75. Worcester Archive, The Hive, BA 1531/69 (A and B).
76. Manor of Halesowen Birmingham Archives/ Wolfson Centre, MS 3279/ to MS 3279/.

Bibliography

Primary Sources

Halesowen Court Rolls, Birmingham Library and Archives, Wolfson Centre, MS 3279.

Records of the Manor of Elderfield: Worcester Archive, The Hive, BA 1531/69 (A and B).

J. Amphlett, ed., *Court Rolls of the Manor of Halesowen 1270–1307* (Oxford, Printed for the Worcestershire Historical Society by James Parker, 1912).

P. Foden, ed. and trans., *Records of the Manor of Norton in the Liberty of St. Albans, 1244–1539* (Caxton Hill, Hertford: Hertfordshire Record Publications, vol. 29, 2014).

J. Lister, ed., *Court Rolls of the Manor of Wakefield, vol. iv, 1315–1317* (Leeds: Yorkshire Archaeological Society, 1930).

R. Lock, ed., *The Court Rolls of Walsham le Willows, 1303–50* (Woodbridge: Boydell & Brewer and Suffolk Record Society, vol. xli, 1998).

R. Lock, ed. and trans., *The Court Rolls of Walsham le Willows, 1351–1399* (Woodbridge: Boydell Press and Suffolk Record Society, vol. xlv, 2002).

D. Noy, *Winslow Manor Court Books, Part I 1327–1377*, (Amersham: Buckinghamshire Record Society, no. 35, 2011a).

D. Noy, *Winslow Manor Court Book, Part II 1423–1460*, (Amersham: Buckinghamshire Record Society, no. 36, 2011b).

L.R. Poos and L. Bonfield, eds., *Select Cases in Manorial Courts 1250–1550 Property and Family Law* (London: Seldon Society, 1998).

K.M. Troup, ed., *Court Rolls of the Manor of Wakefield October 1338 to September 1340* (Leeds: Yorkshire Archaeological Society, 1999).

Secondary Sources Books

M. Aston and C. Gerrard, *Interpreting the Medieval Village; Landscape and Community in Shapwick, Somerset* (Oxford: Oxbow Books, 2013).

M. Bailey, *The Decline of Serfdom in England; From Bondage to Freedom* (Woodbridge: Boydell Press, 2014).

H. Dawson, *Unearthing Late Medieval Children, Health, Status and Burial Practice in Southern England* (BAR British Series 593, 2014).

C. Dyer, *Standards of Living in the Later Middle Ages, Social Change in England c. 1200–1520* (Cambridge: Cambridge University Press, 1989).

C. Dyer, *Making a Living in the Middle Ages the People of Britain 850–1520* (New Haven and London: Yale University Press, 2002).

R. Gilchrist, *Medieval Life; Archaeology and the Life Course* (Woodbridge: The Boydell Press, 2012).

C. Klapisch- Zuber, *Women, Family and Ritual in Renaissance Italy* (Chicago: University of Chicago Press, 1985).

J. Mullan and R. Britnell, *Land and Family; Trends and Local Variations in the Peasant Land Market on the Winchester Bishopric Estates, 1263–1415* (Hatfield: University of Hertfordshire Press, 2010).

A. Musson, *Medieval Law in Context, the Growth of Legal Consciousness from Magna Carta to the Peasants' Revolt* (Manchester: Manchester University Press, 2001).

Z. Razi, *Life, Marriage and Death in a Medieval Parish Economy, Society and Demography in Halesowen 1270–1400* (Cambridge: Cambridge University Press, 1980).

P.R. Schofield, *Peasant and Community in Medieval England 1200–1500* (Basingstoke: Palgrave Macmillan, 2002).

S. Shahar, *Childhood in the Middle Ages* (London and New York: Routledge, 1992).

S. Wrathmell, *Domestic Settlement 2: Medieval Peasant Farmsteads; Wharram, a Study of Settlement on the Yorkshire Wolds, VI* (York: York University Archaeological Publications 8, 1989).

Secondary Sources Articles and Chapters

N.W. Alcock, 'The Meaning of Insethouse', *Vernacular Architecture*, vol. 27, no. 1 (1996), pp. 8–9.

L. Bonfield and L.R. Poos, 'The Development on Deathbed Transfers in Medieval English Manor Courts', in: Z. Razi and R.M. Smith, eds., *Medieval Society and the Manor Court* (1996), pp. 117–142.

C. Briggs, 'Manorial Court Roll Inventories as Evidence of English Peasant Consumption and Living Standards, c. 1270–c. 1420', in: A. Furio and F. Garcia-Oliver, eds., *Pantas de Consumo y niveles de vida en el mundo rural medieval* (Valencia, forthcoming).

N.M. Burt, 'Stable Isotope Ratio Analysis of Breastfeeding and Weaning Practices of Children from Medieval Fishergate House York, UK', in: *American Journal of Physical Anthropology*, vol. 152 (2013), pp. 407–416.
E. Clark, 'The Custody of Children in English Manor Courts', in *Law and History Review*, vol. 3, no. 2 (Autumn 1985), pp. 333–348.
E.A. Clark, G.D. Gaunt, with milling stones by S. Watts, 'Stone Objects', in: S. Mays, C. Harding, and C. Heighway, eds., *The Churchyard, Wharram, a Study of Settlement on the Yorkshire Wolds, XI* (York: York University Archaeological Publications 13, 2007) pp. 294–299.
C. Dyer, 'Documentary Evidence', in: N. Alcock and D. Miles, eds., *The Medieval Peasant House in Midland England* (Oxford and Oakville: Oxbow Books, 2013), pp. 105–152.
C. Dyer, 'Living in Peasant Houses in Late Medieval England', in *Vernacular Architecture*, vol. 44 (2013), pp. 19–27.
R. Faith, 'The Class Struggle in Fourteenth Century England', in: R. Samuel, ed., *People's History and Socialist Theory* (London: Routledge & Kegan Paul, 1981), pp. 50–60.
D.L. Farmer, 'Some Livestock Price Movements in Thirteenth Century England', *Economic History Review*, 2nd series, vol. 22 (1969) pp. 1–16.
R.K. Field, 'Worcestershire Peasant Buildings, Household Goods and Farming Equipment in the Later Middle Ages', in: *Medieval Archaeology*, vol. 9 (1965), pp. 105–145.
B.A. Hanawalt, 'Economic Influences on the Pattern of Crime in England 1300–1348', *American Journal of Legal History*, vol. 18 (1974), pp. 281–297.
B.A. Hanawalt, 'The Child in the Middle Ages and the Renaissance', in: W. Koops and M. Zuckerman, eds., *Beyond the Century of the Child: Cultural History and Developmental Psychology* (Philadelphia, PA: University of Pennsylvania Press, 2003), pp. 21–42.
D.A. Hinton, 'Deserted Medieval Villages and the Objects from Them', in: C. Dyer and R. Jones, eds., *Deserted Villages Revisited* (Hatfield: University of Hertfordshire Press, 2010), pp. 85–108.
I. Kershaw, 'The Great Famine and Agrarian Crisis in England 1315–1322', in: *Past & Present*, no. 59 (May 1973), pp. 3–5.
C. Lewis, 'Children's Play in the Later Medieval English Countryside', in: *Childhood in the Past*, vol. 2, no. 1 (2009), pp. 86–108.
A.G. MacGregor, 'Bone and Antler Objects' with a note on wooden objects by E.A. Clark in: P.A. Stamper and R.A. Croft, eds., *The South Manor Area, Wharram, a Study of Settlement on the Yorkshire Wolds, VIII* (York: York University Archaeological Publications 10, 2000), pp. 121–124.
P. Mahoney, et al., 'Deciduous Enamel 3D Microwear Texture Analysis as an Indicator of Childhood Diet in Medieval Canterbury, England', in: *Journal of Archaeological Science*, vol. 66 (2016), pp. 128–136.

S. May, 'The Human Remains', in: S. May, C. Harding, and C. Heighway, eds., *Wharram, a Study of Settlement on the Yorkshire Wolds, XI, The Churchyard* (York: York University Archaeological Publications 13, 2007), pp. 77–192.

M. Müller, 'Seigniorial Control and the Peasant Land-Market in the 14th Century: A Comparative Approach', in: L. Feller and C. Wickham, eds., *Le Marché de la Terre au Moyen Âge* (Rome: Collection de L'École Française De Rome -350, 2005), pp. 197–313.

M. Müller, 'Peasants, Lords and Developments in Leasing in Later Medieval England', in: B. van Bavel and P. Schofield, eds., *The Development of Leasehold in Northwestern Europe, c. 1200–1600*, vol. 10 (CORN Series, Turnhout: Brepols, 2008), pp. 155–178.

M. Müller, 'Food, Hierarchy and Class Conflict', in: R. Goddard, J. Langdon, and M. Müller, eds., *Survival and Discord in Medieval Society Essays in Honour of Christopher Dyer* (Turnhout: Brepols 2010), pp. 231–248.

M. Müller, 'Arson, Communities, and Social Conflict in Later Medieval England', in: *Viator, Medieval and Renaissance Studies*, vol. 43, no. 2 (2012), pp. 193–208.

M. Müller, 'Le genre en théorie et en pratique: le statut des femmes, la question des espaces genrés, publics et privés dans le village anglais médiéval', *Cahiers électroniques d'histoire textuelle du LaMOP*, vol. 8 (Paris, 2015).

N. Orme, 'The Culture of Children in Medieval England', in: *Past and Present*, vol. 148, no. 1 (1995), pp. 48–88.

P. Slavin, 'The Great Bovine Pestilence and Its Economic and Environmental Consequences in England and Wales 1318–50', in: *Economic History Review*, vol. 65, no. 4 (2012), pp. 1239–1240.

CHAPTER 4

Looking After Underaged Heirs

1 The Children

At manors which recorded underaged heirs systematically, and where we are fortunate enough to have long-term data for underaged heirs, it is possible to plot numbers of minors for whom, and for whose inheritance, guardians had been found. It is striking that overall underaged heirs were not a common, but certainly a regular occurrence. It is principally during periods of crises, associated with high, and unusual, levels of mortality, that we see greater numbers of minors appearing in manorial records. So, who were the children we encounter in manorial records, what can we learn about them and what can they tell us about other children and young people in their villages as well as the views their adults had about them? We have already seen that it was by no means only wealthy families whose children appear in court records, but they would certainly have to have been set to inherit property in order to be mentioned as underaged heirs. Children of landless cottagers are therefore less likely to make an appearance than children who were due to inherit a lot of lands. This begs once again the question of the position of non-inheriting siblings in the eyes of the community. It has been suggested that non-inheriting siblings were not considered very important, but is it safe to make such assumptions? Were they really neglected? Examining the evidence of underaged heirs, especially their ages, in village societies also sheds light on other, wider social structures within their localities. The nature of peasant family compositions has been the matter of some debate but

M. Müller, *Childhood, Orphans and Underage Heirs in Medieval Rural England*, Palgrave Studies in the History of Childhood,
https://doi.org/10.1007/978-3-030-03602-7_4

research revealed that poorer families had fewer children who survived into adulthood. Typically English peasant families were mainly nuclear in character. That is, the core of the typical English peasant household was made up of a couple and their children.[1] While this may conjure up images of the modern western European family characterised by husband, wife, two kids and a dog, in reality peasant family arrangements were a lot more eclectic and flexible than this image suggests.[2] We know that at least sometimes other relatives also lived within the parental family household. Occasionally therefore one can find extended family set-ups, both laterally and horizontally.[3] Additionally some peasant household would have included servants at least periodically or seasonally. Such servants would often have been young people or adolescents and, as we will see, this was a very common entry into paid work by young villagers. We know as yet quite little about the effects of crisis like famine or the Black Death on family structures, especially the effect on children and the degree and extent of step-parentage. Similarly, how old were children typically when they were left orphaned and what does this tell us about household structures. Additionally, the frequency with which girls were recorded as heirs gives us important insights into inheritance customs and the level to which male primogeniture inhibited or circumscribed access to land by young women.

The youngest heir recorded at the manor of Winslow was baby Agnes, who was only 15 days old when she was handed over with her land to Master John, chaplain of the manor in April 1349. Agnes had lost both her parents, presumably due to the Black Death and the chances of her surviving would have been slim at the best of times, unless John had been able to find a wetnurse with a ready supply of breastmilk.[4] However with the plague still claiming victims in the manor those chances were lower still and the court book notes accordingly that 'within a short time after the grant, [of the wardship] both the aforesaid Agnes and the aforesaid Chaplain died'. The land then went to Agnes' closest heir Richard son of John ate Hall, who was 12 years old and was himself orphaned and taken in by fellow villager Richard Martyn.[5]

The ages of orphans were often, though not always recorded alongside other details of cases of wardships. The main reason for this would have been to correctly identify—in cases of future disputes—the exact point upon which an heir reached the age of majority and was hence able to hold their tenement in their own right. Babies as young as Agnes were, however rarely recorded. That is to say, as far as we can tell, considering the not uncommon occurrence of no age for an heir being recorded; for example, at Winslow 7 wardship cases recorded no ages of the heirs in question, at Halesowen no less than 18 cases give no information on the ages of the minor. However, in many cases it is possible to work out the approximate age of the child, if the accepted age of majority of the manor is known alongside information of how long a wardship lasted. Some studies of wardship, especially in London, have identified the typical ages of wards, with Tarbin for example noting that in the fourteenth century the 'average age of orphans' was 'between 7 and 10 years'.[6] Elaine Clark has similarly found that in Bristol and London in the fourteenth century 'two out of three orphans… were younger than ten; nearly twenty-one percent were no older than three'.[7]

However, the patterns which emerge if we consider the ages of orphans across the manors of Winslow, Norton, Halesowen, Walsham le Willows and Brandon, manorial communities for which we have significant data across a representative chronology, are slightly different. Across the entire period from the end of the thirteenth century to the end of the fourteenth, there are significant numbers of cases for which the ages of wards are unknown (Table 1).

The low number of heirs aged 16 or over can be partly explained by the low age of majority 16 at the manor of Walsham. It is also the case that during the crisis of the Black Death some young people, who had not reached the normally customary age of majority were allowed to inherit their holdings prematurely. A fundamental problem however is the significant number of young heirs whose age cannot be determined, amounting to over 21%. This unknown factor is considerably lower especially during the Black Death, but also in the post-Black Death period. It is possible that lords realised that it was important to keep more accurate records in the face of the administrative chaos caused by the arrival of the Black Death, and therefore took care to include the ages of heirs more systematically.

Table 1 Ages of wards upon arriving at court at the manors of Walsham le Willows, Halesowen, Norton, Brandon and Winslow, from 1270 to 1400 in per cent

Age unknown	21.3%
5 years old and under	29.2%
6–10 years old	27.3%
11–15 years old	16.3%
16 years old and over	5.9%

If we split our figures into pre-Black Death, Black Death and Post-Black Death categories some interesting changes emerge (Table 2).

While the majority of orphans were aged below 11 years, this would only reflect the fact that this age group represented the largest category. Both before and after the Black Death the age groups are proportionately fairly evenly split, indicating that the children under the age of 11 were roughly equally likely to be orphaned, whichever age they were. An interesting exception is the 5 years and under category, who shoot up in prominence during the plague year with over 48% of wards appearing in manorial courts in this age group. It is difficult to account for this anomaly, as one would expect the Black Death to be equally deadly across all age categories of both parents as well as children. One might even expect a higher mortality rate among the very young—as well as the elderly—as immunity in these groups either not fully developed or often vulnerable and in the elderly compromised. Nonetheless one would similarly expect that in pre- and post-Black Death years fewer adults aged between about twenty and mid-thirties would have died prematurely, precisely the age group which one would expect to be most likely to have young children. Additionally, not all of these young children would have survived to the end of the plague year or if they lived beyond that into adulthood, and as we have seen in the case of baby Agnes, many would have perished very young.

When it comes to determining the sex of the child heirs we are on somewhat firmer ground. Overall across all manors 26% of underaged heirs were girls (see Chart 1). These figures are interesting as they are a little higher, but not significantly more, than the proportions found in other studies examining the incidence of female inheritance. Richard Smith, for example, found that 'roughly twenty per cent of families

Table 2 Ages of wards at Walsham, Halesowen, Norton, Brandon and Winslow in per cent across the period

Age of ward	*Pre Black Death (%)*	*During the Black Death year (%)*	*Post the arrival of the Black Death (%)*
Unknown	27.8	7.1	23.7
5 years old and under	19.4	48.2	28.9
6–10 years old	25.9	32.1	23.7
11–15 years old	20.4	7.1	18.4
16+years old	6.5	5.4	5.3

Chart 1 Sex ratio of heirs at the manors 1270–1400

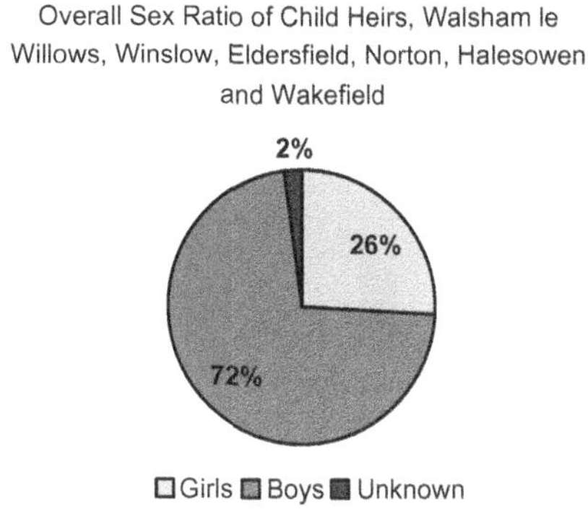

would have only surviving daughters and no sons at the father's death'.[8] Therefore, while male primogeniture or male partible inheritance ensured that most landed properties went to boys, and the lions share to older boys, girls represented a rather significant minority of heirs.

If we break these figures down to individual manors where we have significant information we can also see that there is in general no significant difference between manors in these male to female proportions. The exception is Norton where an unusually high proportion of female child heirs can be observed, despite the predominant inheritance custom at the manor being male primogeniture (Chart 2).

Manorial courts were concerned to safeguard the inheritance of a young heir, as well as the heirs themselves. It is not always immediately apparent what happened to the siblings of heirs, especially in manors where male primogeniture was the dominant inheritance custom, which could have left younger sons and daughters potentially without anything unless parents had already made provisions for them premortem. Conversely, in cases where partible inheritance applied, typically in freehold tenure, and all co-inheriting children were of the same sex, no potential problems of non-inheriting children could arise. Their status as heirs equally in waiting would thus, theoretically at least, accord them a degree of protection from neglect. Such was the case with the four sons of Nicholas Kembald of Walsham le Willows, who died in 1335. Although his holding was in villein tenure, the implication is that his four sons were to inherit equally, as they were described as underage as well as coheirs.[9] Similarly, when Alex Canalar died at Heacham in Norfolk in 1285, his two sons who inherited equally, were both handed into the

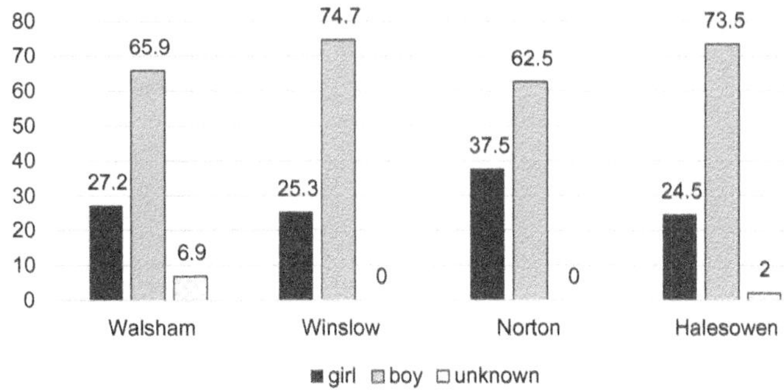

Chart 2 Proportion of male and female heirs in per cent

custody of Roger du Boys.[10] It is easily possible to underestimate the role and importance of non-inheriting siblings. However, this would be misleading. It has been argued, that courts were primarily, or only, concerned with the fate of the orphans who were determined to be the main heirs of a tenement, with Elaine Clark, for example, going so far to suggest that 'only minors who were actually heirs had guardians'.[11] Indeed, non-inheriting siblings make very rare appearances in manor courts in cases dealing with guardianship. However, some cases make it quite clear that non-inheriting siblings were also trusted into the care of guardians, alongside the principal heir.

The question concerning the residence or status of non-inheriting siblings would not have arisen in about 40% of wardship cases, as in these the recording of the guardian was a formality as the appointees were considered a surviving parent of the child heir, either a mother, stepmother, or more rarely, a father or stepfather. In such cases the heirs were already residing with their surviving parent or step-parent, as were their siblings. For the remaining 60%, the kind of children whom we would consider to have been orphaned in a modern, western sense, in having neither surviving parent, the position of siblings raises important questions which ultimately go to the heart of the motivations for accepting guardianships with all these entailed.

Non-inheriting—usually younger—siblings are often hidden from the records, but not always. Where they are mentioned it is indicated that they could sometimes be viewed as next heirs in line, should the eldest child die prematurely. At Halesowen this is made quite explicit in

1338, when Roger de Walloceshale, 'a villein of the lord', died and left behind his four daughters, aged between 2 and 10 which were placed into the guardianship of his widow until one of them was to reach maturity.[12] One reading of the sources might view the orphaned, especially younger, child as an inconvenient adjunct to valuable land. An inconvenience, which guardians were prepared to accept if it meant access to precious landed resources. From this perspective one might expect perhaps step-parents or mothers to offer homes to non-inheriting siblings, but equally expect reluctance to offer a home to siblings or half-siblings who did not come with any landed status. This is indeed a well-known topos found across a myriad of folk stories and Märchen.

However, there is significant evidence that even in cases where the guardians do not appear to have been close relatives, younger siblings were taken in. At the manor of Norton in 1312 Laurence de Blaseworth accepted the guardianship of three teenagers who were the children of Sibyl the widow of John Norton. It is unclear what inheritance practice was associated with the holding, but as the teenagers were all girls, Joan being the eldest at 17, followed by Agnes aged 15 and Margaret aged 13, it is possible that the young women were expected to inherit equally upon reaching majority.[13] In cases where partible inheritance was practised, such as on some holdings at Walsham le Willows, guardians sometimes quite explicitly offered a home to all children who were seen as potential heirs. In 1329, Hilary, the widow of the unfree tenant William Lene of Walsham, was granted guardianship over William's two sons, William, aged 10 and Robert aged 6.[14]

However, there is also evidence of guardians who took on wardships over both heirs and their siblings when these were clearly not in line of inheritance. Thus John Deepslough—to whom we shall return later, took on the guardianship of Thomas Silby's heiress Johanna, while also taking care of 'two boys'. It is notable that the heiress was the daughter, and not the boys in this case. While we generally associate medieval society with patriarchal landholding and inheritance structures, such cases may have been more common than we might think. At the root of this lies the very elasticity and eclectic nature of medieval peasant households. The two boys may have been younger half-brothers or illegitimate half-brothers of Johanna, as they were not considered to be Silby's direct heirs.[15] They may also have come via a second marriage to Silby. As boys they would normally have taken precedence over Joanna's claim if they had been Silby's sons by blood. Whatever their situation may have been, their guardian Deepslough promised to feed and clothe the two boys until they were able to look after themselves.

In another case found at the Worcestershire manor, Henry le Parklere took on the guardianship of 7-year-old John, the son and heir of John Geralt who died as a villein of the lord. Henry did not merely agree to look after John, but also four other children 'the brothers and sisters of the said John'.[16] This is a very interesting case, as it would be almost impossible for all these four children to be both biologically from the same mother as John, and younger than him. Considering the lengthy period of breastfeeding practised in peasant societies, as we have seen, a child almost per year would probably have been an unlikely scenario. Accordingly, once again, it seems likely that at least some of these children were either illegitimate or half-brothers and sisters or step-siblings brought into the marriage with John Geralt. None of them were in direct line of inheritance, a point perhaps underlined by the expressed relationship of John to his son John, who is described as the 'closest heir by blood of John Geralt'. In other words, while the other four children were certainly seen equal to the boy John in familial terms, as his brothers and sisters, they were not viewed as having an equal right to inheritance.

Consequently, in cases such as this, it becomes evident that the acceptance of wardships was not merely a calculation by guardians concerning their aim of economic improvement. There is plenty of evidence that medieval communities were concerned about those among their midst who were poor and needed support and help.[17] It is true that wardships cannot be divorced from complex economic and sociopolitical considerations, including, for example, desires by individual families or kinship networks to politically align themselves with other family networks in the village, aimed at a long-term gain in status. However, such considerations should not be seen as the sole motivators in accepting wardships in medieval villages.

The importance of mutual aid and concepts of charity and caregiving are particularly pertinent if we consider the ages of the children involved. As over 56% of heirs were 10 years old or younger, and across our entire period nearly 30% of heirs were 5 years old or under, the argument that guardians accepted wardships as this may have provided additional free labour also has to be dismissed, as no child of 5 years of age, or younger can make a productive worker. Instead young children represent a negative labour input, as they cost more, both in food, clothing and supervision, than they could possibly contribute. Such considerations were important, for example for theorists such as Chayanov, whose analysis of peasant household economics stressed that peasant families tended to increase their holdings at the point in time when their children reached ages when their productivity increased.[18] Young children, however, encouraged holdings to be smaller, as so much time has to be spent looking after them and they were as yet unable to contribute to the household's economic activities. Chayanov went as far as to argue that there was a clear relationship between acreages sown by individual peasant households and the overall age of the familial unit. On the one hand, in his own words, 'those that sow small areas consist of young families with a large number of young children, and those that sow more consist of older families in which small children do not play such a great part'.[19]

As peasant households represented the core of all productive processes in rural societies, the composition of the household had a profound impact on its ability to exploit and manipulate the available natural resources. To stay with Chayanov, his argument that below the age of fourteen or fifteen the potential of labour input from any offspring was, while not non-existent, especially after the age of about 6, still very limited is sensible, especially when seen in the context of slowly increasing earning power of young teens at Glastonbury manors discussed earlier. Instead it was only when the age of a household or familial unit came to 14 or 15, with maturing offspring that the proportion of workers to consumers shifts away from the burden of the number of consumers in the household to workers.[20] Therefore, unless plenty of experienced labour was already available in the guardian's household, taking on the wardship of a younger child, especially one who came with siblings, would have made very little economic sense for the guardian indeed.

Complex wardship cases involving siblings also illustrate that we should review the generally accepted position that daughters inherited only in the absence of sons. Rather, as in the Silby case, at least in some manors girls inherited in the absence of biological sons, not sons per se. Conversely, in such cases boys only inherited if they were the closest blood relation of the head of the household, the official tenant, whether male or female. These distinctions were clearly important as the phrase 'closest heir by blood' is also used in cases of disputes over inheritance. This means that peasant communities must therefore have drawn a distinction between different categories of children living in any given household. Considering the significant fluidity prevalent in medieval peasant households, the question of who was a son by blood or not would have been a common occurrence. Such stratifications can also be observed when tenants made provisions for their children which may have included illegitimate children.

An example for this is William Lene of Walsham le Willows, who in his will in 1329 not only provided for his principal heirs, his two legitimate sons, but also his two daughters, by leaving them £4 in cash and his illegitimate son William who inherited a mare valued at 6s. 8d and three ewes valued 6s.[21] Clearly William was not seen to have the same category of rights as even Lene's daughters, but it still would not have been appropriate to provide nothing for the boy, even if he had no legitimate right to any inheritance. The ordering of rights to inheritance was therefore hierarchical, according to bloodline and in relation to marriage.

Regional and local differences in customs often prevailed in such matters. At Hatfield Chase in Yorkshire, acknowledging implicitly the complexity of such inheritance matters, and peasant family structures, the manorial court concluded an inquiry of 24 jurors in 1336 that 'sons or daughters begotten within marriage of one father, although they had various mothers, will have the inheritance, the half – blood notwithstanding'.[22]

As we shall see, in some instances siblings could be split up and sent to live with different guardians. Especially in cases where tenants held land in both free and unfree tenure, the lord himself could take on the responsibility of the child deemed to be the freehold heir. However, such cases are rarely recorded. Generally, the preference appears to have been to house orphaned children together, even if they were not blood relatives.

Chart 3, shows data gathered from manors with exceptionally good records, Winslow, Norton, Halesowen and Walsham le Willows, where several peaks of recorded orphans can be observed. The first notable spike occurs during the period of the Great Famine in the early fourteenth century, which witnessed repeated crop failures between 1316 and 1321. The years 1317 and 1318 in particular stand out with several underaged heirs recorded at the manor of Halesowen. As we have seen previously, the very small holdings these children were set to inherit can be seen as further indication of the poverty of their families. Several child heirs were also recorded between 1325 and 1331, and certainly poor barley and wheat harvests were recorded in 1331 to 1332. The largest peak is of course associated with the arrival of bubonic plague in 1349, when over

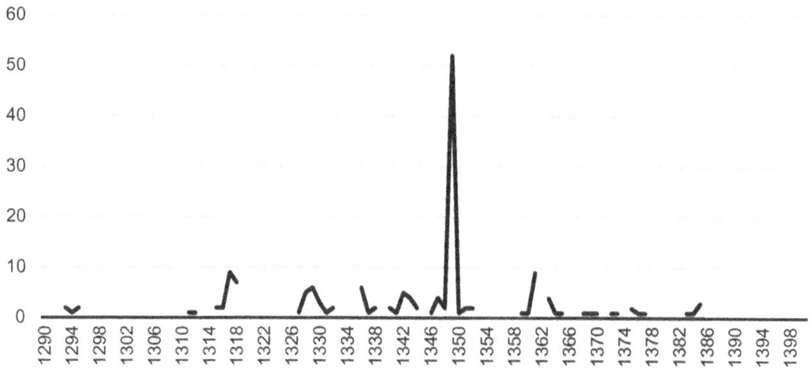

Chart 3 Recorded number of underaged heirs at the manors of Winslow, Norton, Halesowen and Walsham le Willows 1290–1400. Note that records for Winslow only commence in 1322, and for Walsham in 1308. No underaged heir is recorded for the remainder of the fourteenth century at either manor post 1385

50 child heirs were recorded across the manors, attesting to significant mortality levels. Another peak can be seen in 1361 to 1362, coinciding with yet another poor harvest as well as the return of the plague.[23]

It is notable that subsequent plague outbreaks in the 1370s and 80s do not appear to have made an impact on the number of child heirs presented in court. Instead the self-evident scarcity of recorded underaged heirs from the second half of the fourteenth century onwards is evidence for the declining importance of the formal recording of guardianship arrangements in rural communities into the manor court roll, in tandem with the changing patterns of tenure discussed earlier.

Moments of crisis put communities under intense social as well as economic strain and pressure. Mass mortality brought with it a host of practical as well as psychological challenges. Chroniclers tell us about mass graves, manorial records tell us about sudden increased availability of land, and the resultant increased bargaining power of workers and tenants who survived the catastrophe.[24] The extent of the psychological impact caused by events like the Great Famine or the Bubonic Plague are more difficult to assess. Small, generally tight-knit communities which may have constituted of anything between 200 and 500 inhabitants would undoubtedly have been severely traumatised by the death of about half of the village or in some places more, in a fairly short space of time in 1349. While we know that people grieved their dead, manorial documents are silent about the emotional world of these young heirs, whose fates were decided by the manorial court. Their trauma, sense of confusion and dislocation, or indeed any stigma they might have experienced for coming from a plague affected household especially among the very young children can only be guessed at.[25]

The only reason these underaged heirs appear in manorial records is that they were connected to land—either as heirs or potential heirs and because they were assigned a guardian. As we have already seen, motivations for guardianship were complex and very much dependent on individual circumstances—family connections, social status, potentially political ramifications and, of course, economic considerations of wealth and size of landholding. It is clear that many guardians took on the responsibility of looking after younger, non-inheriting siblings or very young heirs not due to economic calculations, but presumably because they cared about the children of their neighbours and kin. While the process of guardianship has sometimes been represented as a rather cold-blooded affair, if we look beyond the unemotional language of the manorial court, it becomes clearer that the rationale behind guardianships was not. In turning to take a closer look at the guardians themselves it will be possible to unpick some of these motivations and also examine the social structures in villages which allocated wardships.

2 The Peasant Guardians

Lords played an important role, at least notionally in the process of finding guardians and awarding wardships. Indeed, the subject of guardianship especially involving unfree tenements cannot really be adequately explored without considering the roles and motivations of lordship. Ultimately all unfree land and holdings belonged to the local lord. As such, the rituals associated with handing over land from a deceased head of the household, the legal tenant in the eyes of manorial custom and law, to their heir via the hands of the lord were also reflected in the awarding of wardships. The ritual recognised the dominion and rule of the lord, and as such it was formally from the hands of the lord that an heir and/or their guardian received the land. The lord's interest in such matters of inheritance was accordingly cemented and reaffirmed in the manorial court.[26] The ritualistic transmission of land to the guardian also represented a check by the lord as well as the community, that lands, chattels and ward were in reliable hands until the heirs came of age. In almost all cases, barring some exceptions where lords assumed the role of guardian themselves, which will be discussed below, this is the point at which such formal seigniorial involvement ended.

In most cases, courts awarded guardianship to the closest living relatives of the heir in question. It is important to bear in mind that the minors in this study were both orphaned children as well as children whose guardians died who had been manorial tenants of the lord, but not necessarily the direct or biological parent of the child. Therefore, while in almost all cases those who died were a parent or both parents of the child, the deceased were not always fathers, mothers or step-parents. Still, in the vast majority of cases the adult carer who had died and left their holding to the minor were their fathers or stepfathers.

It has been argued that in medieval England feudal relationships dictated that upon the 'death of the tenant and father', land automatically 'returned to the overlord', leaving the mother with 'no right to the guardianship of her child'.[27] However the manorial records speak of very contrasting conditions. In a tradition which appears to have been already established in the seventh century under King Ine of Wessex, the guardianship of a child should go to the mother upon the death of the father.[28] In the thirteenth and fourteenth centuries, similarly the default policy of the manor court was to look first to the closest relative to act as a guardian. The most commonly named guardian were mothers or stepmothers accounting together for over 39% of appointed guardians at the manors of Walsham le Willows, Norton, Winslow and Halesowen. Stepmothers and their children would not have been blood relatives, although there may well have been half-siblings in the household. Yet they were still seen as the closest relative of any minor in the absence of the father, and if a mother or stepmother was alive, the guardianship was always awarded to them almost automatically.

However, at times of serious crisis, punctuated by high mortality, during famine or much more acutely, upon the arrival of the Black Death, such systems were placed under intense stress. The resultant provision for the care of rural orphans shifted at such times, and high mortality had a centrifugal effect on familial care structures. In a pattern which has also been recognised in other studies, children were sent to homes of more distant relatives. Clark has argued that while the lord would first turn to the closest relatives of the deceased tenants, the 'usual procedure involved paternal kin in the wardship of paternal inheritance, maternal kin to the wardship of maternal inheritance'.[29] If all else failed, the lord and court would turn to neighbours who had no apparent direct or indirect kinship ties to the minors.[30] The situation can be compared to shifting patterns of orphan care in African communities initiated by the Aids crisis—or more recently—the Ebola outbreak, where structures of traditional care for orphans were under great stress.[31]

As we have seen, orphan care in medieval society was seen as a communal matter; children were not merely considered a matter of concern for their biological parents. This meant that at crisis points communities stepped into provide for vulnerable youngsters, and the recording of guardianship arrangements into manorial court rolls were not merely a convenience of record keeping on the movement of land, but also a practical way of recording contractual obligations on the part of the guardian to take care of the orphan until their age of majority. In this sense medieval communities also embedded their orphaned children and other underaged heirs within communal affairs (Chart 4).

Women clearly played a predominant role as mothers and stepmothers in looking after underaged heirs and hence in preparing future tenants for their roles for the lord and the village communities. These women would have been looking after the heirs and their inheritance in their own name, at least while they remained unmarried.

However, the largest single category of guardian are people grouped under 'other'. These are individuals, who were named in the court records but for whom no direct relationship to the heir can be established. This does not mean that they were not related to the child heir,

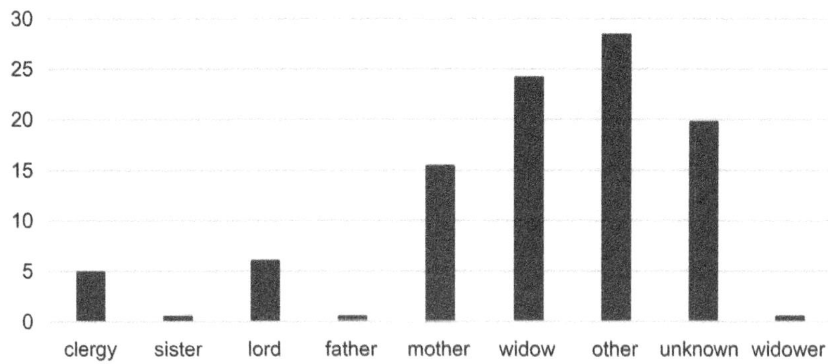

Chart 4 Guardians recorded at Winslow, Halesowen, Walsham le Willows and Norton from 1290 to 1400 in per cent

but merely that a familial relationship cannot be proven or shown. It is therefore to be expected that a number of 'others' include uncles and more distant relatives connected through kinship ties horizontally by marriage. As such these statistics offer a guidance to general patterns, but will necessarily include errors. It is also probable that among the 'others' are also godparents of the heirs. Godparents are very rarely mentioned in manorial records as such, and while occasionally guardians are described as 'kinsman', 'uncle' or even 'sister', no indication of the role of godparents in orphan care can be ascertained through these present sources. Only one godparent relationship is mentioned across the entire chronology and all the manors under study. In June 1427, Joan Watts at Winslow mentioned her godson William Childe in her will, leaving him '1 bushel of malt'.[32] However, it was not Joan who was looking after William Childe, who appears to have been an underaged heir in his teens at the time, and in service with John Kyng, until he inherited his father's holding of one virgate of land in 1444.[33] However, it is the only entry which shows that godparents did have some element of a caregiving role to their godchildren.

Where uncles are mentioned as guardians, the relationship seems to have been patrilinear.[34] At Halesowen in 1279 Richard the son of William Putteneye was placed under the guardianship of Thomas Puteneye, as it was noted that 'the boy shall be in the custody of his uncle for the said term'. Judging by the shared surname, Thomas is therefore likely to have been the deceased father's brother.[35] Similarly at the manor of Norton in 1336, the 14-year-old Richard son of William Bate was placed with his 'uncle' Henry Bate, who, again, if we can trust the shared surname, appears to have been the brother of William's father.[36] Conversely, however, no explicit case of an aunt acting as guardian could be found. That does not mean that aunts did not act as guardians, but that if this happened it was not expressly stated.

The category of 'unknown' guardians is also significant, and these include cases where the identity of a guardian is not known. Such cases are most common in periods of dislocation, especially during the first arrival of the Black Death. In Walsham le Willows John Goche died in 1349 leaving his two sons, aged 10 and 2 a smallholding containing half a messuage and 6 acres of land. No guardian is recorded, only that the boys 'have entry'.[37] The phrase should not be mistaken to mean that the boys were expected to hold the tenement in their own right at the rather tender age of 2 and 10 years, but rather that it was acknowledged that the holding was legitimately theirs. In the same month another member of the Goche family, Peter Goche succumbed to the plague leaving behind his 4-year-old son John, who, it was noted 'has entry', before adding that the holding was granted to Robert Man and his wife Catherine until John came of full age.[38] In other words therefore, the Goche sons must have had a guardian, even if the information regarding their identity is missing from the court record. Such missing data is by no means uncommon especially in the plague years when mass mortality led to a degree of confusion and hasty decisions which were not always clearly written down. Similarly, even if it was not explicitly made clear, Peter Goche's son John must have been placed under the guardianship of Robert Man and Catherine—as is implicit in their tenure of his lands.

Chart 5 demonstrates a strong correlation between crisis points with elevated levels of mortality and the incidents of unknown guardians or guardians who were more likely to be more distant relatives or have no known kinship relationship. In 1349 the situation was so acute that over 52% of guardians at the manors of Winslow, Walsham and Halesowen could not be identified as close relatives of the heirs. The figure is higher at over 57% if we include members of the clergy who acted as guardians for minors. Outside of periods of high crisis only 40% of children were placed into the guardianship of 'others' or whose guardian was unknown.

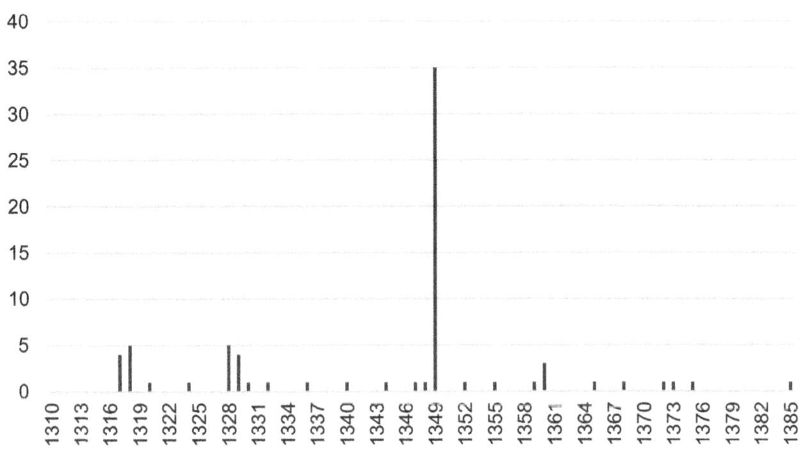

Chart 5 Incidents of 'Other' and 'Unknown' guardians at the manors of Walsham le Willows, Winslow and Halesowen

The role of the clergy in taking on guardianship of minors is surprisingly marginal in these rural communities, considering that fatherless children were viewed as deserving the special protection of the church.[39] Members of the clergy only seemed to have stepped in as guardians as a very last resort, mainly during the crisis of the first arrival of the Black Death, and predominantly only at one manor of our sample, Winslow. Master Geoffrey the vicar of the village of Greneburgh which was under the manorial jurisdiction of Winslow took over the guardianship of several minors and their lands, ranging in age from 8 to 12 as well as their siblings. In the case of the 12-year-old Ralph son of William King who died in the plague year of 1349 this included at least one younger brother Walter and a sister called Agnes.[40] In total between 1342 and before the end of the first attack of the plague in 1349 he took in 6 children we know of.[41] It is unclear how Geoffrey looked after the children and their holdings with \ll their obligations. But, given that he must have had some help, it is likely that this was arranged through parish structures which are hidden from the manorial records. It is highly unlikely—again—that economic motivations were the main or any reason for accepting so many orphans as wards. Instead we can understand Geoffrey's actions primarily as charitable. Since we have no evidence that the lord excused any servile dues which were attached to the holdings of these orphans, we have to conclude that any villagers who would have helped to perform such dues similarly did so out of charitable motivations.

It is possible that some of the couples who agreed to accept wards did so due to their own childlessness or because their own children had died, but we have no evidence for this in our records. In this context it is important to note that guardianship and the acceptance of wards was not the same as adoption. Adoption has received some attention by historians, especially in continental Europe. Kerstin Gager has, for example, highlighted the prejudices and difficulties which surrounded early modern adoption in France. The roots of some of the contemporary concerns Gager identified, such as practical matters including blurring of the lines of inheritance or bloodlines, alongside perceptions of adoption as a practice contravening the will of god—for childless couples to remain childless—for examples—did not apply in the case of guardianships.[42]

The way guardianship was conceptualised was not that a ward was seen to transfer to other parents, even in cases where the child was orphaned and not merely fatherless; rather the guardians acted in loco parentis. They might be told to treat their ward like their own child, but the ward came with their own inheritances, bloodlines and networks, which might be more or less socially or economically significant than the guardian's own standing. The ward was however never, and certainly not automatically, entitled to any chattels or lands from their guardians. As such guardianship agreements could not confuse lines of inheritance. Accordingly, the care for fatherless children and orphans could be viewed entirely positively in the community, as charitable acts, as economically fruitful, or as socially beneficial, without any of the threats implicit or explicit to such structures in the case of adoptions.

Siblings make only very rare appearances as guardians. In Wakefield a very interesting case involving the granting of wardship to a brother also sheds some rare light on the obscure ritual often referred to in manorial documents by the phrase 'to hold by the rod', indicating unfree tenure at the will of the lord. In 1275 a tenant named William had granted one bovate of his land to his son Thomas, his firstborn and one bovate of land was granted to Richard, his younger son. Upon William's death, the sons came to court to pay for their land. Thereupon the steward of the manor proceeded to ritually hand over the land to the heirs holding the rod, symbolising the link between tenant and lordship. Thus, 'holding a rod in his hand, of which one end was black and the other white, gave seisin to Richard with the white end, because he was fair in colour, and gave seisin to Thomas with the black end'. The Steward then realised that Richard was not of full age to 'hold or keep the land', and he appointed Thomas as the guardian of his brother, until his coming of full age.[43]

While such cases of guardianship between siblings are rarely made explicit, it is possible that some have not been identified and are grouped among 'others'. We do know from the study of Coroner's rolls that siblings did play an important role in looking after younger brothers and sisters in medieval society, it is unclear to what extent this continued into the adulthood of especially older siblings.[44]

Occasionally relatives worked together to look after an heir and their inheritance in order to share the burden of looking after a holding, which might have caused particular problems to a household headed by a single parent who had other younger dependent children. When William the 14-year-old son of J. [full name unknown] Steinwulf of Halesowen was set to inherit an unknown amount of land, the custody of the boy was taken on by his mother, but half the land was entrusted to his uncle William for a period of 6 years in return for an allowance of grain and clothing.[45]

If we consider the distribution of heirs (Table 3) by sex to guardian we find that for the most part there is no significant gendered differences in the allocation of heirs to specific guardians. While we have a very small number of male heirs being placed under the guardianship of brothers and sisters, where we have none for girls, the numbers are too small to be statistically significant, especially as we have far fewer girl heirs than boy heirs, as we have seen. Where we do have significant data, as for the main categories of guardians, including, mothers, stepmothers, others, unknowns and the lord, gender differences are practically absent.

Therefore, it is safe to conclude that communities did not make a conscious decision to send boys or girls to different type of guardians due to their sex. All court rolls carefully differentiated between guardians who were described as mothers of the heirs and guardians who were described as 'wife' or 'widow' of the deceased male tenant and head of the household. In 1343 Christina was described as 'the mother of Roger' who was the son of Thomas le Peer who had died and as such was also described to be as 'closest in blood relation of the same Thomas' accordingly Roger was designated Thomas' heir and the guardianship was handed to Roger's mother.[46] However, two years later, when Roger Huwlot died leaving his young son John, aged six and a half as his closest heir, the guardianship was granted to Margery, who 'was the wife of the said Roger'.[47] Considering the care which was taken in the wording of guardianship cases, it is hard to conclude that this distinction was anything else except deliberate. Therefore, the distinction in these records may well allow us a rare glimpse into the prevalence of step-parentage in later medieval rural societies.

Table 3 Allocated guardians according to gender at Winslow, Halesowen, Norton, Walsham le Willows

Guardian	*Girl (%)*	*Boy (%)*
Clergy	2	5
Father	4	–
Lord	9	5
Mother	12	16
Widow	20	21
Other	37	33
Unknown	16	17
Brother	–	1
Sister	–	1
Widower	–	1

We know that due to mortality levels the experience of step-parentage would have been common in medieval society and here we have confirmation for this.[48] The importance of step-parents is clear and may have had significant social and cultural consequences. The prevalence of step-parents in medieval society has long been recognised, as the frequency of remarriages in some cases more than once has been well documented.[49] However, due to lack of sources allowing us direct insights into familial compositions, it has proved to be much more difficult to ascertain the true incidence of step-parent families, especially in the countryside. Cunningham has argued that the effects of premature deaths of parents in medieval society would be highly comparable to the effects of divorce on familial constitution in the twenty-first century.[50] In reality, however, the incidence of step-parentage in medieval rural society was probably considerably higher.

According to the Office of National Statistics, in 2011 a total of 12.7% of all families in the UK were step-families.[51] While we do not have any manorial sources stating such census information, we might be able to gain some approximate insights, by exploring the way guardians were allocated to underaged heirs. If we take the number of orphans or wards who were allocated to either their mother or the widow of their fathers as wards at the manors of Walsham le Willows, Norton, Winslow and Halesowen, and if we read the term 'widow' as against 'mother' as de facto step-parent, then we are led to the conclusion that of the child heirs requiring guardians at these manors, 59% of those who were looked after a surviving parent, were looked after by stepmothers. 'Widows' represented nearly 25% of all guardians overall. If 25% can be read as roughly representative of the incidence of stepmothers in rural society as a whole, this would mean that the experience of stepmotherhood alone was nearly twice—as common in later medieval English society than step-parentage in recent contemporary society. The true incidence of step-parentage (including therefore stepfathers) would have been even greater. This is not only interesting information on the nature of family compositions, but as we have seen, also causes our perhaps rather simplistic image of simple, linear and patriarchal inheritance patterns to founder.

On the one hand, such statistics underline the notion of a permanent nuclear family with one father and one mother in a stable long-term relationship as only a mythologised, modern political construct, with little basis in historical realities; on the other, it demonstrates the significant malleability and eclectic nature of medieval rural family structures. The significant level of elasticity which has been observed in rural household and familial structures which has, for example also been noted by Hanawalt, therefore finds confirmation in these figures.[52] We have already seen how rural societies might view step or half-brothers as indeed 'brothers' even if they might have no rights on inheritance. However, the attitudes regarding step-parentage are more difficult to gauge.

The theme of the 'wicked stepmother', is well known, and a common trope in folklore. Shahar has similarly pointed out that problematic characters of unpleasant stepmothers are also common in the Life of Saints.[53] She suggested that the trope of the wicked stepmother might have been more prominent than that of the stepfather due to the greater prevalence of children 'raised in the parental home by a second wife (and not by paternal or maternal relatives) than of children raise by re-married mothers'.[54] It is likely that widowers often married younger spouses than widows, which would explain why such stepmothers were perhaps more likely to survive their husbands.

The image or representation of the evil stepmother who prefers her own biological children over any others acquired by marriage has inspired evolutionary biologists led by Martin Daley and Margo Wilson, to explore underlying biological, rather than cultural factors responsible for the often conflictual relationships between stepmothers and their children. They have argued that a 'Cinderella effect' can be identified whereby children are far more likely to be killed, abused or neglected by non-biological guardians. Other sociocultural and economic factors, including social class and poverty, were found to play only a marginal role in step-relationships.[55] The research has since been broadened to other areas and socio-economic contexts and seems to find widespread verification.[56] The underlying argument which is advanced is that from a Darwinian point of view the preference to expend more intensive parental care and affection on biological offspring makes evolutionary sense, as concern over the survival of biological children will lead to discrimination over that of step-children.[57] If cultural factors are truly peripheral to the experience of step-relationships, this research would have important implications for the experience of medieval family life. On the face of it, it would indicate potentially rather fractious and difficult family relationships, fraught with problems and conflict, if indeed step-parentage was as common and prevalent as our statistics indicate. A crucial question in this context therefore must be the extent of communal regulation and involvement in such familial relationships. As we have seen, communities as a whole played important roles in ensuring the well-being of underaged heirs, by effectively turning the awards of wardships into contractual relationships, the details of which were written down in manorial court rolls, so that in case of dispute they could be easily referred to in the future. The very fact that they existed in contract form is indicative of the recognition of at least the potentiality of a prevalence of problems. Furthermore, the widespread exhortations to look after the ward and inheritance adequately are similarly a reflection of such concerns by communities. The real problem for the theory of the Cinderella effect however, lies in the interesting fact that widows were almost as unlikely as mothers to be warned to feed and clothes their wards adequately, as we have seen in Chapter 2. This would mean that communities did not routinely associate wilful neglect of heirs with stepmothers.

In this context the frequency of stepmothers and very eclectic and frequently shifting family structures may well have contributed to the normalisation of the experience of step-parentage. In other words, a widespread cultural acceptance of stepmotherhood may have inhibited negative or even hostile behaviour from stepmothers. Fundamentally, Märchen are narratives of the aberrant, fears of the abnormal and marginal behaviour. Accordingly, we cannot conclude or even suspect the widespread ill-treatment of stepchildren, as this was not anticipated in communities, despite—or probably because—of the eclectic family structures in medieval villages which would have frequently contained several step-relationships.

The guardians were always chosen with care and as far as we can tell, deliberation, communities tried their best to keep families together and children with close relatives, the church only stepped in in extraordinary circumstances. The evidence of the guardians is indicative of a culture which cared about its young people and their future well-being. It also shows culturally quite different familial experiences to our own, evidencing family structures which appear quite informal and inclusive of half-siblings and step-parents and step-kin.

3 The Roles of Lords; Guardians and Profiteers

Lords played an important role as guardians, but generally and predominantly only in cases of freehold tenure. On some manors the only types of guardianships recorded were those which involved freehold land, as was the case at the manor of Brandon in Suffolk, held by the

Bishop of Ely. Here the default position of orphans, as well as underaged heirs and their free land seems to have been to be assigned to the responsibility of the lord. Thus when John son of John de Metefeld of Brandon died in 1347, leaving behind his 7-year-old son John, who was due to inherit 2 messuages and 7 acres of land in free tenure, the court noted that 'the lord owes to have wardship of the said heir therefore it is ordered to seize the holding and the body of the said heir'.[58] The holding was accordingly 'seized' thus effectively taken possession of by the lord and transferred into the hands of the lord. The 'body' of the heir himself likewise. The choice of words is significant here. The body designated that child, very distinctly from his rights to the inheritance. The implication is that the lord too had direct and clear responsibility of the child heir himself; on the other hand the term also indicated ownership and possession. In this case the future of the relationship between the lord and the Metefeld family soured. We do not know why relationships broke down, but they certainly did, as a later generation of the Metefelds turned out to be very active local and regional rebels in the 1381 revolt, and William Metefeld emerged as a local rebel leader, who was also later pardoned for his role in the rising.[59]

However, even when lords had rights or duties of guardianship, it was comparatively rare for lords to actually act on these. In most cases of underaged heirs among freeholders, if the mother of the ward was alive the custody was subsequently granted to her. In 1371, for example Nicholas, the son of Robert Smith who had died, was 12 years old when the court was ordered to take his holding into the lord's hands 'together with the body of the said heir due to him being ward of the lord'. However, 'afterwards Agnes the mother of the said Nicholas came' and found pledges and wardship was thereby transferred from the lord to the mother.[60] The phrase that 'the body of the heir' was to be taken to the lord indicates once again that lords did actually assume the responsibility of looking after the child and their physical needs, as well as their landed inheritance. Brandon was not the only manor where lords assumed direct responsibility over the heirs of freehold tenants. In some cases this custom of direct seigniorial intervention could lead to siblings being split up if a tenant died holding both free and unfree land. When William le Swon died in 1344 at the manor of Winslow, he held from the lord a smallholding comprised of a messuage, four acres and one rood of free land as well as two and half acres of unfree, villein land.[61] The court split the custody over the land and William's two heirs. John, his eldest son aged 11 was considered 'nearest heir to the free land and will remain in the lord's custody', his 8-year-old younger son John was considered 'his nearest heir to the villein land', and his custody was handed over to Bartholomew Wethege.[62]

The case shows not only that lordship was more closely associated with free land, but also that free land had a higher status than unfree land, where under male primogeniture the eldest son was to inherit the free land and the younger the unfree land, as if they were separate holdings, with no relationship to each other.

Occasionally land was ordered to be taken into the lord's hands if no guardian for a young heir could be found. This can be observed most commonly in times of high mortality, such as the Black Death. At Walsham le Willows for example in 1349 upon the death of John Pynfoul it was ordered to take his holding of 2 acres into the hands of the lord, and to 'report of the profits', that is the reeve was to account for any profits gained from the land while in the lord's hands. What is not clear in this and similar cases is what became of John's heiress, his 5-year-old daughter Hilary.[63] In such cases the point at issue is not responsibility over guardianship but rather land, which was not tilled on account of having no tenant, being taken into the lord's hands until a tenant could be found. This is even spelled out in a Court in Walsham le Willows in 1384, where 13 acres and 3 roods of land which 6-year-old Lucy Bretonn was due to inherit was taken into the hands of the lord until Lucy was to reach majority, 'because nobody came to receive the said tenement'.[64]

A fiduciary relationship between lord and tenant thus only existed in the context of freehold tenure, when lords assumed a special role of protector and guardian over the heir and his prospective inheritance. While it has been argued that such relationships only occurred in the case of tenure in socage, this does not seem to be the case in all manors.[65] The Custumal of the manor of Laughton in Sussex dating from 1292, noted that some of the freeholders were not entitled to seigniorial wardship. Accordingly John de Monceus, who held from the lord 200 acres of woodland was told that 'even if his heir be under age he shall not be in custody of the lord because he holds by Socage'.[66] Therefore seigniorial protection of the ward and their land could be a privilege, and in the same custumal is mentioned as a clear perk in relation to the tenancy of Robert de Byreche. Robert held a very substantial 69 acres of land in addition to some meadow. He was also a forester and the custumal noted that 'the lord shall have ward and the marriage right of his heirs' should he die.[67]

The notion that lords had a special responsibility to the heirs of freehold property might be rooted in structures of the feudal order.[68] There may be several reasons why lords very rarely assumed direct responsibility for wards and their inheritance in the case of unfree tenures within their manorial jurisdiction. It could be argued that the sale of wardships represented too lucrative a prospect for lords to pass over. It has been noted that wardships could be profitable for lords, both in the sense of gaining financial income from selling wardships and by gaining profits from holdings under their ward.[69] However, while selling wardships was certainly a source of profit, it is unconvincing that assumption of guardianships by the lord over, especially smaller, peasant holdings was seen by lords as particularly profitable. Lords held far more substantial acreages than their peasant tenants, including their freeholders, in most ordinary years the additional income from, say the seven acres of land held by Brandon's Metefeld family, would appear pitiful next to the lord's demesne at the manor of several hundred acres.

Furthermore, while the wardship of a teenager may well be seen as supplying additional labour power, including in the lord's own household, the same cannot be said of very young children, like, to stay with our example, 7-year-old John Metefeld. In the case of much more substantial tenants, such as Robert de Byreche, profits from the tenement might have been more lucrative, but this does not explain while wardships of large holdings such as those of John de Monceus were also sometimes shunned.

Interesting corroborating evidence can be found in the behaviour of lords post-Black Death. We know that lords felt particularly threatened by the rising wages and highly mobile labourers in the post-Black Death decades. Various manorial evidence alongside legal evidence like the Statute of Labourers attests to this fact. The land to labour ratio had shifted considerably due to the demographic collapse. A ready supply of land with limited labour meant that labour became a precious commodity, something peasants and labourers were only too aware of. In response, well-known attempts were made to freeze wages to pre-plague levels and hamper worker mobility, which helped to create competition between lords for sparse and expensive labour. Considering these circumstances, it is perhaps striking that there is no sign of a trend by lords to gather wards, even older wards under their authority.[70] In principle older wards should have been viewed as easy and cheap labour, but clearly they were not. This must tell us something about the low value associated with the labour of younger teenagers or older children.[71]

Similarly, the nature of exploitation of the resources which came with an heir's holding might be limited as heirs could, as we will see later, sue their guardians in cases of mismanagement—which could also include freeholders, though not villeins, who could—at least in theory—have tried to sue their lord. More importantly, such guardianships were by their nature only for limited periods after which they had to be returned to the heir upon them reaching majority.

When lords did take on wardships over minors, they often, rather unsurprisingly considering the circumstances, just leased the land and holdings out to other tenants for a fixed term. The Petworth Minister's Accounts in Sussex thus note several properties leased out at farm. In the accounting year of 1347–48 for example, at Petworth 10s. 6d. were received 'from the farm of land in Imbehagh, being in the lord's hands by reason of the minority of Roger son and heir of John de Shelvestrode'.[72] By 1352–53, after the Black Death added to the toll of minors, a total of 4 wardships yielded a rental income of no less than 81s. 4d. per annum.[73] This clearly represented a significant income, however, the annual farm rent of the cottage 'in the lord's hands because of the minority of Thomas Dawtrey' at Duncton in 1352–53, was at 12d., hardly the most profitable source of income.[74]

One important way for lords to profit from wardships was the collection of fines from their tenants upon being granted the guardianship over an heir and their holding. Across all manors examined, some lords appear to have been much more systematic in extracting payments for wardships than others. The sums considered in this context are not heriots or indeed entry fines to the holdings, which were recorded as well, but rather separate sums of money which went to the lord and are often accompanied by explanatory phrases such as 'to have the wardship' or 'for the wardship'. In many cases this sum also included a licence for the heir to be allowed to marry, thus purchased in some cases many years in advance of any actual marriage. Such marriage licences, or merchets were usually fairly systematically extracted from unfree, villein tenants by lords, not least as they represented a clear test of villeinage. Free tenants had no obligation to ask their lord's permission to marry, and hence paid no merchets.[75]

There was significant local variation in the consistency of the extraction of payments for wardships. No financial returns for any wardships are recorded at all at the manor of Brandon, even when the lord handed wardships over to the mothers of local freehold heirs. At Walsham le Willows, similarly only a very small handful of guardianship cases involved any payment. At the manor of Eldersfield only one payment for a wardship is recorded.

We do have a good set of data from the manor of Halesowen. Here some interesting patterns and changes across time can be observed in the payments made for wardships. Average payments made at the manor in the later thirteenth century, from 1270 to 1300 are 13s., with the lowest payment recorded in this period of 6s. 8d. and the highest of 20s. From 1300 to 1348, before the arrival of the Black Death the average payment was higher at 15s., this time with some considerable variation in individual payments extracted, ranging from 10d., collected during the famine years, to 50s and even in one case 5 Marks, amounting to over 66s., demanded for a wardship in 1320. Total profits in the first half of the fourteenth century amounted to £14, 4s. 5d. After the Black Death, however the average rate of payment for a wardship fell to 10s. 8d., reflecting once again a falling demand for land and increasing seigniorial and perhaps also communal difficulties in finding families willing to take on the responsibilities associated with wardships. Similarly, the overall profits derived from wardships also fell very significantly from the arrival of the Black Death onwards. Amounting to merely £4, 5s. 5d.

The most dramatic data comes from the St Albans manor of Winslow. At this Buckinghamshire manor the lord very conscientiously collected cash for wardships, perhaps not surprising for a lord who was happy to collect pots and plates as heriots from his plague-stricken tenants. Before the Black Death had made its way to Winslow, from 1327 to 1348 the lord had collected a total of £24, 6s. 6d. across this period. Payments made by tenants for wardships varied significantly and appear to bear little relationship to the size of the holding in question. The lowest payment collected was 4d. for a cottage and the highest 46s. 8d. for a larger holding containing a virgate of land. However, in the same year Agnes, the widow of Ralph Rolf paid only 33s. 4d. to have the wardship over a virgate of land, and in 1342 Alice, paid a rather hefty 8s. for the wardship over her son's smallholding of 5 acres.[76] Some variation may have been due to factors affecting the overall value of the holding, additional buildings present on the messuage, soil quality and location of arable land. However, as variations were quite pronounced in some cases, such factors on their own can probably not account for them. Instead it has to be accepted that the lord exercised a degree of arbitrariness in assessing the value of wardships. While in general larger acreages tended to yield higher payments, a wardship for a virgate could cost as little as 26s., or 30s. while the wardship of a smallholding could cost 4d., 40d., 8s., or as much as 13s. 4d. The average payment for a wardship in this pre-plague period was 15s. 8d.

The value of average payments for wardships dropped significantly in the post-plague period. Despite many more cases of wards being recorded in the manor court at the manor post-Black Death, the community was clearly struggling to accommodate the minors and their inheritances at the manor. As we have seen before, we have 7 recorded cases of wardship where payments were expressly excused by the lord, in addition to a total of 14 cases where no payment has been recorded. These latter have been excluded from calculation of averages as we do not know for certain that there were not scribal oversights. We are left with a total of 34 sales of wardship in this period which did record the nature of the financial transaction. These again show a significant arbitrary element to the sums demanded. Ranging from 4d. to over 26s. However, wardships were substantially less profitable in the post-Black Death period up to 1377, and in total the lord only made £15, 9s. despite the peak of wardships recorded in the plague year. The reason for this relative decline in the profitability of wardships is that the average payment made for wardships also dropped. If we include those where payments were excused the average payment was 7s. 7d.; if we exclude the excused payments from our calculations the average payment was 9s. 1d. No less than 6s. 7d. lower than the average payment collected prior to the Black Death.

At the St Albans manor of Norton similar, though not quite as dramatic, patterns can be discerned. Before the Black Death the lord made a total of £5, and 8d. from the same of wardships, after the Black Death the recording of the payments for wardships is more haphazard, and in one case of a holding containing a quarter of a virgate one messuage, a croft and a toft, the lord accepted in payment 2 hens instead of cash.[77]

The average payment collected before the Black Death amounted to 8s. 5d. After the Black Death it is higher at 10s. 3d. However, this average is skewed due to the recording of one exceptionally high payment for a wardship of no less than 60s. for a holding in 1350, the size of which is unknown.[78] Of the remaining payments for wardships the lowest payment is 12d. and the highest 7s., underlining how unrepresentative a 60s. payment is for this period. If we therefore exclude this one payment from our calculations, we reach a more representative average payment of merely 2s. 4d. per wardship. It is striking that the profitability of wardships declined, even though, as we have seen, the number of underaged heirs looking for guardians peaked significantly in the year of the first arrival of the Black Death. The decline in income for lords was therefore real as well as pronounced.[79]

The level of profitability of wardships for lords is accordingly highly variable, and from the sample examined it appears to be the case that stronger lordship—as can be seen at St Albans, is associated with higher profitability of the sale of wardships, while some lords appear to have gained no, or barely any, profit at all from wardships. Rates for wardships were influenced by three key factors. The price of wardships was to some degree market sensitive. Generally speaking, wardships were more expensive at times of higher demand for land that is in the later thirteenth and early fourteenth century, and less expensive post-Black Death. However, this was also influenced by a second factor, namely the ability of individual lords to exact in some cases very high payments. Finally there was some relationship to the size of holding, but the influence of this seemed tempered by the dynamic of negotiation between lord and tenant, This was influenced to some degree, as we have seen by ability (or inability) to pay on the part of the guardian, but also their willingness or not to take on an additional plot of land, which might be an asset during land scarcity or a burden when land was abundant.

Research of the post-Black Death economic developments has neglected wardship developments. However, as we have seen, wardships could be lucrative for lords, and the decline in their value post-Black Death thereby diminished an important stream of income. In other respects lords had a more distant relationship to wards. They were not particularly interested in looking after the offspring or the land of their peasants. They did, however, play an important role in regulating and to some extent overseeing the wardship system.

This chapter has focused primarily on the social and economic relationships surrounding wardships. It demonstrated the work of the rural communities in regulating and intervening in families which left children orphaned or an heir at too young an age. While children were recognised to be vulnerable and inexperienced, the way wardships were organised within manors shows the practical solutions to the problem of underaged heirs at work in the localities, in association with, and under the auspices, of lordship. At the same time, examining the children and their guardians more closely allows important insights into peasant mentalities, structures of family households, in particular, the importance of step-relationships, which are so very richly demonstrated in the examples of underaged heirs. As we have seen, it can hardly be overemphasised how common step-relationships within individual peasant family households were. Moreover, the nature of the dynamics which underpinned these communal relationships themselves were deeply influenced by a backdrop of demographic, social and economic change, creating an intricate dialectical relationship between families, land and lordship, brought into focus through the examination of the children in their communities.

Notes

1. The literature on this is quite extensive. See for example: B.A. Hanawalt, *The Ties That Bound, Peasant Families in Medieval England* (New York, Oxford: Oxford University Press, 1986), p. 91; Z. Razi, *Life, Marriage and Death in a Medieval Parish Economy, Society and Demography in Halesowen 1270–1400* (Cambridge: Cambridge University Press, 1980); C. Dyer, *Making a Living in the Middle Ages; The People of Britain 850–1520* (New Haven and London: Yale University Press, 2002), esp. pp. 156–158.
2. A similar point was made by C. Dyer, *Making a Living in the Middle Ages*, p. 158.
3. B.A. Hanawalt, *The Ties that Bound*, p. 83 and p. 91.
4. For a discussion of nursing, and the dangers medieval commentators already correctly associated with feeding infants with non-human milk, see: S. Shahar, *Childhood in the Middle Ages* (London and New York, 1992), esp. pp. 53–57.
5. *Winslow Manor Court Books, Part I 1327–1377*, p. 232.
6. S. Tarbin, 'Caring for Poor and Fatherless Children in London, c. 1350–1550', in: *Journal of the History of Childhood and Youth*, vol. 3, no. 3 (2010), p. 394.
7. E. Clark, 'City Orphans and Custody Laws in Medieval England', in: *The American Journal of Legal History*, vol. 34, no. 2 (April 1990), p. 176.
8. R.M. Smith, 'Women's Property Rights under Customary Law: Some Developments in the Thirteenth and Fourteenth Centuries', in: *Transactions of the Royal Historical Society*, 5th series, vol. 36 (1986), p. 165.
9. R. Lock, ed., *The Court Rolls of Walsham le Willows, 1303–1350* (Woodbridge: Boydell & Brewer and Suffolk Record Society, vol. xli, 1998), p. 183.
10. NRO MS DA1, June 1285.
11. E. Clark, 'The Custody of Children in English Manor Courts', in: *Law and History Review*, vol. 3, no. 2 (1985), p. 336.
12. Halesowen Court Rolls, Birmingham Library and Archives, Wolfson Center, MS 3279/346279.

13. P. Foden, ed. and trans., *Records of the Manor of Norton in the Liberty of St Albans, 1244–1539*, p. 61.
14. R. Lock, ed. and trans., *The Court Rolls of Walsham le Willows, 1303–1350* (Woodbridge: Boydell & Brewer and Suffolk Record Society, vol. xli, 1998), p. 132.
15. J. Amphlett ed., *Court Rolls of the Manor of Halesowen 1270–1307*, p. 330.
16. Halesowen Court Rolls, Birmingham Library and Archives, Wolfson Center, MS 3279/346307.
17. See for example: J.M. Bennett, 'Conviviality and Charity in Medieval and Early Modern England', in: *Past and Present*, no. 134 (1992), pp. 19–41; E. Clark, 'Social Welfare and Mutual Aid in the Medieval Countryside' in: *Journal of British Studies*, vol. 33, no. 4; *Vill, Guild and Gentry: Forces of Community in Later Medieval England* (Oct 1994), pp. 381–406; E. Clark, 'Some Aspects of Social Security in Medieval England', in: *Journal of Family History*, vol. 7, no. 3 (1982), pp. 307–320.
18. A.V. Chayanov, *The Theory of Peasant Economy*, D. Thorner, B. Kerblay, R.E.F. Smith, eds. (Homewood, IL: American Economic Association, R.D. Irwing, 1966), pp. 53–61.
19. Chayanov, *The Theory of Peasant Economy*, p. 66. A similar point has been made by B.A. Hanawalt, *The Ties That Bound Peasant Families in Medieval England* (Oxford University Press, 1986), p. 157.
20. Chayanov, *The Theory of Peasant Economy*, pp. 58–59.
21. R. Lock, ed., *The Court Rolls of Walsham le Willows 1303–1350*, p. 135.
22. L.R. Poos and L. Bonfield ed., *Select Cases in Manorial Courts 1250–1550; Property and Family Law* (London: Selden Society, 1998), pp. 148–149.
23. For lists of harvest failures across the period see: J.E. Thorold Rogers, *A History of Agriculture and Prices in England*, 7 vols (Oxford, 1866), p. 102; C. Dyer, *Standards of Living in the Later Middle Ages* (Cambridge University Press, 1993), pp. 262–263.
24. A plethora of studies have examined the socio-economic conditions in the post Black Death decades. See for example for an excellent summary of main developments: C. Dyer, *Making a living in the Middle Ages; The People of Britain 850–1520*, esp. pp. 271–362.
25. The only modern comparison of a similarly traumatic event of a deadly disease—causing mass mortality resulting in thousands of orphans is the Ebola outbreak in Sierra Leone. Here the organisation Street Child identified trauma as a 'major issue' among all orphans, resulting not just from the grief of losing parents and siblings, but also due to the uncertainty of their precarious and vulnerable situation. Stigma was also a widely observed problem, whereby many Ebola orphans experienced isolation and communal rejection. *The Street Child Ebola Orphan Report* (Jan–Feb 2015), pp. 12–13.

26. See also on this E. Clark, 'The Custody of Children in English Manor Courts', p. 335.
27. S. Sheridan Walker, 'Widow and Ward: The Feudal Law of Child Custody in Medieval England', in: S. Mosher Stuard ed., *Women in Medieval Society* (Philadelphia: University of Pennsylvania Press, 1976), p. 160.
28. H. Cunningham, *The Invention of Childhood* (2006), p. 23.
29. E. Clark, 'The Custody of Children in English Manor Courts', in: *Law and History Review*, vol. 3, no. 2 (Autumn 1985), p. 337.
30. B.A. Hanawalt, 'Narratives of a Nurturing Culture: Parents and Neighbours in Medieval England', in: B.A. Hanawalt, *Of Good and Ill Repute, Gender and Social Control in Medieval England* (New York, Oxford: Oxford University Press, 1989), pp. 170–171.
31. G. Foster, 'The Capacity of the Extended Family Safety Net for Orphans in Africa', in: *Psychology, Health and Medicine*, vol. 5, no. 1 (2010), pp. 55–62; B.J. Beard, 'Orphan Care in Malawi: Current Practices', in: *Journal of Community Health Nursing*, vol. 22, no. 2 (2005), pp. 105–115.
32. D. Noy, ed. and trans., *Winslow Manor Court Books, Part II 1423–1460*, p. 503.
33. D. Noy, ed. and trans., *Winslow Manor Court Books, Part II 1423–1460*, p. 498; pp. 621–622.
34. This evidence does not reply on surnames alone but the clear expression that the guardian was the 'uncle'.
35. Manor Records Halesowen, Birmingham archives, Wolfson Center, 1279, MS ....
36. P. Foden, ed. and trans., *Records of the Manor of Norton in the Liberty of St Albans, 1244–1539*, p. 111. The use of surname evidence is indeed problematic, as some men adopted the surname of their properties wives. However, this is unlikely to be a problem in these cases as it was the men who shared the same surnames, thus the evidence points to patrilinear kinship ties. See M. Müller, 'Peasant Women, Agency and Status in Mid Thirteenth to late fourteenth—Century England', some reconsiderations', in: C. Beattie and M.F. Stevens eds., *Married Women and the Law in Premodern Northwest Europe* (Boydell Press, 2013), p. 108.
37. R. Lock, ed., *The Court Rolls of Walsham le Willows, 1303–1350* (Woodbridge: Boydell & Brewer and Suffolk Record Society, vol. xli, 1998), p. 325.
38. R. Lock, ed., *The Court Rolls of Walsham le Willows, 1303–1350*, p. 325.
39. S. Shahar, *Childhood in the Middle Ages* (Routledge: London and New York, 1992), p. 155.
40. D. Noy, *Winslow Manor Court Books, Part I, 1327–1377*, Buckinghamshire Record Society, no. 35 (2011), p. 221.
41. See also E. Clark, 'The Custody of Children in English Manor Courts', p. 344.

42. K. Gager, 'Adoption Practices in Sixteenth and Seventeenth-Century Paris', in: M. Corbier, ed., *Adoption et Fosterage* (De L'Archéologie à L'Histoire; De Boccard, Paris, 1999), pp. 183–198. For the examples discussed see especially pp. 183–184.
43. W. Baildon, ed., *Court Rolls of the Manor of Wakefield vol. 1; 1274–1297* (Yorkshire Archaeological Society, 1901), pp. 118–119.
44. P.J.P. Goldberg, 'Childhood and Gender in Later Medieval England', in: *Viator*, vol. 39, no. 1, esp. p. 260.
45. R.A. Wilson ed., *The Court Rolls of the Manor of Hales 1276–1301 and Romsley Courts 1280–1303*, Part III (Oxford: Warwickshire Historical Society, 1933), p. 52.
46. Halesowen Court Rolls, Birmingham Library and Archives, Wolfson Centre, MS 3279/346302.
47. Halesowen Court Rolls, Birmingham Library and Archives, Wolfson Center, MS 3279/346314.
48. See also on this for example: B.A. Hanawalt, Childrearing Among the Lower Classes of Late Medieval England', in: *Journal of Interdisciplinary History*, vol. 8, no. 1 (1977), p. 6.
49. S. Shahar, *Childhood in the Middle Ages* (Routledge: London and New York, 1992), p. 160.
50. H. Cunningham, *The Invention of Childhood* (BBC Books, 2006), p. 22.
51. Office for National Statistics, Source 2011 census. Based on Table 1.
52. See for example for her discussion of these issues, especially concerning the effects of premature mortality due to accidents: B.A. Hanawalt, 'Childrearing Among the Lower Classes of Late Medieval England', in: *The Journal of Interdisciplinary History*, vol. 8, no. 1 (1977), p. 6.
53. S. Shahar, *Childhood in the Middle Ages*, p. 160.
54. S. Shahar, *Childhood in the Middle Ages*, p. 161.
55. M. Daly and M. Wilson, '"The Cinderella Effect" is No Fairy Tale' in: *Trends in Cognitive Sciences*, vol. 9, no. 11 (November 2005), pp. 507–508.
56. G.A. Tooley, M. Karakis, M. Stokes, and J. Ozanne–Smith, 'Generalising the Cinderella Effect to Unintentional Childhood Fatalities', in: *Evolution and Human Behaviour*, vol. 27 (2006), pp. 224–230.
57. M. Daly and M. Wilson, 'Child Abuse and Other Risks of Not Living with Both Parents', in: *Ethology and Biology*, vol. 6 (1985), pp. 197–210; esp. p. 197 and p. 209.
58. Brandon Court Rolls Sourced from Microfilm, Bacon collection, University of Chicago 1307–1400, MS291, no. 15.
59. M. Müller, 'Conflict and Revolt: The Bishop of Ely and His Peasants at the Manor of Brandon in Suffolk ca. 1300–1381', in: *Rural History*, vol. 23, no. 1 (April 2012), pp. 1–19. See also: C. Dyer, 'The Rising of 1381

in Suffolk: Its Origins and Participants', in C. Dyer, *Everyday Life in Medieval England* (London and New York, 2000 edition), pp. 191–220.
60. Brandon Court Rolls Sourced from Microfilm, Bacon collection, University of Chicago 1307–1400, MS291, no. 55.
61. D. Noy, ed., *Winslow Manor Court Books Part I 1327–1377*, p. 145.
62. D. Noy, ed., *Winslow Manor Court Books Part I 1327–1377*, p. 145.
63. R. Lock, ed., *The Court Rolls of Walsham le Willows 1303–1350* (Woodbridge: Boydell & Brewer and Suffolk Record Society, vol. xli, 1998), p. 325.
64. R. Lock, ed., *The Court Rolls of Walsham le Willows 1303–1350*, p. 145.
65. L.R. Poos and L. Bonfield, eds., *Select Cases in Manorial Courts 1250–1550 Property and Family Law* (London, Seldon Society, 1998), p. cxxx.
66. *Custumals of the Manors of Laughton, Willingdon and Goring* (Sussex Record Society, vol. LX, 1961), pp. 2–3.
67. *Custumals of the Manors of Laughton, Willingdon and Goring*, p. 5.
68. L.R. Poos and L. Bonfield, eds., *Select Cases in Manorial Courts 1250–1550 Property and Family Law* (London, Seldon Society, 1998), p. cxxx.
69. B.A. Hanawalt, 'Narratives of a Nurturing Culture: Parents and Neighbours in Medieval England', p. 169; S. Tarbin, 'Caring for Poor and Fatherless Children in London, c. 1350–1550', in: *Journal of the History of Childhood and Youth*, vol. 3, no. 3 (2010), p. 394.
70. For the threat to seigniorial incomes after the Black Death see for example: C. Dyer, *Making a Living in the Middle Ages; The People of Britain 850–1520* (New Haven and London: Yale University Press, 2002), esp. pp. 278–286.
71. See also on this S. Bardsley, 'Women's Work Reconsidered; Gender and Wage Differentiation in Late Medieval England', in: *Past and Present* (Nov 1999), vol. 165, pp. 3–29.
72. L.F. Salzman ed., *Petworth Minister's Accounts 1347–1553* (Sussex Record Society, vol. LV, 1955), p. 1.
73. L.F. Salzman ed., *Petworth Minister's Accounts 1347–1553*, p. 63.
74. L.F. Salzman ed., *Petworth Minister's Accounts 1347–1553*, p. 80.
75. For discussions of marriage Licences see for example: M. Müller, 'The Function and Evasion of Marriage Fines on a Fourteenth Century English Manor', in: *Continuity and Change*, vol. 14, no. 2 (1999), pp. 169–190.
76. D. Noy, *Winslow Manor Court Books Part I 1327–1377*; These examples can be found on p. 62 and p. 125.
77. P. Foden, ed., *Records of the Manor of Norton in the Liberty of St Albans, 1244–1539* (Caxton Hill, Hertford: Hertfordshire Record Publications, vol. 29, 2014), pp. 166–167
78. P. Foden, ed., *Records of the Manor of Norton in the Liberty of St Albans, 1244–1539*, p. 147.

79. Such declines in income post Black Death fit into a wider pattern-observed elsewhere in the country, of lords struggling to maintain their incomes. See for example for a general discussion of the kinds of problems lords faced in this period: C. Dyer, *Making a Living in the Middle Ages*, esp. pp. 330–340.

Bibliography

Primary Sources

Brandon Court Rolls, Sourced from Microfilm, Bacon collection, University of Chicago 1307–1400; MS 291.

Halesowen Court Rolls, Birmingham Library and Archives, Wolfson Centre MS 3279.

Heacham Court Rolls, Sourced from Microfilm held at the Norfolk Record Office Le Strange Collection.

J. Amphlett, ed., *Court Rolls of the Manor of Halesowen 1270–1307* (Oxford, Printed for the Worcestershire Historical Society by James Parker, 1912).

W. Baildon, ed., *Court Rolls of the Manor of Wakefield vol. 1; 1274–1297* (Yorkshire Archaeological Society, 1901).

Custumals of the Manors of Laughton, Willingdon and Goring (Sussex Record Society, vol. LX, 1961).

P. Foden, trans. and ed., *Records of the Manor of Norton in the Liberty of St Albans, 1244–1539* (Caxton Hill, Hertford: Hertfordshire Record Publications, 2014).

R. Lock, ed. trans., *The Court Rolls of Walsham le Willows, 1303–1350* (Woodbridge: Boydell & Brewer and Suffolk Record Society, vol. xli, 1998).

D. Noy, *Winslow Manor Court Books, Part I, 1327–1377*, Buckinghamshire Record Society, no. 35 (2011).

United Kingdom Office for National Statistics, Source 2011 census. https://www.ons.gov.uk/census/2011census.

L.R. Poos and L. Bonfield ed., *Select Cases in Manorial Courts 1250–1550; Property and Family Law* (London: Selden Society, 1998).

L.F. Salzman ed., *Petworth Minister's Accounts 1347–1553* (Sussex Record Society, vol. LV, 1955).

R.A. Wilson ed., *The Court Rolls of the Manor of Hales 1276–1301 and Romsley Courts 1280–1303*, Part III (Oxford: Warwickshire Historical Society, 1933).

Secondary Sources Books

A.V. Chayanov, *The Theory of Peasant Economy*, D. Thorner, B. Kerblay, and R.E.F. Smith, eds. (Homewood, IL: American Economic Association, R.D. Irwing, 1966).

H. Cunningham, *The Invention of Childhood* (London: BBC Books, 2006).
C. Dyer, *Making a Living in the Middle Ages; The People of Britain 850–1520* (New Haven and London: Yale University Press, 2002).
B.A. Hanawalt, *The Ties that Bound, Peasant Families in Medieval England* (New York, Oxford: Oxford University Press, 1986).
Z. Razi, *Life, Marriage and Death in a Medieval Parish Economy, Society and Demography in Halesowen 1270–1400* (Cambridge: Cambridge University Press, 1980).
S. Shahar, *Childhood in the Middle Ages* (London and New York: Routledge, 1992).

Secondary Sources Articles and Chapters

S. Bardsley, 'Women's Work Reconsidered; Gender and Wage Differentiation in Late Medieval England', in: *Past and Present*, vol. 165 (Nov 1999), pp. 3–29.
B.J. Beard, 'Orphan Care in Malawi: Current Practices', in: *Journal of Community Health Nursing*, vol. 22, no. 2, (2005) pp. 105–115.
J.M. Bennett, 'Conviviality and Charity in Medieval and Early Modern England'. In: *Past and Present*, vol. 134 (1992), pp. 19–41.
E. Clark, 'Some Aspects of Social Security in Medieval England', in: *Journal of Family History*, vol. 7, no 3 (1982), pp. 307-320.
E. Clark, 'The Custody of Children in English Manor Courts', in: *Law and History Review*, vol. 3, no. 2 (Autumn 1985), pp. 333–348.
E. Clark, 'City Orphans and Custody Laws in Medieval England', in: *The American Journal of Legal History*, vol. 34, no. 2 (April 1990), pp. 168–187.
E. Clark, 'Social Welfare and Mutual Aid in the Medieval Countryside' in: *Journal of British Studies*, vol. 33, no. 4; *Vill, Guild and Gentry: Forces of Community in Later Medieval England* (Oct 1994) pp. 381–406.
M. Daly and M. Wilson, 'Child Abuse and Other Risks of Not Living with Both Parents', in: *Ethology and Biology*, vol. 6 (1985), pp. 197–210.
M. Daly and M. Wilson, '"The Cinderella Effect" is no Fairy Tale' in: *Trends in Cognitive Sciences*, vol. 9, no. 11 (Nov 2005), pp. 507–508.
C. Dyer, 'The Rising of 1381 in Suffolk: Its Origins and Participants', in C. Dyer, ed., *Everyday Life in Medieval England* (London and New York: Hambledon and London, 2000 edition), pp. 191–220.
G. Foster, 'The Capacity of the Extended Family Safety Net for Orphans in Africa', in: *Psychology, Health and Medicine*, vol. 5, no. 1 (2010), pp. 55–62.
K. Gager, 'Adoption Practices in Sixteenth and Seventeenth-Century Paris', in: M. Corbier, ed., *Adoption et Fosterage* (De L'Archéologie à L'Histoire; De Boccard, Paris, 1999), pp. 183–198.
P.J.P. Goldberg, 'Childhood and Gender in Later Medieval England', in: *Viator*, vol. 39, no. 1 (2008), pp. 249–262.

B.A. Hanawalt, Childrearing Among the Lower Classes of Late Medieval England', in: *Journal of Interdisciplinary History*, vol. 8, no. 1 (1977), pp. 1–22.

B.A. Hanawalt, 'Narratives of a Nurturing Culture: Parents and Neighbours in Medieval England', in: B.A. Hanawalt, ed., *Of Good and Ill Repute, Gender and Social Control in Medieval England* (New York, Oxford: Oxford University Press, 1989), pp. 158–177.

M. Müller, 'The Function and Evasion of Marriage Fines on a Fourteenth Century English Manor', in: *Continuity and Change*, vol. 14, no. 2 (1999), pp. 169–190.

M. Müller, 'Conflict and Revolt: The Bishop of Ely and His Peasants at the Manor of Brandon in Suffolk ca. 1300–1381', in: *Rural History*, vol. 23, no. 1 (April 2012), pp. 1–19.

M. Müller, 'Peasant Women, Agency and Status in Mid Thirteenth to Late Fourteenth – Century England', Some Reconsiderations', in: C. Beattie and M.F. Stevens eds., *Married Women and the Law in Premodern Northwest Europe* (Woodbridge: Boydell Press, 2013), pp. 169–190.

S. Sheridan Walker, 'Widow and Ward: The Feudal Law of Child Custody in Medieval England', in: S. Mosher Stuard ed., *Women in Medieval Society* (Philadelphia: University of Pennsylvania Press, 1976), pp. 159–172.

R.M. Smith, 'Women's Property Rights under Customary Law: Some Developments in the Thirteenth and Fourteenth Centuries', in: *Transactions of the Royal Historical Society*, 5th series, vol. 36 (1986), pp. 165–194.

S. Tarbin, 'Caring for Poor and Fatherless Children in London, c. 1350–1550', in: *Journal of the History of Childhood and Youth*, vol. 3, no. 3 (2010) pp. 391–410.

The Street Child Ebola Orphan Report (Jan–Feb 2015).

G.A. Tooley, M. Karakis, M. Stokes, and J. Ozanne-Smith, 'Generalising the Cinderella Effect to Unintentional Childhood Fatalities', in: *Evolution and Human Behaviour*, vol. 27 (2006), pp. 224–230.

CHAPTER 5

Plotting Out a Living

1 Kinship Networks and Match Makers

The work of the guardians was not concluded with merely maintaining their wards and their land. Guardians were very much aware of the fact that the role they entered into also entailed the active involvement into their ward's education and potentially also their marriage and wider social networks. Guardians were looking after young people who were moving through adolescence into young adulthood, where growing autonomy and independent agency could result in conflict with their younger charges. At the same time, guardians undoubtedly had significant control and influence over young people who might hold the key to large holdings and their exploitation could be a tempting prospect.

The aim of this chapter is therefore to explore these difficult and at times—potentially at least—conflictual ramifications of the guardian–ward relationship. At the same time, the analysis of the relationships which families of underaged heirs and orphans forged allows us detailed insights into how some families created kinship associations and networks of mutual support. In the case of orphans who had no living parents, guardians acted as the surrogate family of the ward; but even in cases where wardship was handed over to a step-parent, or surviving single mother, an important role of the guardian was to prepare the ground for fruitful familial, kinship and social networks for the future of the ward.

M. Müller, *Childhood, Orphans and Underage Heirs in Medieval Rural England*, Palgrave Studies in the History of Childhood,
https://doi.org/10.1007/978-3-030-03602-7_5

While medieval English peasants did not normally operate within extended families, they still drew on the support of wider kinship and other networks when it suited them, while mutual neighbourly support was also of great importance in a society in which some of its members occasionally led a rather precarious existence along the economic margins.[1] From the perspective of an orphaned child, or any underaged heir for that matter, establishing supportive networks was a crucial protective mechanism, both in the short and in the long term. How such supportive networks were forged is often elusive from manorial records, but the reconstitution and reconstruction of the lives of some of the young heirs allow some valuable insights into such mechanisms of mutuality in peasant society.

An integral part of the guardian's role involved setting up the young people under their care for life, involving training, as well as occasionally arranging suitable matches or at the very least helping to set up suitable marriage partners. As we have seen, a wardship covered both material and emotional interests of the child. Using manorial court rolls where long series of rolls are extant, it is possible to reconstruct the life cycles of a number of young heirs who had appointed guardians. Underaged heirs are sometimes well-recorded across their entire life. As we often have the age when they were first being recorded as children requiring guardians, reconstructing their lives can provide valuable insights into their ordinary life cycle, including at what age they married, inherited their holding and became fully involved in a myriad of village affairs. Additionally, such reconstructions give important clues regarding the typical experiences of young people who had lost at least one of their principal guardians.

In particular, as I will show, it is notable that among some of the families which experienced guardianship strong ties and economic as well as connections of kinship were forged, especially between the affected children. Such connections can be seen to have acted as supportive networks, which were themselves cemented into wider communal relationships and structures.

In 1314, Agnes Goche, daughter of Adam Goche was born at the manor of Walsham le Willows to smallholding villein parents. At the age of three, Agnes's father Adam died, holding 8 acres of arable and half a rood of meadow. Agnes was the closest heir. It is not entirely clear who was appointed a guardian over Agnes, but it seems to have been the case that her mother was still alive as Agnes was to recover land from her in years to come. In the meantime, the lord took a heriot consisting of a cow, which was judged to be worth 13s. 4d., while the land was—initially at least—ordered to be taken into the hands of the lord, with the bailiff ordered to 'report the profits' which were accrued on the land.[2] This was probably done until the nature of the guardianship was resolved, and does therefore not imply that the lord acted as guardian, but rather asserted his rights over the land.

In the court held in December of 1329, when Agnes would have been around 15 or just turning 16, she was noted alongside some other fellow orphans and underaged heirs to have 'received' her inheritance without fine, following the custom of the manor, and she swore fealty.[3] At the same time, she was granted by the court, presumably following a dispute over her inheritance, the right to recover from Simon Peyntour as well as her mother 'half of all the land sown at 1 August'. The implication, therefore, is that Agnes' mother and Simon held the land jointly, which raises the possibility that Simon was Agnes' stepfather and her mother's second husband. Agnes thereafter proceeded to participate fully in village affairs, and recovering the land from Simon Peyntour and her mother does not appear to have soured any relationships between them as Simon acted as Agnes' pledge in May 1336, when Agnes admitted in court to the 'unlawful detention of 16d. from Henry Albry', for which she was amerced 3d.[4] The conflict over the debt was settled in the same court when Agnes bought a licence to agree with Henry over the matter of the debt. Two years later, when Agnes would have been about 24 years of age, Agnes paid the lord 6s. 4d. for a licence to marry the very same Henry Albry, and once again Simon Peyntour was one of the named pledges acting as surety for the payment.[5] The marriage lasted 10 years, as Henry died in 1348, leaving Agnes widowed at the age of 34.[6] Agnes herself did not get the chance to remarry, as was recorded as having died in June 1349, very probably from the plague which had arrived by then in the village. Upon her death, she held 12 acres of land and had no surviving children.[7]

The case of Agnes is illustrative of a number of things. Once again it shows the communal intervention—against the backdrop of the lord—in arranging her guardianship. It shows her slowly assuming adult responsibilities in the manorial court, and thereby also getting into conflict with her presumed stepfather. Her life illustrates also some important supportive networks, again via her presumed stepfather and mother, despite the conflict in her adulthood. Agnes herself married when she entered her mid-twenties, thereby confirming a pattern observed elsewhere that peasant women married quite late into their twenties.[8] She also paid her own marriage licence, indicating a degree of economic independence and certainly agency.[9] We do not know whether Agnes had ever given birth, but she certainly died without any surviving offspring.

Another person of that group of young heirs listed in 1329 was Walter Qualm, one of the children left orphaned in the famine year of 1317. He would have been 15 years old upon entering his smallholding, which contained merely one and a half acres of land. As we have seen in part I, he would have been unusually young to enter his inheritance at the manor, and strictly speaking, it was against custom, as at least in theory he would not have been considered to be of full age.[10] However, clearly the community had made the decision that Walter had shown himself to be mature enough to handle his own affairs. In July 1339, Catherine, the daughter of William Typetot, paid the lord 6s. 8d. to marry Walter, when, like Agnes, he would have been 25 years old.[11] Walter also succumbed to the plague in June 1349 at the age of 35. He left no living children, and the declared heir to his smallholding of 2 messuages and 4 acres of land was his nephew Richard.[12] Catherine, Walter's wife, herself was the daughter of Phillippa and William Typetot. William, Catherine's father, had also died in the famine year of 1317, leaving his son and heir Peter, then aged 6 a total of 6 acres of land, in the guardianship of his mother. Catherine also had a sister, Alice. No further mention of Peter can be found in the court records, and it may well be the case that he also died.[13] This would have left Catherine and Alice as the heiresses, although initially, they would have been non-inheriting siblings of an underaged heir. They had not just been looked after well enough to reach adulthood, despite their backgrounds as smallholders, but it seems to have been the case that children with shared experiences of growing up as underaged heirs forged networks of support, friendship and even marriage.

Another character in this group of 7 heirs and heiresses is William son of Walter Patel. We do not have a record of his parent's death and how old he was when he was orphaned, but he was clearly stated as having been 'in the custody of Walter the Cooper and his wife for the past six years' in December 1329.[14] This means that he can't have had any surviving biological parent or step-parent. As he swore fealty in that year, he must have been at the very least 15 years old—like some of his fellow peers, or older, but not above 21. In 1334, he was accused of having brought a false testimony against another villager and was excused.[15]

In 1341, he was elected to the office of Hayward, when he must have been between 28 and 33 years old.[16] His election must be seen as testimony to the respect and social standing in his community, both from his neighbours and his lord; his perhaps rather difficult childhood start notwithstanding. William died a smallholder in 1349, holding a messuage and a little over 2 acres of land. He had no surviving children and his heiress was declared to be his sister Christina, again a non-inheriting orphaned sibling, who was not however granted entry as the lord ordered his possessions to be seized due to debts accrued during his office as Hayward to the lord.[17] The earliest we hear of Christina is in 1329, when she had to pay childwite for giving birth out of wedlock. We do not know her age, but considering her illegitimate pregnancy, and the then age of her brother, she may well have been in her teens as well.[18] We can not know if it was due to her own free will that it was over 10 years before she formally married, or if her illegitimate child harmed her marriage prospects, but in 1341 Robert Typetot paid an amercement of 3d. to the lord for having failed to tell the lord that he had married Christina, while Christina herself paid 5s. to the lord for a licence to marry Robert.[19] Her child, if it was still alive, would have been around 12 years old upon her marriage.

Robert Typetot, in turn, was the brother of William Typetot who died in 1317, and hence uncle to the orphans Catherine and Peter Typetot. This would have made Christina and Robert uncle and aunt of Catherine née Typetot, who married Qualm. In other words, the underaged heirs of the Typetot, Qualm and Patel families were all interlinked through marriage. What we can therefore see quite clearly, though the reconstitution of at least partial biographies of underaged heirs and their families are extensive familial networks, especially among families who were affected by having underaged heirs. This indicates that peasant families forged associations due, at least in part, to shared experiences. The court seems to have reflected this, in recognising shared links by listing the seven underaged heirs together in a group. This gave these young men and women a shared identity on which they drew solidarity and built mutually supportive networks.

While some of the intricate familial and kinship relationships between the Qualms, the Patels and the Typetots are difficult or impossible to reconstruct, not least due to gaps in the record, it is clear that some families affected by the experience of being underaged heirs forged links of kinship and alliances which emerge also in other dealings in the manorial courts. In 1349, for example, the Qualms, the Patels and the Typetots also held some meadowland jointly, which they agreed to surrender to John Tailor and his son.[20]

Other alliances were created much more purposefully. In some cases, non-parental guardians actively used their positions to create family alliances through directing the marriage of the ward. Such social engineering by guardians may have been tempting in particular economic circumstances. In times of land scarcity, such as in the late thirteenth century or the early fourteenth century, it could have been an attractive prospect to forge alliances via orphaned children to secure permanent access to land. In 1295, John Deepslough of Halesowen, for example, was appointed a guardian over Thomas Silby's heiress Joan, whom John had promptly married 'by licence of the lord to his son Thomas'. This means that the lord had given his permission for the match. The result of this was that, with the approval of the court, Thomas was placed in charge of Joan's holding. However, he was only able to exercise this right until the coming of age of Joan, when she would have regained the authority over her holding despite being married.[21] In other words, the marriage could not override Joan's rights over her land. In Winslow upon the death of Simon le Newman, his son Robert was left orphaned and Walter Wilkin paid his entry fine to have the custody over the 'land and the aforesaid heir until the coming of age of the said heir'. He also paid for a licence to 'marry the said heir to the daughter of the said Walter'.[22]

In some cases, guardians arranged the marriage of their wards when these were still extremely young. When John le Shepherd of Norton died in 1342, holding a rather substantial half a virgate of land, his heir was 3 years old Helen (whom we shall refer to as Helen A to avoid confusion), whose guardianship was handed over to John's widow, Helen (Helen B), who is not explicitly stated to have been the heir's mother, and may therefore have been her stepmother.[23] It seems to have been the case that Helen B did sell, or at the very least arrange, her ward's marriage only two years later, in 1344, when Helen A would have been aged 5. In May that year, the lord granted the marriage of Helen A the daughter of John Shepherd to Walter Broun, who appears to have had two children, Geoffrey and Agnes. Walter was not granted the marriage of Helen A for himself, but for 'the use of Geoffrey the son of the said Walter'. Due to this agreement Geoffrey was to hold Helen's inheritance, to 'hold to him and to the aforesaid Helen', presumably in joint tenure, and in villeinage. Thus, Geoffrey was granted 'permission to marry' Helen A by the lord, for which he paid to the lord 20s.[24] The potential implications of this are interesting, but not explored in the sources. We do not know what, if anything Helen B received from Walter for this arrangement. Similarly, we cannot be sure whether this meant the effective surrender of the guardianship of Helen B over Helen A, but this seems unlikely as such a matter would in all probability have been noted. Nonetheless, as in the case of Joan in Halesowen, Helen's Rights to her holding were not lost due to the marriage arrangement. Helen's rights are retained in terms of the tenurial agreement. That is, she was not de facto disinherited. However, Helen A did not live long enough to be married. She died in July 1349, presumably of the Black Death, aged about 7, when Matilda her aunt received her land.[25]

The case also highlights the risks some families were prepared to take in order to secure holdings for their own children which could come with a young heir. The marriage licence of a rather substantial 20s. was presumably lost to Walter Broun and his son Geoffrey, as without any legitimate marriage his family had no rights to the land; instead, it remained with Helen's patrilinear side of the family. It is important to stress that, at Norton at least, the right to arrange a marriage could be granted at any age of the child, yet the actual marriage, through which full access to the inheritance was granted, was, by implication only recognised as valid upon the heir reaching the age of majority. In addition, had Helen lived to full age, she would have had the right according to canon law at the age of 12 to refuse the arranged marriage, even if one might expect that significant pressure was exerted on wards for whom marriages had already been arranged.[26] Yet, while we have no evidence for instances of such non-cooperation by heirs, it must have represented an additional risk factor for the adult match makers.

The right to find a marriage partner for the underaged heir could also be granted by the lord. In 1317, at the manor of Eldersfield, Peter Bastyng and Joan his wife were granted the custody of half a virgate of land containing 20 acres which belonged to John, the 16-year-old heir of Walter Haliday. Peter and his wife, the court roll made explicit, thereby had the 'custody of the tenement and marriage of the heir granted' to them, until he was judged to be of a lawful age.[27]

Especially at times of relative land scarcity or high prices of land, the prospect of gaining additional land by joining one's own child with a ward in marriage would have looked attractive. In addition, landed resources came with familial connections and kinship networks, which might increase political or economic influences in the community, and thus could turn wards into socio-economic assets as well as tools. Historians have noted that the sale of marriages of wards could be very lucrative, and it has been argued that the evidence of urban medieval wardship shows that prospective marriage partners could be found to offer guardians significant financial rewards in return for marriages.[28] It may indeed be the case that one reason why licences to marry were usually acquired by guardians upon accepting a ward and their holding, was to ensure that the heir could be married off to whomsoever the ward or the guardian wished, including, as we have seen in the examples above, to their own children.

However, while it may be tempting to view the acceptance of wardships as a calculated financial transaction, this would be an over-simplistic reading of the evidence. In medieval English manors lords had the right to demand marriage licences from their unfree, villein tenants upon their marriage. Lords could—and occasionally did—use this right to actively attempt to influence the choice of their tenants' marriage partner. As such, therefore, many lords were not averse to engaging in some social engineering in their own villages either. Typically lords could attempt to encourage endogenous marriages by demanding much higher payments for marriage licences outside their own manorial estates.[29] The tenant planning to marry outside the manor was not stopped from doing so as such, but a financial disincentive was imposed. In the case of wardships in some manors, the right to arrange a marriage of an underaged heir by the lord seems to have been granted as a privilege to the tenants concerned. The Custumals of the manor of Laughton in Sussex of the year 1292 thus note that 'the lord shall have ward and marriage right of' the forester Robert de Byreche's heir should Robert die.[30]

In reality, many marriage licences were purchased well in advance of the intended marriage, and were noted down as such in manorial court rolls. Heirs themselves often paid for licences to marry, for example, upon entering their holding when they reached majority. As such the point at which a licence was purchased was only occasionally the actual time when a given couple married.[31] Theoretically licences to marry could be purchased for the child heir to use as they wished in adulthood or, indeed to be sold on or used in various ways to one's own advantage.

However, it is striking that the use of marriage licences in such a way appears to have been comparatively rare. Even when it was clearly noted that at least in theory parties other than the heir involved had a say in matters of marriage, the choice of a marriage partner was often left to the ward. In 1329, John the son of William Typetot was due to inherit a smallholding in free tenure from his father. The court roll notes that the boy was underage and accordingly under guardianship, 'until he marries at the lord's discretion and pays a relief to the lord and does as he ought'. The implication is close seigniorial scrutiny or input into John's marriage arrangements, however, it was then also noted that 'afterwards seisin of the land is granted to the heir, and the lord's leave to marry as he wishes'.[32]

At the manor of Halesowen, less than 8% of wardships recorded in the court rolls include explicitly a recorded licence to marry for the ward between 1270 and 1400. Although interestingly all licenses to marry at this manor were recorded before the arrival of the Black Death, representing 10% of the total recorded wardship cases in this period. At Winslow, we have enough data on marriage licences to allow a more substantial pre- and post-Black Death comparison. Again, pre-Black Death it was much more common for guardians to acquire marriage licences for their wards. A total of 51% of guardianship arrangements included marriage licences for the ward. After the Black Death, this number again fell significantly to 10.9%. At Norton, only 14% of pre-Black Death wardship agreements note marriage licences, and only a single one is recorded post-Black Death. At Walsham le Willows, no marriage licences at all are recorded in extant wardship arrangements across the entire fourteenth century.

In other words, in cases where no marriage licence was purchased in advance, the heir would have been left to choose and purchase their own licences to marry in adult life. Which means that between about half and 90% of all underaged heirs at Halesowen and Winslow were free to exercise their own agency in their choice of marriage partners, or at least they were in full control over the purchasing of their own marriage licence. This is important, as, by definition, this would only have been possible to occur when the heir was considered of full age to enter their holding and thus set up their own households, removed, therefore, physically at least, from the influence of their guardians. Therefore it is safe to conclude that in most localities, direct intervention by guardians into their wards' marriages through the purchase of marriage licences was uncommon, and became positively rare post-Black Death.

It is similarly important to note, that in cases where a marriage licence was purchased in advance for a child heir, this did not necessarily involve a marriage arranged by the guardian. When in April 1349 William and his wife Alice Harry lay on their deathbed and surrendered a portion of their land pre-mortem to their youngest son John, they ensured not only to entrust his guardianship to Ralph Harry but also that in paying for the custody a licence to marry for John was included, even if he was only 8 years of age.[33] When John formally entered his holding aged 16, and his guardian stood as his surety for his entry fine to half a virgate of land in 1357, it was noted that he had already acquired a marriage licence through the fine paid previously—for the guardianship.[34]

The purchase of marriage licences in advance becomes far less common after the first arrival of the Black Death. Three main factors may have been responsible for this development. It is possible that the potential ability to sell the marriage of a landed underaged heir was a more attractive temptation at a time of relative scarcity of land before the Black Death, conversely post-Black Death guardians may have been less inclined to pay upfront for marriage licences as landed heirs were a less attractive marriage prospect when many tenants were saturated with land. In addition, especially during the Black Death and immediate post-Black Death years, guardians may have been reluctant to pay for a marriage licence in advance for an heir who may well not survive long enough to marry.

One can therefore conclude, that far from representing a common and lucrative way to exploit underaged heirs, marriage seems to have played a minor role in decisions to take on the guardianship of an underaged heir, especially in the second half of the fourteenth century. At the same time, the active agency of the young heirs can be seen at work in their life-cycle experiences. Most seem to have been able to choose whom to marry. And even where marriages were arranged the young heir retained their rights over their inheritance. In addition, we can discern rural societies which placed great value upon building supportive networks. Accordingly, there was a tendency among underaged heirs to form associations and kinship ties with each other.

2 Learning to Make a Living: Education at Home, Independence and Service

Marriage was the most important aspect, aside from reaching the age of majority, of stepping into the role of the tenant with the full assumption of adult responsibilities as well as setting up an independent household.[35] Many underaged heirs did not experience arranged marriages and found different routes into full adult independence. In 1312–1313, Sybil the widow of John Norton of the manor of Norton died, leaving behind three teenaged daughters of John's, Joan (17), Agnes (15) and Margaret (13). The wardship was handed to Laurence Blaseworth.[36] We do not know how much land was involved, but it is clear that in this case partible inheritance was practised. In June 1316, the oldest daughter Joan would have been 19 or 20 when she came to the court to assume full responsibility to the lord as a tenant. Accordingly she swore fealty to the lord and entered her holding, acknowledged to the lord that she owed to pay 12s. 8d. rent per annum, and perform boonworks on the lord's fields with one additional man during the harvest season as well as to attend the halimot manorial court twice per annum.[37] By 1320–1321, Joan's sisters also appear to have entered their holdings, as Agnes and Margaret, by then aged about 23 and 21 respectively, were amerced 6d. for being in arrears by one boonday at harvest time, which they owed to perform for the holding which used to be their father's.[38] There is no record of either of Agnes and Margaret ever to have married, and they seem to have run their holdings alone in their own right.

How did young people like Agnes and Margaret learn how to run a peasant holding? Education in any peasant household started from the day a child was born. We have seen that the entire holding, including the main living quarters of peasant families, was functional and used in economic productive processes. Whether this was brewing, spinning, weaving, dyeing, baking or indeed storing agricultural tools. There is a pictorial evidence that infants were often swaddled and sometimes taken into the fields, where their parents and perhaps also older siblings worked. Evidence suggests that they were often placed on the ground or even hung in a tree.[39] It is however also possible that very young children were also carried in slings, leaving the parent's arms free to work (Fig. 1).[40]

Experiences of working cycles and household chores could also have been acquired by older children left in charge of younger siblings, or other women in the community who may have engaged in communal nursing practices, to pacify infants, even if they no longer lactated anymore, as is evidenced, for example, in early modern sources of witchcraft trials.[41]

Fig. 1 Royal 2AXXII f.220v. 'The Westminster Psalter', Westminster or St. Albans, England mid-thirteenth century. St. Christopher carrying Christ child in a sling (© British Library Board. All Rights Reserved/Bridgeman Images)

Sayings, songs and poetry could also have didactic purposes, and several rhymes surviving from the later medieval period may well have been taught to children to educate them about various aspects of rural life. The seasonality of agriculture, for example, is central to this lyric dating from the fourteenth to fifteenth century.

Januar By thys fyre I warme my handys;
Februar And with my spade I delfe my landys
Marche Here I sette my Thynge to sprynge;
April And here I here the fowlis synge
Maij I am as light as byrde in bowe;
Junij And I wede my corne well I – now.
Julij With my sythe my mede I maw;
Auguste And here I shere my corne full lowe
September With my flayll I erne my brede;
October And here I saw my whete so rede.
November At Matynmasse I kylle my swine;
December And at Christesmasse I drynke redde wyne.[42]

Other texts discuss various skills including how to pick the best plot of land to purchase. Considering the extensive involvement of peasants in the market of land, both free and unfree, such knowledge was crucial. Thus in one poem a young person would have been warned to check prior to purchase whether the land was free or unfree, to take care that all the dues and rents owed on the land are known beforehand, and indeed to avoid future problems, by making sure that the seller is of full age and that the land does not come with any debts:

Se that þe seller be of age,
And yf the land be not in mortgage…[43]

It could be argued that acceptance of a young ward was often intertwined with the concomitant enticement that the ward themselves would represent an additional pool of labour the guardian would be able to draw on freely. In particular in the years following the Black Death, when labour was in high demand, servants were very highly valued, while in turn servants were able to take advantage of the changed land-labour ratio and effectively bargain for better conditions and higher wages.[44] While additional labour would have been an undoubted bonus to any peasant household, whose entire productivity—after all—resided from within the houseful, we ought to be careful not to make the problematic assumption that such welcome labour would equate to the acceptance of wards on purely economic grounds. After all, the labour of servants was not free, they were paid in food and lodging, training, as well as in cash in many circumstances.[45] Not too dissimilar from families burdened with more consumers of their labour output, in the shape of young children, than skilled and able workers, who are able to drive up productivity and potentially contribute to the ability of households to expand their landed holdings; families with adolescent servants would, initially at least, have faced the prospect of only limited labour output from their young employee in comparison to an adult, strong and skilled worker.[46] While young, they would also have required more supervision and training before becoming more productive assets. Unless we follow Ariès' view that medieval society failed to recognise childhood as a distinct state in human development, and accept the rather illogical idea that concomitantly medieval people would not have recognised that young people were unable to make as efficient a workforce as older people, we have to accept that labour cannot have been a prime motivator in accepting wards.[47]

The idea that peasant children worked productively from a young age is very persistent. It was re-iterated, for example, in 2007 when Handel, Cahill and Elkin argued that '… peasant parents put them to work around the age of 7'—and, in some respect echoing Ariès, they felt that 'Peasant children were incorporated into adult society at an early age'.[48] As everybody who has ever looked after very young children knows, below a certain age, 8 or 9 a child's required input of supervision, feeding, clothing and other care, by far outweighs any potential gain they might bring in labour output. The issue may well be amplified in agricultural work, which requires strength, skill and endurance. Analysis of Coroner's Rolls has indicated occasionally children performing tasks which were work-related; so between the ages of 6 and 12, children were tasked with certain small jobs, such as collecting nuts, while younger adolescents were also entrusted to watch over sheep and pigs.[49] However, it is difficult to ascertain just how common work practices for children were, as the incidents of work-related accidents in the younger age groups as examined by Hanawalt was still comparatively rare as a proportion of all Coroner Roll Cases.[50] While a child might be sent to perform certain tasks, such as looking after smaller livestock, scaring birds away, fetching things, helping with general tasks, they do not have the strength or skill to make a significant saving on the labour force probably until they are in their teens. It would certainly not be correct to view young children working like adults or fully 'integrated' into the adult working world.

If we consider that up to 48% of wards could be aged 5 years or under, we have to discard the notion that families primarily were motivated to accept wards as servants.[51] That does not mean however, that young people who were wards were never accepted as servants, but rather that we should not view such motivations or circumstances as the default position.

Service should also not merely be understood in terms of labour provision on the part of the young person, but also as a time of skill acquisition.[52] Medieval education for the lower classes was primarily driven by the focus on the learning of a significant range of skills. In the countryside, this included all aspects of animal husbandry, agrarian production as well as—potentially depending upon the locality, woodland management, management of drainage systems and fishing. One could add a whole host of by—industries, from brewing to malt making, pottery, spinning, weaving, baking or indeed thatching, carpentry and many other trades which may have been engaged with on a full or part-time basis in individual households. As a result, different households would have been able to offer different specialised sets of skills for young people to learn, mainly by doing and helping. Accordingly, as Orme has rightly argued, the medieval household in itself represented 'an educational institution'.[53] The importance of learning skills in targeted household settings therefore set young people up to become responsible, skilled and productive members of their communities, and thereby acquire the knowledge and intellectual tools necessary for eventually entering their own households and becoming heads of households themselves. In this context, Goldberg has stressed the importance of placing orphans in London into apprenticeships in order to provide them with a family environment, which could also offer them valuable training to provide for their futures.[54]

William Coppelowe became an underaged heir in 1328, aged 2, when his guardianship was handed over to his mother. When William was only 5 years old, his widowed mother Matilda had remarried a certain Geoffrey Rath, and had surrendered William's 'custody and care' with her dower into the lands of the lord. It is then noted that John of Stoneham had been granted entry into William's lands for annual services to the lord. What is not clear however is whether John also took in the boy, or only the land. We do hear from William again in 1348, when his sister died and left a tiny holding of 1 and a half roods to him as she had no other heirs, but which William never came to enter, even though he would have been of full age then according to the custom at the manor.[55] However, in 1353, William Coppelowe, by now aged 25, was clearly in the lord's service, when he was amerced 5d. for having caused damage in the lord's crops, while employed as a 'servant of the manor'.[56] It is most likely that William was in the service of his lord since childhood and that he found it well enough rewarded in the post-Black Death period not to enter a holding, but instead continue with salaried labour.

Explicit expressions that a ward was coming to live with guardians to go into service are very unusual. A rare case dates from 1279 in Halesowen, when Henry the son of John le Fremen, aged around 15, was handed into the joint custody of John and William, to 'live with them in service', although, as we have seen previously Henry was also accorded sufficient agency to quit their service, if he so wished.[57] This level of agency accorded to Henry is also notable in the context of accepted norms of household structure. The accepted view of the position of servants or apprentices in the household economy was one of subordination to and dependency of the head of the household, the master, who held a patriarchal upper hand, which in turn lay at the root of conflict as well as, occasionally very firm, social control.[58] However, such a relationship is not in evidence in Henry's case. It may well be that underaged heirs whose de facto employer was also the guardian found themselves in a stronger hierarchical, if not a more protected position due to their officially sanctioned and witnessed contract of wardship.

In 1353, the court rolls of the manor of Walsham le Willows notes a memorandum, stating that 'Agnes Hulke is living in the house of Robert Herning, Alice Tailor in that of John Spilman, Hilary Pinfoul in that of William Elys and Christina Rampolye in that of Robert Rampolye'.[59] Once again we have an example of the court of Walsham implicitly recognising the shared identity and potential mutuality in the shared experiences of underaged heirs, but listing affected young people in a group. Accordingly, reconstruction reveals at least some of these residents were orphans, and the implication is that they may have been residing in their guardian's houses as servants or labourers.

Hilary Pinfoul was orphaned in the Black Death aged 8 years old. Her father, John Pynfoul held 2 acres of land for which he rendered to the lord a service of half a pound of pepper per annum. The land was taken into the hands of the lord.[60] In 1359, when Hilary would have been 18 years old, she purchased a licence to marry Walter Franceys, paying 3s. 4d.[61] In 1381, Hilary Pinfoul is noted as holding 2 acres of land for which she pays half a pound of peppercorn as relief, swears fealty and agrees to pay half a pound of peppercorn annually at Christmas for rent.[62] Therefore when Hilary is noted as residing with William Elys, she would have been around 12 years old, and while in his wardship may well have been in his service. Very little can be reconstructed of the life of Alice Tailor. In 1353, she was residing with John Spilman, presumably as his ward or servant, but by 1361 she was noted as having married William Margery.[63] By 1368, she had died leaving a messuage and a smallholding of 5 acres to her two young children and her husband, who it was judged, should have a life-long right to her holding.[64]

Agnes Hulke does not appear to have ever married or entered any holding. It seems that she was one of the unnamed heirs of Walter Hulke, noted in 1318, who had all been taken into custody of Adam Noble.[65] By 1353, she lived with Robert Herning, a freeholder at the manor, who is occasionally noted as trespassing on the lord's lands with his livestock.[66] Agnes was not married to Robert, as she paid childwite to the lord repeatedly for having born children out of wedlock in 1354, 1361 and 1366.[67] Therefore Agnes must have been Robert's life—an employee, at least for a while. After 1366 nothing more is known of her. She certainly does not seem to have either married or entered a holding.

While we have little direct, and only scattered, evidence of orphans being employed as servants, we should expect this to have been the common route towards economic independency for heirs and their siblings before they were in a position to enter their holdings. If we turn, once again, our attention to the garciones lists of Glastonbury Abbey manors, we find further indications of young people entering service in their teens in village societies. In 1346, Walter son of Gilbert Godefrey was entered for the first time on the garciones lists, so he must have been 12 years of age. As he was noted as residing with his mother, his father must have died, and his mother acted as his guardian.[68] He subsequently survived the plague and in 1348 noted as paying 8d. head tax for the lord as his economic viability grew with his earning potential.[69] Manorial evidence therefore seems to confirm that many young people in their teens worked as servants or labourers for their lord or their neighbours. Such activities should be understood not merely in terms of earning wages but also in collecting and gaining experiences and learning important practical skills in the wider agricultural economy, Ranging from the handling of livestock, and associated skills—such as dairying—over to annual cycles of sowing, growing, harvesting and storing crops. As a young person's skills and knowledge increased, so their economic value was considered to rise as well, reflected in, for example, wages they could draw, and accordingly—the size of payments they were expected to be able to make to their lords.

3 Attending Grammar School

It was possible for boys, but not very often for girls, to be sent to attend formal schooling.[70] Attendance of clerical school could specifically lead to entering a career, and for boys to potentially become a member of the clergy. While the route of such formal education is generally more associated not just with urban societies but also with the wealthier classes, especially the aristocracy, scholars from more humble backgrounds were not unknown where local opportunities of schooling were available, especially as the availability of schools grew in the later middle ages.[71] The importance of formal schooling of children in peasant societies has been somewhat neglected, despite the potentially far-reaching ramifications schooling of poorer children represented. To consider formal schooling in peasant societies is not merely important for us in order to gain insights into the lives of children in medieval villages, and potentially rates of literacy or semi-literacy, but offers an interesting avenue of research into the activities and live choices of children and young people who were not due to inherit any or the lion's share of the family's lands and holdings.

Recent research indicates that schooling in later medieval England may well have been a lot more common and widespread than has previously been assumed, for which monastic houses, including their lesser institutions, were largely responsible.[72] For the poor in particular, the route of schooling was likely to be much more locally at variance depending on the existence of schools within the vicinity. While the better off might be able to pay for board and lodging to reside at schools, due to the expense involved the poorer were more reliant on schools in closer proximity to their homes.[73]

We can gain insights into peasant boys attending schools, as unfree tenants were required to seek a formal permission from their lord to send their sons to school. Such permissions, or licences, were entered into manorial court rolls. The rationale behind demanding such licences was based on attempts to control the movements of local peasant populations. Fundamentally, lords wanted to control the comings and goings of their various assets, and as far as manorial lords were concerned, their tenants and dependants constituted such assets. Children did not merely represent assets as potential future rent-paying tenants but they were also potential assets as part of the labour force, even where children were not due to inherit land. Lords typically drew their labour from two main sources, and their respective prominence and importance varied according to locality and style of lordship. The first was the unfree and unpaid labour of villein tenants, and the second was from paid labourers who were at least in part drawn from the local manorial population.

Younger siblings who were not due to inherit due to primogeniture for example, other landless residents or smallholders represented an important pool of labour which could be drawn upon at times of acute need, such as during the very busy harvest periods. In this respect, a licence to send a son to school acted in a similar way as seigniorial demands for cheavage payments from tenants who left their manorial demesnes, or marriage licences especially from unfree tenants who were planning to marry outside the manor.[74] Additionally, attending clerical school also opened up the possibility of the long-term loss of the seigniorial asset of a potential tenant and labourer, by the scholar entering a clerical career or leaving the manor to pursue other designs. However, on the other hand, allowing some tenants to attend schooling could also represent a seigniorial opportunity. Lords relied on officials to help manage the daily running of manors and the agricultural productions on the seigniorial demesne, the part of the manor the lord farmed for himself. Reeves, in particular, must have been schooled in at least conducting tallies as they were expected to render the seigniorial accounts at the end of the year, detailing incomes through rents, sales, court perquisites as well as other local assets, alongside debts and financial outgoings through purchases of livestock, for example.[75]

Manorial officials tended to be drawn from the unfree tenantry, and often benefited from a range of perks as a result of their responsibilities to the lord.[76] The position of such officials in their own communities could be problematic, as like Chaucer's reeve introduced in his *Canterbury Tales*, they could be feared by their neighbours, and loyal to their lord, or they could also be found leading local revolts and ally with the community against their lord. The potential conflicts of interest caused by such office holding are also reflected in the didactic text 'How the Wise man taught his Son', in which the author warns the boy against office holding, for he will end up either 'displeasing' his neighbours or not fulfilling the duties of his office adequately.[77] However, despite such conflicts and problems, office holding in rural communities would have increased the social and political standing of office holding families in their localities, while families were also able to reap benefits through perks, as well as, less legally perhaps, ill-accounting and corruption.

That some of these local officials had at least some formal schooling is entirely plausible and likely, and it has been suggested that some lords even drew clerks who drafted the manor court rolls from local tenants. As such, allowing promising peasant families to send their sons to a local school, especially when that school was run by lords themselves, such actions can be seen as helping to foster loyalties and ties to the lord. In this sense, it was also in the interest of the lord to monitor the schooling activities of his tenants carefully. Considerations of faithfulness and loyalty of individual families were probably more important than simple academic ability of a peasant child. The licensing system therefore facilitated the policing of which peasant families were allowed some schooling, and which were not. Such issues mattered, as we know that knowledgeable peasants sometimes turned to law and hired lawyers to plead their freedom or proceed otherwise against their lords.[78]

The manors of St. Albans certainly found themselves within a fairly close proximity to a school which accepted poorer scholars. The Abbey had run its own grammar school since at least 1286 in the town of St. Albans.[79] It is therefore not surprising that much evidence of peasants attending school comes precisely from the manors of the Abbey, including the manors of Winslow and Norton. Such evidence comes to us in two ways. Firstly, through the purchasing of licences before the child commenced schooling, or in cases involving financial penalties, in the shape of amercements imposed on families in the manorial court, who had sent their son to school before seeking seigniorial permissions. Occasionally we can therefore find cases of tenants having sent their sons to school illegally. In 1339, in Winslow, Richard Ponteys was thereby accused of sending his son Geoffrey to be schooled 'without a licence', and he was amerced 3d.[80] At other manors sending a son to be schooled could arouse suspicion that this had been arranged without the lord's permission, and at Wakefield in 1286, the manor's jury launched an inquiry to establish if Peter Tyrsi had 'put his sons to book-learning' with the lord's permission or not.[81]

However, such cases are rare, and especially so in connection with orphaned, underaged heirs, as, by definition, their perceived and stated role was to enter their inheritances in due course as full tenants, and hence not seek alternative career options. However, occasionally it was their non-inheriting siblings who were sent to school instead. In this way, peasant practice appears to echo aristocratic and noble practices regarding non-inheriting sons, who can often be observed to have been sent to school and university to pursue careers within and outside the church.[82] At the same time, the late medieval founding of grammar schools has sometimes been clearly associated with local monastic desires to educate poor, foundling children.[83]

Sending a son into formal education was not cheap. On the one hand, the lord had to be satisfied to gain his permission, and fees had to be paid to the school, while the lost labour power of especially older children could also be felt in individual households. In addition, if the school was far enough away from the village, board and lodging had to be paid for the child, unless other kin living more closely to the school could offer lodging.[84] Such matters were clearly on the mind of John Bradeway of the manor of Norton, when he left no less than 40s. in his will, recorded in the manor's court book in 1405, to his grandson John, 'to support him at school'.[85]

At St. Albans, as in other monastic institutions, which were concerned about the education of the poor and the orphaned, structures were also in place to help poorer scholars with the cost of their studies.[86] In 1328, John of Langley left a house located in the town of St. Albans to the 'Grammar school in the same place' to help support financially the 'poor scholars' of the school, by freeing them from contributions.[87]

At the Manor of Norton seeking permissions to send boys to school was particularly popular before the arrival of the Black Death, with 17 recorded permissions between 1300 and 1348, with the first extant recorded case in 1303. Thereafter, however, recorded permissions drop off significantly, with only 3 recorded until 1412. None of these permissions are associated with the underaged heirs. At Winslow between 1327 and the end of 1349, a total of 15 cases of permissions to send a son to attend school can be found, of which three are specifically associated with younger non-inheriting orphaned sons, as far as one can tell. Another two are associated with boys who became orphaned after they had commenced clerical schooling. After the Black Death until, and including 1377, sending a son to be educated at school seems to have still been seen as a viable and potentially attractive option at Winslow, as 11 permissions for boys were acquired in this period, none of which however can be associated with orphans.

The permissions to send boys to school were generally purchased when the children were between the age of 6 and 8, which accords with the typical age upon which children started clerical schooling.[88] For example in January 1332, John Mayn of Winslow paid his lord the substantial sum of half a mark to send his son Richard to clerical school.[89] Two years later, in 1334 John Mayn died and his holding was handed to his nine-year-old son John. Richard, presumably his younger son, was not mentioned, and it is likely that he was actually in residence at the school in St. Albans. A similar case emerges at the same manor in May 1336, when Ralph Rolf had died, leaving his holding to his then two-year-old son. The tenement was not insubstantial, containing one messuage and a virgate of land.[90] It seems, however that he had another younger son, as in 1343, Richard, the son of Ralph Rolfs was granted a seigniorial licence to 'go and attend clerical school where and when he wishes', and a fine of 12d. was duly paid.[91] It is possible that Ralph's wife Agnes was pregnant when her husband died, which may also explain her rapid remarriage in November 1336, when she was presented in court for having married without a licence.[92] Therefore Richard can't have been older than 7 or 8 when he was sent to school. John, Ralph's principal heir did not live long enough to enter his holding though as he died during the first arrival of the plague in 1349, then aged 13 years, and the holding was handed over to his aunt.[93]

An unusual permission by the lord of Winslow to one of his tenants is recorded in 1342, when John, the son of Richard atte Welle of little Horwood is granted a licence 'to get married and be apprenticed or attend clerical schools if and wherever he wishes, and to serve outside the lordship or inside it, where and whom he pleases for his whole life', as long as he was to ensure that his tenement was in the hands of active cultivators, who would also attend the manorial court for him. At the time when this blanket permission was granted for a fine of 40d., John, unless he had a younger brother of the same name, or a clerical error was made in recording their names, would have been far too old to commence schooling, as he was at least 27 years old. He had been left orphaned in 1328, aged 13, named as John the son of Richard atte Welle of Little Horewood, due to inherit half a virgate of land.[94] No other Richard atte Welle of Horewood was recorded, making it therefore highly likely that this was the same John. As a result the permission should not be interpreted literally, but rather as a blanket licence to John to do as he pleases with his life. Perhaps John just wanted to leave the manor or felt ill-suited for an agricultural life, as long as the lord could be reassured that the lands would not fall into decline and waste.

Clerical life and education could also run in families. In November 1343, William Kyng paid the lord 12d. for a permission to send his son Ralph to clerical school.[95] Just a few years later, in 1349 William Kyng died, leaving his son Ralph, then aged 12, to inherit his holding of over one virgate of land. Ralph would therefore have been 6 upon commencing clerical school. The guardianship over Ralph and his holding were granted to none other than Geoffrey Kyng, then vicar of the vill of Greneburgh.[96] It therefore may well be the case that Ralph Kyng was by now considered to be well on the path towards a clerical career. On the other hand, while Geoffrey Milcent was granted permission to marry off his daughters Agnes and Matilda in 1345, as well as send his son Geoffrey to clerical school in the same year, the lord stipulated that Geoffrey was not allowed 'to take orders among the clergy', even if he was allowed to attend the school.[97] When a few years later in 1349, Geoffrey Milcent died in the plague year, his son Geoffrey was aged 12 and placed under the guardianship of William atte Lane.[98] This means that Geoffrey attended clerical school from the age of 8. Such stipulations provide evidence of peasant negotiations with the lord; each boundary laid upon the unfree which circumscribed their free agency had to be tested, pushed and re-negotiated. In this case the boy was allowed to study, but the circumscription was imposed upon the conclusion of basic studies. Seigniorial motivations behind such decisions were not dissimilar from those which led lords at times to encourage marriages within his manorial demesne and hence within his jurisdiction. Yet other factors may also have been at play. Thinking ahead, a lord may want to encourage a steady trickle of peasants educated to a fairly basic level to serve as officials, but local priests may already have been present in sufficient numbers.

Upon their arrival at the school the young boys lived under the rules of the school, and also, for the time, were placed more directly under the authority of the church. The symbolic ritual which signified this transition was that 'immediately' upon admission the boys' hair was cut, and they were tonsured 'in the manner of choristers and clerics', as school rules dating from the early fourteenth century state.[99] By the fourteenth century, the use of English in translations from Latin in schools became more common, thereby implying a growing literacy in both Latin and English.[100] Indeed, as Orme has shown, Chaucer's own largely urban-based perception of his society appears to have been one which was largely literate.[101] Unless we make an assumption of an educational gulf between urban and rural children, the importance of peasant boys attending school for a few years where this was available locally, should not be underestimated. On the one hand, they would have provided an educated pool of tenants for the lord to draw manorial managers from, while from the perspective of the village community they represented individuals who would have been able to help with drawing up charters in transfers of land, or even more complex legal issues.

Corporal punishment was considered to be part of the education process, and the heartfelt late medieval lament of a schoolboy testifies to the harsh beatings sometimes meted out to pupils, as they tested and provoked him.

> Ffor ofte sore we abye
> Þe twynkelinges of his hye,
> Þe maystur us to bete;
> For he & þu are at asent,
> Al day ȝyuen agagement
> To ȝyuen us strokes grete.[102]

Indeed laments of the at times apparently sadistic inclinations of school masters are far from rare, in another poem probably dating from about 1500, the author complaints that it would rather do other things than go to school, where his master 'looked as if mad' and sharp birch sticks instilled the boy with terror, making him wish that his master were a hare and his book a cat, and all the master's books dogs, to which hunt the school boy himself would blow the hunting horn, wishing his master dead: 'ffor if he were dede I wold not care'.[103]

However, despite such images of fear and brutality, the rules of the St. Albans school stressed the importance of peaceful and studious behaviour by both students and their masters. In 1339, it was stipulated that neither the scholars nor the teacher were allowed to bear arms within the school or outside, under pain of excommunication as it was feared that the 'peace and tranquility of the said school may be disturbed'. Fighting and any kind of noisy behaviour were not tolerated and any scholars found involved in serious wrongdoing, fighting or being noisy could expect to be 'chastised' for their actions.[104] It was also stressed that behaviour which would disturb scholars or anyone found guilty of wandering around at night time could be expelled.[105]

We cannot say with any certainty for how long these peasant boys attended school. Orme suggests that a few years attendance at a grammar school would have provided the 'basic skills required to follow a trade or business'.[106] The school rules of St. Albans' state that 'admittance for a duration of five years at most' was considered 'sufficient time for proficiency in grammar'.[107]

While the attendance of grammar schools were the basic prerequisite for further studies and eventually entering the priesthood, it is unlikely that this would have been the aim of all the rural boys who attended schools as children, not least because further schooling and potentially attending university would have been a rather costly undertaking as fees as well as bed and board had to be paid for.[108] Therefore it is quite likely that in most rural communities which were located in close enough proximity of a school, some tenants did possess a basic level of literacy.[109]

This also has ramifications for the spread of dissenting ideology in popular revolt, for example attested by the cryptic letters which were found on captured rebels in the rising of 1381, and indicate a degree of background literacy.[110]

Nonetheless, the level of literacy in rural communities should not be exaggerated. The numbers recorded as involved in attending school, while important, represented little more than a steady trickle, even if some of those who had attended school subsequently passed some of their knowledge on to others. Additionally, considering the geographical spread of schools in later medieval England, such levels of literacy would be significantly at variance according to locality.[111] This is also confirmed by the complete absence of any permissions sought or granted in the manorial court rolls of the manors of Longbridge and Monkton Deverill, held by Glastonbury Abbey, between 1300 and 1338, and apparently nowhere near a suitable school for poorer rural boys.[112] Similarly at Wakefield, the mention of study or schooling for local boys are almost unheard of, despite the clear expectation that tenants had to gain the lord's approval for the education of their sons. Between 1274 and 1297, the extant court records mention no case of schooling, bar one in 1286, while between 1313 and 1316 similarly no cases are recorded. Clearly an education at Wakefield was exceedingly rare at least among the unfree population.[113]

Where suitable schooling was available locally, it could represent a viable option to ensure training and a livelihood for non-inheriting younger sons in rural households. As such the importance of the impact of schooling in some peasant communities should not be underestimated, and may indicate locally stronger ties between the lord and certain peasant families from whom more privileged officials including scribes could be drawn from. However, the level of local literacy among peasant boys was significantly dependent upon the availability of accessible and cheap schooling. Such schooling represented important avenues for the acquisition of skills by non-inheriting children whose families have sufficient means to send them to school for a few years.

4 Problems and Conflict

Peasant families were far from harmonious institutions.[114] Common squabbles and arguments over land in particular in medieval English rural societies might conjure up images of Emil Zola's fictional dissection of the nineteenth-century peasant strife in *The Earth*, and at times this comparison might not seem far-fetched either. Standing central to a myriad of human interactions, from the lord–tenant relationship, to village hierarchies and social status, land and associated holdings and connected rights therefore represented a key axis of conflict and disagreement, yet also of mutuality and cooperative ties within communities. Intra-familial conflict has therefore been frequently linked to land, as have disputes over debts, trespass and transfers of land.[115] Inheritance thereby represents the core of landed relationships in the English medieval village, tying and intertwining interests of kinship, neighbourhood as well as lordship.

As we have seen, communities were very much aware that guardianship could cause problems and friction. Maintenance agreements of underaged heirs in themselves can be read as an acknowledgement of potential problems and conflict arising from wardships, which made such contractual depositions in the court necessary in the first place. Theoretically therefore at least the problems observed in familial households, hinging on land and inheritance, should have been magnified in disputed wardships.

However, while peasant families were no strangers to conflicts and arguments, it has been noted that medieval peasant families appear to have been surprisingly congenial. In fourteenth century England, Hanawalt found that only 8% of homicides occurred within families, a figure significantly lower than modern comparable statistics.[116] It might also be considered surprising how comparatively infrequently conflict over wardships surfaced in manorial court rolls. In general communities worked hard to avert discord, and when it did occur, mechanisms were in place to facilitate—where possible—amicable solutions. This comparative rarity of conflict over wardships has also been observed in the case of urban societies. In London, Hanawalt found that only 5% of cases concerning orphans in the letter books of London between 1309 and 1428 dealt with complaints of abuses of wardships.[117]

In manorial records conflict in relation to wardships falls broadly into two main areas. Firstly, we find complaints concerned with the failings of guardians, and secondly, problems associated with certain actions of underaged heirs themselves the validity of which could be called into question, including once they reached the age of majority. These problems and conflicts can be grouped into four main categories, namely (a) retained inheritance, (b) deforcement or effective disinheritance, (c) subletting of an inheritance and lastly, and (d) waste or degradation caused to the inheritance during the period of the wardship.

Occasionally custodians were loath to let go of potentially lucrative holdings, and conflicts arose especially after the heir came of age, and they tried to reclaim holdings or money owed to them. In such cases, heirs were not averse to taking even their own relatives to court to enforce their rights. Respect for their elders or gratitude for their upbringing was certainly no barrier to resorting to law. Such matters often came to a head once the heir planned to establish their own household and marrying. Entering a holding was seen as a portal to full tenant responsibilities and social status. As such, the blocking of this transition could be considered a serious matter by the court. At the manor of Winslow, Christina Porter was about 19 years old when she married John Chonneson in 1335. In the previous year, Christina had gone to court claiming that her father had unjustly retained certain lands and holdings which should have been hers by right for a total of 'two years beyond her coming of age'. Her father was amerced 3d. for the offence, but allowed to hold unto the holding until Michaelmas, presumably to allow sufficient time to gather any crops growing on the land during the upcoming harvest season. Such crops would have been considered his by right, as he had invested the seed grain as well as his labour into their production. In the intervening period, he was ordered to provide Christina with 'food and other necessaries in his house' should she wish to reside there, and if not, he was to provide her with 'two quarters of grain'.[118]

Christina's status was implicitly recognised as liminal by the court, and her case exemplified her transitional limbo. Her place of residence was considered to be her choice, while a clear message was sent to her father that it was her right to leave with her inheritance. He may have hoped that she would stay, perhaps with her husband 'in his house', all reaping the fruits of the total lands and the couple's labour. To Christina, this however amounted to disinheritance, and her father was amerced and ordered to pay Christina in grain, effectively a portion of his harvest. It is highly likely that Christina's named father would have been her step-father, presumably of a subsequent marriage of her mother, as Christina would have gained her inheritance from her biological father only after his death. Such cases also indicate that children could not have been perceived as a straightforward investment for future care in parental old age. Anthropologists have highlighted the importance in some cultures of the role of children in caring for their parents in their old age, even residing in their elderly parent's residence or considering the parental care invested in their children as a repayable debt.[119] In peasant societies of medieval England, we certainly find maintenance contracts between children and their retired parents, but we do not appear to have an implicit understanding of grown-up children owing their parents a debt. The relationship was rather defined by independence and while mutuality existed, it was not apparently based primarily on the parent–child interdependence. Instead, the aim was for young people to become their own persons, to which path it was the responsibility of guardians and parents to direct the child.

While cases such as the latter amount to disinheritance or deforcement, such cases of retained inheritance are very rare. Much more common are cases where either the guardian or the underaged heir themselves alienated permanently or temporarily part or all of the inheritance to a third party. At the manor of Wakefield in January 1297, Thomas the son of Matthew de Heppewrth, pleaded against William concerning a bovate of land, which Thomas claims was his 'by rights of inheritance after the death of his father'. The land, so Thomas argued, was taken from him while he was still underage.[120]

The issue of deforcement became more problematic if it was the underaged heir themselves who had alienated the land before reaching the age of majority. In June 1339, again at Wakefield, Agnes, who was the daughter of Thomas Bateson accused Robert Alot of having 'unjustly deforced her of 1½ acres of land and a rood of meadow'. Answering the accusation, Robert came to court and explained that Agnes herself had come before the court and 'surrendered the land to Robert and his heirs'. Robert is, therefore, claiming that Agnes herself had not only conducted the land transfer through the proper channels of the manorial court, and thereby, by definition, in front of plenty of witnesses but that she therefore also consented to the transfer. Agnes returned to this that she was underage at the time, and Robert claimed that she was not, but of full age. Both parties turned to the court to launch an inquiry into the question of her majority and conclude the matter.[121] It only took the court one month to reach a verdict in this case, and in July 1339 the court concluded that 'Robert Alot unjustly deforces Agnes daughter of Thomas Bateson of 1½ acres and a rood of meadow in Crigeleston as acknowledged in the full court. He is amerced 6d'.[122]

In other words, the court concluded that Agnes was indeed underage when she made the transfer, which, while validly and properly conducted, could be declared null and void if the plaintiff, in this case Agnes, was not satisfied with the arrangement anymore upon reaching majority. As we have seen in chapter one, as minors were perceived as incapable of making a fully informed decision, transfers of land conducted by them were insecure. It was not the case that such transfers were not considered valid, but rather that the heir in question was at liberty to change their minds upon reaching full age. Moreover, by definition, in this case at least, the ultimate responsibility to ensure that the land-transfer is consented to or conducted by a person of full age resided with the party acquiring the holding.

Similar problems were encountered by John Spanle of Heacham in Norfolk, when in 1278, Alan de Ponte with his wife Matilda claimed from him 5d worth of land and a messuage, which had been held by Matilda's father Reynard Freyche upon his death.[123] John Spanle was therefore accused of unjust deforcement, of which the couple claimed damages amounting to half a mark. John claimed that Matilda had come to court together with her sister Sabina and had surrendered the land into the hands of the lord for his benefit. An inquiry was immediately launched into the matter which returned that Matilda and her sister Sabina were not of a legitimate age to sell land or indeed, even to consent to such a transaction. The plaintiffs and defendant were granted a 'love day' to come to an amicable solution to their problem.

A slightly different set of circumstances emerge from a case concerning William Lene of Hatfield Chase in Yorkshire in 1336. In October of that year, John, son of Adam Wilcok, had gone to the manorial court to claim from William a messuage and 9 acres of land. William Lene argued, very much like Robert Alot of Wakefield, and John Spanle of Heacham, that John had 'surrendered the aforesaid tenement to him in the lord's court, to hold to himself and his heirs according to custom'. John did not even try to deny this, but like Agnes claimed that 'he was underage' at the time when he alienated the aforesaid tenements to him. In this case, however, the outcome was rather different. John might have considered his actions with hindsight a touch ill-informed or immature, but Hatfield Chase's jurors thought otherwise. The following inquiry concluded that at the time when the transfer was made, John was 16 years of age, which was deemed to be the age of majority.[124] Accordingly, the transfer was considered valid and therefore inalienable.

While custody arrangements were often at pains to guard inheritances against being wasted and run down, occasionally complaints about letting a ward's inheritance go to waste do surface. The concept of a wasted holding could encompass a number of different problems. Such waste may be associated with the land itself, if arable land was not tilled and made productive for example and left unduly fallow. Wasted holdings could also refer to the buildings associated with a tenement, and hence such waste also became an issue of concern for the lord, whose objective was to maintain his assets to a high and therefore profitable standard. Such wasted holdings became, in particular, a problem in the decades after the Black Death, when demand for land dropped and population decline meant that fewer buildings were needed to house local populations and their livestock. Instead, peasant communities were actively re-shaping and re-building their buildings, and may well have pilfered building materials from structures, which were no longer required to extend or renew other buildings in their tenements.[125] However, considering the level of concern there was about this issue it is notable how comparatively rarely such cases are mentioned in the context of inheritances. In 1423, at Winslow, there was no complaint from the heir about a wasted holding, but instead the lord intervened directly, by taking all 'the lands and holdings which were entrusted to the custody of John Est' into the hands of the lord, as he had caused waste in the holding. Typical for the period John Est was accused of letting houses fall into ruin and 'felling trees'.[126]

Subletting of land by heirs was also not tolerated, especially not without prior permission of the lord. Thus in 1351, Richard Martyn of Winslow was found to have sublet half a virgate of land over which he held custody without permission.[127] Once again, however problems over such land rights of sublets were significantly complicated when they were due to the actions of underaged heirs. At the manor of Wakefield, the manorial jury was faced with a rather unenviable set of problems in 1339, when an inquiry had been initiated to explore that status and associated rights of an acre of land. Thomas, son of William, had leased the acre to Edmund de Barneside, and now wished to recover the land, as Thomas argued that he had been underage when the transfer had been agreed.[128] The inquiry returned that Thomas was indeed allowed to recover the land, as he had not reached the age of majority when he let the land to Edmund. However the court also argued, which Thomas conceded, that Edmund should continue to hold the land until Thomas was to pay him back the 10s which Edmund had given in payment to Thomas.

Entering inheritances and reaching the age of majority were life events which were potentially fraught with problems and conflict. Rural communities recognised this and established structures to mitigate as far as possible against conflict and the escalation of conflict where it did occur. The aim was not just to help young people on their road to independent adulthood but also to maintain communal relationships. While conflict did occur, it was a comparatively uncommon event in the communities under study.

Notes

1. See also, B.A. Hanawalt, *The Ties That Bound*, p. 83.
2. R. Lock, ed., *The Court Rolls of Walsham le Willows 1303–1350* (Woodbridge: Boydell & Brewer and Suffolk Record Society, vol. xli, 1998), p. 51.
3. R. Lock, ed., *The Court Rolls of Walsham le Willows 1303–1350*, p. 133.
4. R. Lock, ed., *The Court Rolls of Walsham le Willows 1303–1350*, p. 196.
5. R. Lock, ed., *The Court Rolls of Walsham le Willows 1303–1350*, p. 220.
6. R. Lock, ed., *The Court Rolls of Walsham le Willows 1303–1350*, p. 311. Agnes is mentioned as his widow in June 1348, but in August 1347 Henry was still alive as he was accused of causing damage in the lord's grain with his animals, p. 301.
7. R. Lock, ed., *The Court Rolls of Walsham le Willows 1303–1350*, p. 324.
8. See for example: B.A. Hanawalt, *The Ties That Bound*, p. 95ff.
9. For a discussion of the significance of this see for instance: M. Müller, 'The Function and Evasion of Marriage Fines on a Fourteenth Century English Manor', in: *Continuity and Change*, vol. 14, no. 2 (1999), pp. 169–190.
10. R. Lock, ed., *The Court Rolls of Walsham le Willows 1303–1350*, p. 47 and p. 133.

11. R. Lock, ed., *The Court Rolls of Walsham le Willows 1303–1350*, p. 235.
12. R. Lock, ed., *The Court Rolls of Walsham le Willows 1303–1350*, p. 322.
13. R. Lock, ed., *The Court Rolls of Walsham le Willows 1303–1350*, pp. 51–52.
14. R. Lock, ed., *The Court Rolls of Walsham le Willows 1303–1350*, p. 133.
15. R. Lock, ed., *The Court Rolls of Walsham le Willows 1303–1350*, p. 169.
16. R. Lock, ed., *The Court Rolls of Walsham le Willows 1303–1350*, p. 251.
17. R. Lock, ed., *The Court Rolls of Walsham le Willows 1303–1350*, p. 322.
18. R. Lock, ed., *The Court Rolls of Walsham le Willows 1303–1350*, p. 119.
19. R. Lock, ed., *The Court Rolls of Walsham le Willows 1303–1350*, p. 256.
20. R. Lock, ed., *The Court Rolls of Walsham le Willows 1303–1350*, p. 317.
21. J. Amphlett, ed., *Court Rolls of the Manor of Halesowen 1270–1307* (Oxford, Printed for the Worcestershire Historical Society by James Parker, 1912), p. 330.
22. D. Noy, ed., *Winslow Manor Court Book Part I, 1327–1377* (Buckinghamshire Record Society no. 35, 2011), pp. 8–9.
23. P. Foden, ed. and trans., *Records of the Manor of Norton in the Liberty of St. Albans, 1244–1539* (Caxton Hill, Hertford: Hertfordshire Record Publications, 2014), p. 123.
24. P. Foden, ed. and trans., *Records of the Manor of Norton in the Liberty of St. Albans, 1244–1539*, p. 127.
25. P. Foden, ed. and trans., *Records of the Manor of Norton in the Liberty of St. Albans, 1244–1539*, p. 139.
26. References Canon Law etc.
27. Worcester Archives, MS BA 1531/69 (A and B); 1317.
28. B.A. Hanawalt, *Growing Up in Medieval London: The Experience of Childhood in History* (Oxford and New York: Oxford University Press, 1993), p. 101. See also, R.H. Helmholz, 'Marriage Contracts in Medieval England', in: P.L. Reynolds and J. Witte, eds., *To Have and to Hold Marrying and Its Documentation in Western Christendom, 400–1600* (Cambridge University Press, 2007), p. 262.
29. Seigniorial involvement in peasant marriage arrangements and attempts to influence inter peasant marriages have been observed in a number of different studies: See for example: P.A. Brand, P.R. Hyams, and R. Faith, 'Seigniorial Control of Women's Marriage', in: *Past and Present*, no. 99 (1983), pp. 123–148; M. Müller, 'The Function and Evasion of Marriage Fines on a Fourteenth Century English Manor', in: *Continuity and Change*, vol. 14, no. 2 (1999), pp. 169–190; and M. Müller, 'The Function and Evasion of Marriage Fines on a Fourteenth Century English Manor', pp. 169–190.
30. *Custumals of the Manors of Laughton, Willingdon and Goring* (Sussex Record Society, vol. LX, 1961), p. 5.
31. See for example: E. Searle, 'Seigneurial Control of Women's Marriage; the Antecedents and Function of Merchet in England', in: *Past and*

Present, no. 82 (1979), pp. 3–43; P.A. Brand, P. R. Hyams, and R. Faith, 'Seigniorial Control of Women's Marriage', in: *Past and Present*, no. 99 (1983), pp. 123–148; M. Müller, 'The Function and Evasion of Marriage Fines on a Fourteenth Century English Manor', pp. 169–190.

32. R. Lock, ed., *The Court Rolls of Walsham le Willows, 1303–50*, p. 11.
33. D. Noy, ed., *Winslow Manor Court Books, Part I 1327–1377*, p. 230.
34. D. Noy, ed., *Winslow Manor Court Books, Part I 1327–1377*, p. 318.
35. See for example: B.A. Hanawalt, *The Ties That Bound Peasant Families in Medieval England* (New York and Oxford: Oxford University Press, 1986), esp. pp. 90–104.
36. P. Foden, ed., *Records of the Manor of Norton*, p. 61.
37. P. Foden, ed., *Records of the Manor of Norton*, p. 68. The case also illustrates that no distinction was drawn between male and female tenants in the seigniorial expectation to fulfil all responsibilities which burdened tenancies, including labour services. See for a discussion of this: M. Müller, 'Peasant Women, Agency and Status in Mid Thirteenth to Late Fourteenth-Century England Some Reconsiderations', in: C. Beattie and M.F. Stevens, eds., *Married Women and the Law in Premodern Northwest Europe* (Boydell Press, 2013).
38. P. Foden, ed., *Records of the Manor of Norton*, p. 75.
39. B.A. Hanawalt, *The Ties That Bound*, pp. 176–177.
40. We have pictorial evidence of the use of slings, for example, in the mid-thirteenth century image of St. Christopher carrying Jesus in a sling across the water in the Westminster Psalter. Royal 2AXXII f.220v. 'The Westminster Psalter', Westminster or St. Albans, England, mid-thirteenth century. St. Christopher carrying Christ child in a sling.
41. E. Heward, *Matthew Hale* (London: Robert Hale, 1972), pp. 71–72. A mid-seventeenth century case is described where a woman was paid a penny to look after an infant, in which context it was noted that 'it was customary with old women, that if they did look after a suckling child, and nothing would please it but the breast, they did use to please the child to give it the breast, and it did please the child…', p. 72.
42. R.H. Robbins, ed., *Secular Lyrics of the XIVth and XVth Centuries* (Oxford: Clarendon Press, 1961), p. 62
43. Robbins, ed., *Secular Lyrics of the XIVth and XVth Centuries*, pp. 70–71.
44. See especially: P.J.P. Goldberg, *Women, Work and Life—Cycle in a Medieval Economy: Women in York and Yorkshire, c. 1300–1520* (Oxford, 1992).
45. P.J.P. Goldberg, 'What Is a Servant?', in: A. Curry and E. Matthew, eds., *Concepts and Patterns of Service in the Later Middle Ages* (Boydell Press, 2000), p. 16.
46. A.V. Chayanov, *The Theory of Peasant Economy*, pp. 53–65.
47. P. Ariès, *Centuries of Childhood*, ….

48. G. Handel, S.E. Cahill, and F. Elkin, *Children and Society: The Sociology of Children and Child Socialization* (Oxford University Press, 2007), p. 67.
49. B.A. Hanawalt, *The Ties That Bound*, p. 159.
50. B.A. Hanawalt, *The Ties That Bound*, p. 158–160; See also B.A. Hanawalt, 'Childrearing Among the Lower Classes of Late Medieval England', pp. 1–22.
51. See Table 2 in chapter 4 above, p. 122.
52. See for example: P.J.P. Goldberg, 'What Is a Servant?', p. 16.
53. N. Orme, 'Chaucer and Education', in: *The Chaucer Review*, vol. 16, no. 1 (1981), p. 39.
54. P.J.P. Goldberg, 'What Is a Servant?', p. 7.
55. R. Lock, ed., *The Court Rolls of Walsham le Willows 1303–1350*, p. 311 and p. 313.
56. R. Lock, ed., *The Court Rolls of Walsham le Willows 1351–1399*, p. 40.
57. R. Alwyn Wilson, ed., *The Court Rolls of the Manor of Hales 1276–1301 and Romsley Courts 1280–1303* (Warwickshire Historical Society, Part III, Oxford, 1933), pp. 53–54.
58. P.J.P. Goldberg, 'Masters and Men in Later Medieval England', in: D.M. Hadley, ed., *Masculinity in Medieval Europe* (London and New York: Longman, 1999), esp. p. 58 and see, pp. 62–63.
59. R. Lock, ed., *The Court Rolls of Walsham le Willows 1351–1399*, p. 41.
60. R. Lock, ed., *The Court Rolls of Walsham le Willows 1303–1350*, p. 325.
61. R. Lock, ed., *The Court Rolls of Walsham le Willows 1351–1399*, p. 50.
62. R. Lock, ed., *The Court Rolls of Walsham le Willows 1351–1399*, p. 140.
63. R. Lock, ed., *The Court Rolls of Walsham le Willows 1351–1399*, p. 60.
64. R. Lock, ed., *The Court Rolls of Walsham le Willows 1351–1399*, p. 95. Her son Robert, aged 5 at his mother's death was much later noted to be Walsham's Hayward in 1399, when he would have been 36 years old.
65. R. Lock, ed., *The Court Rolls of Walsham le Willows 1303–1350*, p. 77.
66. R. Lock, ed., *The Court Rolls of Walsham le Willows 1351–1399*, p. 41, p. 59, and p. 122.
67. R. Lock, ed., *The Court Rolls of Walsham le Willows 1351–1399*, p. 43, p. 60, and p. 85.
68. There is also a chance that his mother was single and had never married, although that would perhaps been unusual. Glastonbury Abbey Records held at Longleat House, sourced from Microfilm, MS 11251.
69. Glastonbury Abbey Records held at Longleat House, sourced from Microfilm MS 11179.
70. While no examples of girls attending schools have been identified in this study, in some religious houses evidence of the education of girls alongside boys has been identified. See for example: G.M. Draper, 'The Education of Children in Kent and Sussex: Interpreting the Medieval and Tudor Ways', in: *Nottingham Medieval Studies*, vol. 52 (2008), p. 220.

71. N. Orme, *Medieval Schools from Roman Britain to Renaissance England* (Yale University Press, 2006), p. 131 and pp. 190–195.
72. G.M., Draper, 'The Education of Children in Kent and Sussex', pp. 219–220.
73. N. Orme, *Medieval Schools*, p. 132.
74. For a discussion of seigniorial attempts to control peasant movements through marriage licences, see M. Müller, 'The Function and Evasion of Marriage Fines on a Fourteenth Century English Manor', in: *Continuity and Change*, vol. 14, no. 2 (1999), pp. 169–190.
75. For the roles of manorial officials see for example: C. Briggs, 'Monitoring Demesne Managers Through the Manorial Court Before and After the Black Death', in: R. Goddard et al., *Survival and Discord in Medieval Society Essays in Honour of Christopher Dyer* (Brepols, 2010), pp. 179–196.
76. For a recent discussion of such manorial officials, see C. Briggs, 'Monitoring Demesne Managers Through the Manorial Court Before and After the Black Death', pp. 179–196.
77. F.J. Furnivall, ed., *The Babees Book: The Bokes of Nurture* (London: Early English Text Society, 1868), p. 49.
78. See for example: M. Müller, 'The Aims and Organisation of a Peasant Revolt in Early Fourteenth-Century Wiltshire', in: *Rural History*, vol. 14 (2003), pp. 1–20; R. Faith, 'The "Great Rumour" of 1377 and Peasant Ideology', in: R.H. Hilton and T.H. Aston, eds., *The English Rising of 1381* (Cambridge University Press, 1984, reprinted 2007), pp. 43–73.
79. N. Orme, *Medieval Schools*, p. 365.
80. *Winslow Manor Court Books*, Part I, p. 96.
81. J. Lister, ed., *Court Rolls of the Manor of Wakefield, vol. 31 to 1316, and 1286* (Yorkshire Archaeological Society; Record Series, vol. LVII, 1917), p. 133.
82. N. Orme, *From Childhood to Chivalry, the Education of the English Kings and Aristocracy 1066–1530* (London and New York: Methuen, 1984), pp. 69–75.
83. G.M. Draper, 'The Education of Children in Kent and Sussex', p. 238.
84. For costs of schooling, see N. Orme, *Medieval Schools*, pp. 132–134.
85. P. Foden, ed. and trans., *Records of the Manor of Norton in the Liberty of St. Albans, 1244–1539*, p. 216.
86. See for example: C. Rawcliffe, 'The Eighth Comfortable Work: Education and the Medieval English Hospital', in: C. Barron and J. Stratford, eds., *The Church and Learning in Late Medieval Society: Essays in Honour of R.B. Dobson* (Stamford: Shaun Tyas, Harlaxton Medieval Studies xi, 2002), pp. 372–373.

87. T.H. Riley, ed., *Chronica Monasterii S. Albani, vol. II Registra Johannis Whethamstede, William Albon, et Willelmi Walingfords Abbatum Monasterii Santi Albani* (London, 1872), p. 306.
88. S. Shahar, *Childhood in the Middle Ages* (London and New York, 1992), p. 105; N. Orme, *Medieval Schools*, p. 129.
89. *Winslow Manor Court Books*, Part I, p. 30.
90. *Winslow Manor Court Books*, Part I, p. 63.
91. *Winslow Manor Court Books*, Part I, p. 139.
92. *Winslow Manor Court Books*, Part I, p. 70.
93. *Winslow Manor Court Books*, Part I, p. 246.
94. *Winslow Court Book*, Part I, pp. 11–12, and pp. 128–129.
95. *Winslow Court Book*, Part I, p. 143.
96. *Winslow Court Book*, Part I, p. 221.
97. *Winslow Court Book*, Part I, p. 167.
98. *Winslow Court Book*, Part I, p. 236.
99. T.H. Riley, ed., *Chronica Monasterii S. Albani, vol. II Registra Johannis Whethamstede*, p. 315
100. N. Orme, 'Latin and English Sentences in Fifteenth-Century Schoolbooks', in: *The Yale University Gazette*, vol. 60, no. 1/2 (October 1985), p. 47.
101. N. Orme, 'Chaucer and Education', in: *The Chaucer Review*, vol. 16, no. 1 (1981), pp. 38–59.
102. R.H. Robbins, ed., *Secular Lyrics of the XIVth and XVth Centuries*, second edition (Oxford: Clarendon Press, 1952), p. 105.
103. 'The Birched School-Boy', in: F.J. Furnivall, ed., *The Babees Book: The Bokes of Nurture* (London: Early English Text Society, 1868), pp. 403–404 and p. 404.
104. T.H. Riley, ed., *Chronica Monasterii S. Albani, vol. II Registra Johannis Whethamstede*, p. 311.
105. T.H. Riley, ed., *Chronica Monasterii S. Albani, vol. II Registra Johannis Whethamstede*, p. 315.
106. N. Orme, *Medieval Schools*, p. 131.
107. T.H. Riley, ed., *Chronica Monasterii S. Albani, vol. II Registra Johannis Whethamstede*, p. 315.
108. N. Orme, *Medieval Schools*, pp. 131–134.
109. A similar point has been made by Steven Justice, when he argued that just because contemporary chroniclers could not credit rebels in 1381 with literacy, as peasants were generally perceived as too irrational, does not make it a fact. S. Justice, *Writing and Rebellion, England in 1381* (Berkeley California and London: University of California Press, 1994), pp. 16–17; see also footnote 12 on p. 17.
110. S. Justice, *Writing and Rebellion*, pp. 13–66.

111. See for example the maps representing locations of schools in medieval England in N. Orme, *Medieval Schools*, p. 59, p. 190 and p. 194.
112. Glastonbury Abbey Documents at Longleat House, sourced from Microfilm, MS 9629, Skin 2 to MS 96 34 Skin no: 3v.
113. W. Baildon, ed., *Court Rolls of the Manor of Wakefield, vol. I, 1274–1297* (Yorkshire Archaeological Society, 1901); J. Lister, ed., *Court Rolls of the Manor of Wakefield, vol. 3. 1313 to 1316, and 1286* (Yorkshire Archaeological Society; Record Series, vol. LVII, 1917).
114. See for example: B.A. Hanawalt, 'The Peasant Family and Crime in Fourteenth Century England', in: *Journal of British Studies*, vol. 13, no. 2 (1971); M. Müller, 'Conflict, Strife and Cooperation: Aspects of the Late Medieval Family and Household', in: I. Davis, M. Müller, and S. Rees-Jones, eds., *Love, Marriage and Family Ties in the Later Middle Ages* (Turnhout: Brepols, 2001), pp. 311–329.
115. B.A. Hanawalt, 'The Peasant Family and Crime', see esp. pp. 6–8; M. Müller, 'Conflict, Strife and Cooperation', pp. 311–329.
116. B.A. Hanawalt, 'Childrearing Among the Lower Classes of Late Medieval England', in: *Journal of Interdisciplinary History*, vol. 8, no. 1 (Summer 1977), p. 20; B.A. Hanawalt, 'The Peasant Family and Crime in Fourteenth Century England', p. 4.
117. B.A. Hanawalt, *Growing Up in Medieval London* (New York and Oxford: Oxford University Press), p. 100.
118. *Winslow Manor Court Book*, Part I, p. 51 and p. 57.
119. H. Montgomery, *An Introduction to Childhood* (2009), pp. 67–70.
120. W. Baildon, ed., *Court Rolls of the Manor of Wakefield, vol. I, 1274–1297* (Yorkshire Archaeological Society, 1901), p. 260.
121. J. Lister, ed., *Court Rolls of the Manor of Wakefield, vol. IV, 1315–1317* (Yorkshire Archaeological Society, 1930), p. 85.
122. J. Lister, ed., *Court Rolls of the Manor of Wakefield, vol. IV, 1315–1317*, p. 89.
123. Heacham Court Rolls, sourced from Microfilm held at the Norfolk Record Office, MS DA1, 8 June 1278.
124. L.R. Poos and L. Bonfield, ed., *Select Cases in Manorial Courts 1250–1550; Property and Family Law* (London: Selden Society, 1998), pp. 148–149.
125. P.V. Hargreaves, 'Seignorial Reaction and *Peasant* Responses: Worcester Priory and Its *Peasants* After the Black Death', in: *Midland History*, vol. 24 (1999), pp. 53–78.
126. D. Noy, ed., *Winslow Manor Court Books Part II 1423–1460* (Buckinghamshire Record Society no. 36, 2011), p. 471.
127. D. Noy, ed., *Winslow Manor Court Books*, Part I, p. 261.
128. K.M. Troup, ed., *The Court Rolls of the Manor of Wakefield, October 1338–September 1340* (Yorkshire Archaeological Society, 1999), p. 72.

Bibliography

Primary Sources

Manorial documents of the manor of Eldersfield. MS BA 1531/69 A and B; The Hive Worcester Archive.

Heacham Court Rolls, Le Strange Collection; sourced from Microfilm held at Norfolk Record Office, Norwich.

Glastonbury Abbey Records held at Longleat House, sourced from Microfilm held at the University of Birmingham.

R. Alwyn Wilson, ed., *The Court Rolls of the Manor of Hales 1276–1301 and Romsley Courts 1280–1303*, Part III (Oxford: Warwickshire Historical Society, 1933).

J. Amphlett, ed., *Court Rolls of the Manor of Halesowen 1270–1307* (Oxford: Printed for the Worcestershire Historical Society by James Parker, 1912).

W. Baildon, ed., *Court Rolls of the Manor of Wakefield vol. I, 1274–1297* (Leeds: Yorkshire Archaeological Society, 1901).

Custumals of the Manors of Laughton, Willingdon and Goring (Lewes: Sussex Record Society, vol. LX, 1961).

P. Foden, ed. and trans., *Records of the Manor of Norton in the Liberty of St. Albans, 1244–1539* (Caxton Hill, Hereford: Hertfordshire Record Society, 2014).

F.J. Furnivall, ed., *The Babees Book: The Bokes of Nurture* (London: Early English Text Society, 1868).

J. Lister, ed., *Court Rolls of the Manor of Wakefield, vol. 31 to 1316, and 1286* (Leeds: Yorkshire Archaeological Society; Record Series, vol. LVII, 1917).

J. Lister, ed., *Court Rolls of the Manor of Wakefield, vol. IV, 1315–1317* (Leeds: Yorkshire Archaeological Society, 1930).

R. Lock, ed., *The Court Rolls of Walsham le Willows 1303–1350* (Woodbridge: Boydell & Brewer and Suffolk Record Society, vol. xli, 1998).

R. Lock, ed., *The Court Rolls of Walsham le Willows 1351–1399* (Woodbridge: Boydell Press and Suffolk Record Society, vol. xlv, 2002).

D. Noy, ed., *Winslow Manor Court Book Part I 1327–1377* (Aylesbury: Buckinghamshire Record Society no. 35, 2011).

L.R. Poos and L. Bonfield, eds., *Select Cases in Manorial Courts 1250–1550; Property and Family Law* (London: Selden Society, 1998).

T.H. Riley, ed., *Chronica Monasterii S. Albani, vol. II Registra Quorundam Abbatum Monasterii S Albani, Qui Seclo XV mo Floruere Vol. II Registra Johannis Whethamstede, William Albon, et Willelmi Walingfords Abbatum Monasterii Santi Albani* (London, 1872).

R.H. Robbins, ed., *Secular Lyrics of the XIVth and XVth Centuries* (Oxford: Clarendon Press, 1961).

K.M. Troup, ed., *The Court Rolls of the Manor of Wakefield, October 1338–September 1340* (Leeds: Yorkshire Archaeological Society, 1999).

Secondary Sources Books

P. Ariès, *Centuries of Childhood* (New York: Alfred A. Knopf, 1962).
A.V. Chayanov, *The Theory of Peasant Economy*, in: D. Thorner, B. Kerblay, and R.E.F. Smith, eds. (Homewood, IL: American Economic Association, R.D. Irwing,, 1966).
P.J.P. Goldberg, *Women, Work and Life—Cycle in a Medieval Economy: Women in York and Yorkshire, c. 1300–1520* (Oxford: Clarendon Press, 1992).
B.A. Hanawalt, *The Ties That Bound: Peasant Families in Medieval England* (New York: Oxford University Press, 1986).
B.A. Hanawalt, *Growing Up in Medieval London: The Experience of Childhood in History* (Oxford and New York: Oxford University Press, 1993).
G. Handel, S.E. Cahill, and F. Elkin, *Children and Society: The Sociology of Children and Child Socialization* (Oxford University Press, 2007).
E. Heward, *Matthew Hale* (London: Robert Hale, 1972).
S. Justice, *Writing and Rebellion: England in 1381* (Berkeley California and London: University of California Press, 1994).
N. Orme, *Medieval Schools from Roman Britain to Renaissance England* (New Haven: Yale University Press, 2006).
N. Orme, *From Childhood to Chivalry, the Education of the English Kings and Aristocracy 1066–1530* (London and New York: Methuen, 1984).

Secondary Sources Articles and Chapters

P.A. Brand and P.R. Hyams, 'Seigniorial Control of Women's Marriage, I', in: *Past and Present*, no. 99 (1983), pp. 123–133.
C. Briggs, 'Monitoring Demesne Managers Through the Manorial Court Before and After the Black Death', in: R. Goddard, et al., *Survival and Discord in Medieval Society Essays in Honour of Christopher Dyer* (Turnhout: Brepols, 2010), pp. 179–196.
G.M. Draper, 'The Education of Children in Kent and Sussex: Interpreting the Medieval and Tudor Ways', in: *Nottingham Medieval Studies*, vol. 52 (2008), pp. 213–252.
R. Faith, 'Seigniorial Control of Women's Marriage, II', in: *Past & Present*, vol. 99, no. 1 (1 May 1983), pp. 133–148.
R. Faith, 'The "Great Rumour" of 1377 and Peasant Ideology', in: R.H. Hilton and T.H. Aston, eds., *The English Rising of 1381* (Cambridge: Cambridge University Press, 1984, reprinted 2007), pp. 43–73.
P.J.P. Goldberg, 'What Is a Servant?', in: A. Curry and E. Matthew, eds., *Concepts and Patterns of Service in the Later Middle Ages* (Boydell Press, 2000), pp. 1–20.

P.J.P. Goldberg, 'Masters and Men in Later Medieval England', in: D.M. Hadley, ed., *Masculinity in Medieval Europe* (London and New York: Longman, 1999), pp. 56–70.

B.A. Hanawalt, 'Childrearing Among the Lower Classes of Late Medieval England', in: *The Journal of Interdisciplinary History*, vol. 8, no. 1 (1977), pp. 1–22.

B.A. Hanawalt, 'The Peasant Family and Crime in Fourteenth Century England', in: *Journal of British Studies*, vol. 13, no. 2 (1974), pp. 1–18.

P.V. Hargreaves, 'Seignorial Reaction and *Peasant* Responses: Worcester Priory and Its *Peasants* After the Black Death', in: *Midland History*, vol. 24 (1999), pp. 53–78.

R.H. Helmholz, 'Marriage Contracts in Medieval England', in: P.L. Reynolds and J. Witte, eds., *To Have and to Hold Marrying and Its Documentation in Western Christendom, 400–1600* (Cambridge: Cambridge University Press, 2007), pp. 260–286.

M. Müller, 'The Function and Evasion of Marriage Fines on a Fourteenth Century English Manor', in: *Continuity and Change*, vol. 14, no. 2 (1999), pp. 169–190.

M. Müller, 'Conflict, Strife and Cooperation: Aspects of the Late Medieval Family and Household', in: I. Davis, M. Müller, and S. Rees-Jones, eds., *Love, Marriage and Family Ties in the Later Middle Ages* (Turnhout: Brepols, 2001), pp. 311–329.

M. Müller, 'Peasant Women, Agency and Status in Mid Thirteenth to Late Fourteenth-Century England: Some Reconsiderations', in: C. Beattie and M.F. Stevens, eds., *Married Women and the Law in Premodern Northwest Europe* (Woodbridge: Boydell Press, 2013), pp. 169–190.

M. Müller, 'The Aims and Organisation of a Peasant Revolt in Early Fourteenth-Century Wiltshire', in: *Rural History*, vol. 14 (2003), pp. 1–20.

N. Orme, 'Chaucer and Education', in: *The Chaucer Review*, vol. 16, no. 1 (1981), pp. 38–59.

N. Orme, 'Latin and English Sentences in Fifteenth-Century Schoolbooks', in: *The Yale University Gazette*, vol. 60, no. 1/2 (October 1985), pp. 47–57.

C. Rawcliffe, 'The Eighth Comfortable Work: Education and the Medieval English Hospital', in: C. Barron and J. Stratford, eds., *The Church and Learning in Late Medieval Society: Essays in Honour of R.B. Dobson* (Stamford: Shaun Tyas, Harlaxton Medieval Studies xi, 2002), pp. 372–373.

E. Searle, 'Seigneurial Control of Women's Marriage; the Antecedents and Function of Merchet in England', in: *Past and Present*, no. 82 (1979), pp. 3–43.

CHAPTER 6

Conclusion

Manorial records were not primarily concerned about children as such. Children owed no services and owed no rents and were not normally called upon by the lord to help with the harvest or other routine services on the manor. Still, village children were, as we have seen, far from invisible. Yet, we have to look for them, and we have to be willing to see them. Like women, children were often rendered almost invisible not so much merely by medieval commentators, though it is always easiest to blame them, but by historians, who did not spot their agencies and toils, occupations, concerns, and who failed to see snippets of their lives scattered through the myriad of different parchments detailing for us the ins and outs of the daily life in medieval English society.

This book has focused on the lives of children and young people who grew up in the medieval English countryside. There can be no doubt that their experiences would have been quite different from those of children and young people growing up in larger urban centres like London or Norwich, with busy markets, possibilities of formal apprenticeships if their families had the means to pay for them, higher population densities, and exposure to a wider world than most children growing up in rural communities were able to experience or even fathom. This does not mean that peasant children had monochrome experiences of nothing but wide swathe of fields growing crops, isolated from the influences of the worlds of markets and trade and busy towns. We know that rural life was intertwined with urban life, towns relied on their rural Hinterland, peasants travelled into market towns to sell goods

M. Müller, *Childhood, Orphans and Underage Heirs in Medieval Rural England*, Palgrave Studies in the History of Childhood,
https://doi.org/10.1007/978-3-030-03602-7_6

and buy items which were not produced in their villages or hamlets. Some manorial settlements had urban features which placed at least parts of them into an urban category, and each settlement had a different economic base, some more firmly centred around agriculture, some around fishing and others still on other rural crafts. Locality, as we have seen, mattered, while we might be able to determine some overarching common concerns, as revealed in attitudes to mental and physical abilities of growing children and adolescence, we cannot say that the experience of growing up was the same in all of the communities we have explored.

Still, the experiences of the sons and daughters of peasants, would similarly have been worlds apart from those of the children of their masters, the lords and ladies who governed the lives of their free and unfree tenants. They or their representatives would have been encountered perhaps from afar or occasionally within the manorial court, held monthly in the village communities we have encountered in this study. The experiences of growing up of noble and peasant children would have been, however worlds apart, and it was the aim of this book to attempt to explore one part of that world. Peasants made up the vast majority of the population in medieval England, their experiences, and by extension, the experiences of their children therefore mattered.

Rural children were seen to have roles, age—and maturity-determined responsibilities in their local societies, and, above all, they were accorded a secure and protected space in their communities. They started to earn wages and play important economic roles in their teens, which accorded them a wider say in the community and a greater degree of self-determination. They were tasked to help in keeping the peace locally and contain strive and resolve dispute, as soon as boys aged 12 were sworn into tithings. Young women were far from excluded from such communal self-policing mechanisms. Children were already accorded rights as infants, especially if they stood in a direct line towards inheritance, but even if they did not, as potential heirs to be in an age of high child mortality their rights were protected and safeguarded. Children were therefore not figures in the background, and should not be seen by historians as mere appendages to family life. Instead they were central to it, central to their communities and families and kinship networks.

This does not mean that children were revered, or never neglected or abused. Rather it is important to read children and young people back into their records, into their past and for historians to recognise their integral stake in their communal relationships, and indeed vice versa to recognise that communities of adults recognised the integral role and stake young people played and had in their villages, hamlets and fields.

As such children and young adults were not separate from adults, but integral to the adult world, albeit in different capacities. Children and young people drifted through the entire indoor and outdoor spaces of their communities, this is not just confirmed in the records of the manor, but also through studies conducted on legal records, such as Coroner's Rolls. Very young children might have spent more time within the main residential dwelling of the individual peasant family, but there was also a lot of freedom to play and explore the outside world, thereby occasionally getting into trouble and even danger. Younger and older children also helped and learned from their own parents and within the wider local network of kin and neighbours, working in fields, houses and barns. They helped look after animals, learned trades as well as engaged with and learned about local politics and policing. It is very hard indeed to think of a village space which would have been devoid of children.

The integral part children played in their communities places a responsibility upon historians; we cannot and should not write histories which exclude them. Just as historians have made great progress in discovering the lives of the women in medieval village societies, so we are obliged to explore more about the history of children and adolescents in rural and urban communities. The task is not easy however, the sources are problematic and in some respects one might observe that discovering the lives of children in manorial records is like finding the proverbial needles in haystacks. The search for children and the reconstruction of their lives is laborious and fraught with problems, and yet they are there, and ready for us to discover them. The road ahead is surely one of interdisciplinary research, bringing the archaeological and documentary fragments together each bridging gaps the other exposes, leaning on anthropology and other social sciences to guide our steps.

There are no easy answers in the history of childhood. Biology and culture and social structures, ever-changing, shifting and adapting throughout the chronologies and socio-economic contexts make for an elaborate and complex picture of childhood which requires sensitive and careful handling. Attitudes change and are in flux, and single answers are absent.

The history of childhood itself has made great strides forwards, especially perhaps for medievalists who took up the challenge of Ariés's conclusions about childhood in medieval society.[1] Few would still seriously doubt that medieval society did entertain concepts about childhood and child development. Similarly, few would disagree with the notion that parents cared for their children and fretted about their well-being. The evidence that medieval societies entertained various ideas about their young people is simply overwhelming. They debated whether children were born evil or innocent, they had notions about developmental stages and ideas about schooling and training. Medieval society had thoughts about the dietary needs of children, and as we have seen, followed cultural conventions of nursing their babies, which were profound enough to probably impact on fertility and reproductive patterns. Commentators in the Middle Ages debated whether children should be beaten or not, and what adults needed to do in order to ensure the moral well-being of children. What we will not find readily are concepts of childhood which are like ours. We might see familiarity in some of the views and concerns expressed, whether this is concerns about the frivolous or overly exuberant behaviour of adolescents who annoyed their elders probably in recognisably similar ways to contemporary teenager, or in exhortations that babies are precious innocents. We can empathise with the crushing grief and pain expressed by the father whose elegy commemorates the premature death of his beloved daughter, lamenting that 'My grief for her turns wretchedly within me, my tears flow in streams, three times worse than the stab of an arrow sinking into the breast, my heart has been shattered because of her.'[2] Likewise, we can easily recognise the actions of a toddler who begs for apples, coos for wooden swords and a ball in the sad elegy of the death of a young boy.[3] Yet such familiarities, while important, are also deceptive. Childhood was different in Medieval England, and children were perceived differently. Perhaps it is becoming apparent as never before how closely contemporary concerns about childhood are tied to ever-shifting popular culture, and the elaborate, complex dance between our capitalist consumer culture and conceptualisations of childhood which has, after all, itself become a consumer icon. Our western view of children is dominated by stages in schooling, and increasingly perhaps punctuated by the passing of particular exams. We fret about the impact on our children of social media, online games, pornography, x-boxes and too much television, advertising, sugar in the diet, obesity and the narcissism which permeates so much of contemporary popular culture, whether found on facebook or other social media. Such concerns could not have appeared more alien to medieval society if they really did hail from another planet. It is no use attempting to find cultural markers in medieval society to 'find' childhood in the past on a presentist mission.

Instead we have to try to understand medieval society on its own terms. We have to accept that the terms of later medieval people will be different from ours, that their views on education were different from ours and that they did not share many of our concerns and worries. Their social and economic contexts determined different concerns. An additional aspect is that childhood and adolescence did not involve a homogeneous uniform experience. This book has focused on the experiences of medieval peasant children. Some of these children would have grown up in reasonably well to do households, yet others were very poor indeed. We have seen that some owned livestock while others clearly experienced severe hardship especially during famine years when harvests had failed and the price of crops was high. The cultural and social gulf between the families of such children and those of their lords is difficult to imagine. Social class accounted for significant differences in a whole host of experiences in medieval society, as all training, socio-economic engagements as well as leisure experiences were largely determined by social class from birth.

Next to conceptualisation of gender, childhood is probably most prone to presentist bias. The inclination to look for what is familiar is perhaps natural. We might have difficulties explaining what we mean by the term 'child', but we feel pretty confident that we will recognise it when we see it, but do we? Whose idea of 'child' do we recognise really?

Examining manorial records for information on underaged heirs and village orphans has provided a keyhole through which it was possible to shed light on the lives of children and young people in the medieval village more broadly. I hope that I have been able to show that medieval villagers were concerned about the well-being of children who only had one or no surviving parent to look after them. Village communities had systems in place to ensure that children were looked after and that their inheritances were kept in good condition and not left to dilapidation. Guardians had recognised roles in protecting their wards and in many cases their siblings who were not due to inherit. As we have seen, a key element in accepting wards was not simply financial or other economic rewards, but charity and mutuality. Lords and communities were concerned that young people grew up to accept full responsibilities which came along with the status of a tenant and head of the household. In this regard, there was no discernible gendered difference in the treatment of young heirs. There are signs that adults were prepared to go without to ensure the survival of their children. How else did the children of smallholders survive famine years when their parents did not?

There has been a tendency to view medieval society as somewhat ruthlessly practical or even utilitarian. While not devoid of emotion, perhaps still emotionally poorer. Such views—as we have seen, fit into a wider whiggish narrative which sees the development of childhood moving from the misery of the medieval period to—presumably—eventual utopian enlightenment where children are never misused and never experience hardship. From this perspective, it might be difficult to envisage guardians stepping forward to look after an orphan child primarily out of some form of self-interest. Yet, as we have seen, Lords and tenants did not see young heirs primarily as objects of wealth to be exploited, or indeed as free labour to be used. This would have been an almost entirely illogical position to take, considering the large number of children who found themselves orphaned and not even ten years of age, and as such of only limited economic use.

We have looked at some of the items children inherited and the nature of their holdings, which reflected the topographical and economic contexts their home villages found themselves in. I hope that I have been able to show that later medieval children found themselves in a changing material culture, and in societies which tried their best to cope in the face of crises, and the unprecedented devastation caused by the arrival of the Black Death. In 1348–1349 many villages hit such a crisis point that orphans had to be sent in greater numbers to families to whom they were not related, but that despite orphans and their lands representing a burden on the families who took them in, conflict while it certainly did occur, was reasonably uncommon. This was probably in no small way due to the care communities took in setting up careful maintenance contracts for orphans.

As we have seen, while peasant children might have had their social class in common, this does not mean that the experience of children growing up in the medieval English village was the same for every child. Instead, the experiences of peasant children were complex and multi-faceted, due to a number of interlocking social and economic as well as cultural factors. While on the one hand fundamentally different from the experiences of the children of the aristocracy, differences could also be experienced according to familial status in the village. The economic security accorded by a large holding, for example, would have meant a different experience of growing up than for neighbouring children born into the households of smallholders, or indeed artisans. However, ultimately such differences were a great deal more fluid than the more solid class differences experienced between seigniorial and peasant households. A son of a virgaters could slip into smallholdership if partible inheritance led to the break-up of the paternal- or maternal-holding. A young adolescent servant working for wages would in all likelihood become an employer themselves in adulthood.[4] There was little rigidity in the social structures of rural communities, which were nonetheless bound together through common experiences of lordship and labouring for a living—primarily through agriculture. However, as we have seen, occasionally, where local schooling was available, some village boys could be sent to receive some formal education, thus opening doors to clerical careers for example. Other children learned trades while in service in neighbouring households. Some might well have been sent to households where children could learn specialisms, including brewing, cheese making or artisanal trades, like pottery. In effect, such experiences in service are probably better understood as informal and unregulated apprenticeships. Young people were not voiceless in their communities. They had a say in the nature of their training and service, and, as we have noted, such sentiments were occasionally clearly expressed in some of the cases of orphaned adolescents. Young people were thereby accorded significant agency by their communities. We have seen that families were very fluid and in some respects as a result rather informal in their structures and formations, including half- brothers and sisters, step-parents, step-children, as well as, in some cases, illegitimate siblings. The experience of step-parents was so common it was probably completely normalised. Young people were accorded a voice in the manorial court and village affairs, albeit often only indirectly; but we know that they were often presented with choices which the court protected. Most wards were also left to choose their own marriage partner, and the community took care to safeguard their rights in their inherited lands, buildings and chattels. Maturity was judged according to social and economic competences, thus to a degree according to the level of agency a young person was able to exercise rather than according to mere age in years. Children played a role in the local safeguarding and reproduction of culture and social norms, by becoming involved in community politicking activities and local festivities. Yet children were also seen as vulnerable and in need of protection.

Growing up in the medieval countryside was socially, economically and politically complex, and a key aim of parents and guardians was to facilitate young people to navigate these complexities and develop as independent and responsible actors in their communities within a protective and supportive network of kin and other alliances.

Notes

1. P. Ariés, *Centuries of Childhood* (New York, Alfred A. Knopf, 1962). For responses to Ariés see in particular see for example: S. Shahar, *Childhood in the Middle Ages* (London and New York, 1992); B.A. Hanawalt, 'Childrearing among the Lower Classes of Late Medieval England', in *The Journal of Interdisciplinary History*, vol. 8, no. 1 (1977), pp. 1–22; B.A. Hanawalt, 'Narratives of a Nurturing Culture: Parents and Neighbours in Medieval England', in: B.A. Hanawalt, *Of Good and Ill Repute, Gender and Social Control in Medieval England* (New York, Oxford: Oxford University Press, 1989); N. Orme, 'The Culture of Children in Medieval England', in: *Past and Present*, vol. 148, no. 1 (1995); For a discussion of these historiographical developments see also: C. Heywood, 'Centuries of Childhood: Anniversary and an Epitaph?' in: *The Journal of the History of Childhood and Youth*, vol. 3, no. 3 (2010), pp. 341–365.
2. D. Johnson, ed. and trans., *Poet's Grief; Medieval Welsh Elegies for Children* (1993), p. 83.
3. D. Johnson, ed. and trans., *Poet's Grief; Medieval Welsh Elegies for Children* (1993), p. 103.
4. M. Müller, 'A Divided Class? Peasants and Peasant Communities in Later Medieval England', in: C. Dyer et al., eds., *Rodney Hilton's Middle Ages* (Past and Present Supplement 2, Oxford University Press, 2007), pp. 115–120.

Bibliography

Primary Sources

D. Johnson, ed. and trans., *Poet's Grief; Medieval Welsh Elegies for Children* (Cardiff: Tafol, 1993).

Secondary Sources Books

P. Ariés, *Centuries of Childhood* (New York: Alfred A. Knopf, 1962).
S. Shahar, *Childhood in the Middle Ages* (London and New York: Routledge, 1992).

Secondary Sources Chapters and Articles

B.A. Hanawalt, 'Childrearing among the Lower Classes of Late Medieval England', in: *The Journal of Interdisciplinary History*, vol. 8, no. 1 (1977), pp. 1–22.

B.A. Hanawalt, 'Narratives of a Nurturing Culture: Parents and Neighbours in Medieval England', in: B.A. Hanawalt, *Of Good and Ill Repute, Gender and Social Control in Medieval England* (New York, Oxford: Oxford University Press, 1989), pp. 158–177.

C. Heywood, 'Centuries of Childhood: Anniversary and an Epitaph?' in: *The Journal of the History of Childhood and Youth*, vol. 3, no. 3 (2010), pp. 341–365.

M. Müller, 'A Divided Class? Peasants and Peasant Communities in Later Medieval England', in: C. Dyer et al., eds., *Rodney Hilton's Middle Ages* (Past and Present Supplement 2, Oxford: Oxford University Press, 2007), pp. 115–120.

N. Orme, 'The Culture of Children in Medieval England', in: *Past and Present*, vol. 148, no. 1 (1995), pp. 48–88.

Glossary

Amercement Financial penalty payable to the manorial lord for an offence or breach in custom

Boon Works These are works demanded by lords usually only from unfree, villein tenants in addition to regular labour services (see below). The most common boons demanded were associated with the harvest season

Customary Tenant Another term for 'villein' or 'villein tenant'—see below. The term customary tenant highlights the relationship between unfree status and being subjected to the 'customs' of the manorial jurisdiction within which an individual held land

Demesne The land farmed and utilised by the lord for their own purposes. Such as the fields in a given manor which were not tenanted by local peasants. Sometimes the term is also used to describe the local seigniorial jurisdiction, defined geographically as well as legally by a local lord. In some respects, the boundaries of a seigniorial demesne in that sense are defined by a given lord's legal reach

Entry Fine Is usually a sum of money payable to the lord by heirs or other new incoming tenants to a holding. It was payable in addition to any heriot which may have fallen due upon the death of a previous tenant

Essoin An essoin is a proxy, someone who stands in for someone who should be at the manor court

M. Müller, *Childhood, Orphans and Underage Heirs in Medieval Rural England*, Palgrave Studies in the History of Childhood, https://doi.org/10.1007/978-3-030-03602-7

Fine The term 'fine' in manorial documents refers to a payment to the lord usually to be permitted to do something (rather than a financial penalty, as we would understand the term). Examples are entry fines, a sum of money payable to the lord by heirs or other new tenants upon being granted to a holding

Heriot A death duty payable by the heir upon the death of the tenant to the lord. The most common heriot demanded was the household's best animal, but some lords also accepted other goods or cash. Usually only unfree tenants were liable to pay heriots

Holding The lands and buildings pertaining to the tenurial agreement between tenant (both free and unfree) and their lord. Holdings were usually conceived of as distinct units to which obligations in rents and services as well as certain rights—such as the right of inheritance were attached

Labour Services A common manorial custom associated primarily (but not totally exclusively) with villein tenure, whereby unfree villein tenants were obliged to perform a certain number of unpaid labour services—works—on the land of the manorial lord

Licence A licence is a permission sought or granted by the lord to be allowed to do something. Typical examples include licences to marry, to leave the manor, to agree a dispute with someone, or to send a child to attend school. The licence was usually attached to a *fine*

Manor A manor constitutes a jurisdictional as well as geographic unit, falling under the authority of a manorial lord, who could be ecclesiastical or lay. The precise nature of a manor varied regionally and locally. A manor may contain one village, or several, or a village and smaller settlements called hamlets. Some manors had very complex and split lordships, which was more common in East Anglia. Manors were important economic units as they served as significant forms of income for lords. Such income was gained from rents payable by local tenants, as well as the produce gained and harvested from the lords' own fields and livestock in the manor

Manor Court Regular courts held within a given manor in the name of the lord of that manor. Local tenants therefore fell under the legal jurisdiction of the manor court. The precise nature and scope of this private jurisdiction varied from lordship to lordship

Marriage Licence See *Merchet*

Merchet A licence to marry which fell due on unfree (villein) tenants. Local custom varied considerably. In some manors both men and women were liable to pay the licence to the lord, in others possibly not. In essence, it constituted a permission to marry, allowing the lord to vet, and keep track of peasant marriages and hence the movements of his land

Messuage A plot of land within a manor containing the main dwelling of a household, and possibly other associated buildings

Pledge Someone who stood as guarantor for someone else, usually for payments granted in credit by the lord to his tenants. Pledges were used to promise good behaviour or to guarantee the rendering of dues, services and customs by another. Lords usually required pledges to be found to secure de facto loans, involving rent payments or amercements, but also in the case of underaged heirs to guarantee the upkeep of their landed inheritance

Rent Tenants, both free and unfree, paid a rent to their lords. Unfree tenants usually paid a rent comprised of rent in cash, rent in labour and rent in kind (produce), free tenants were more likely to be obliged to just pay a cash rent for the land which they held

Rood A unit of land equivalent to a quarter of an acre

Villein By the thirteenth century, the term was applied to those who were considered unfree in status. While the status of individual tenants was generally attached to the type of land they held from their lord, a person could also become individually associated with the unfree status. The use of the term 'villein by blood' was by no means an uncommon occurrence in thirteenth and fourteenth-century England. It is important to note though, that free tenants were also subject to seigniorial jurisdiction and authority, while at the same time many tenants held both free and unfree land. A tenant may therefore hold unfree (villein) land, for which they had to satisfy seigniorial demands associated with unfree tenure; but did not face such dues for other plots of land held in free tenure for a cash rent

Virgate A unit of land, which could vary significantly according to region. It could contain anything from 25 to 40 acres, but is in any case associated with more substantial tenants

Index

A

Adoption, 20, 80, 135, 136
Age, 2–4, 9, 12–16, 33, 36, 38, 39, 42–49, 58–65, 79, 80, 82–86, 91, 92, 104, 107, 119–122, 125–127, 131, 133–136, 142, 147, 158–163, 165, 166, 169, 170–174, 178, 179, 183–187, 198, 200, 202, 203
  age of majority, 58, 61–65, 86, 90, 120, 121, 132, 163, 166, 183, 184, 186, 187
  full age, 36, 42, 44, 62–64, 79, 82, 85, 104, 134, 136, 160, 163, 165, 169, 171, 185
  underage, 19–21, 33, 38, 41–44, 51, 53, 55, 56, 59, 62, 63, 79, 83–86, 88, 91, 92, 94–98, 100–105, 108, 119, 122, 123, 128, 132, 138, 140, 147, 148, 157–161, 163–167, 171, 172, 176, 177, 182–187, 201, 209
Apprenticeship
  formal, 197
  informal, 203

B

Baby, 39, 120, 122
Black Death, 1, 3, 6, 19, 38–40, 47–49, 64, 67–69, 79, 81, 89, 99–102, 105, 106, 108, 120–122, 131, 133, 135, 142–147, 149, 152, 163, 165, 166, 169, 172, 177, 186, 191, 193, 202
Breastfeeding, 10, 25, 82, 109, 126
Buildings
  grange, 88
  Insethouse, 88
  messuages, 88, 89, 145

C

Clothes, 20, 52–54, 56, 89, 93, 126, 136, 140, 170
  shoes, 53, 55, 56

M. Müller, *Childhood, Orphans and Underage Heirs in Medieval Rural England*, Palgrave Studies in the History of Childhood, https://doi.org/10.1007/978-3-030-03602-7

D
Diet, 14, 25, 82, 109, 200
Disability, 42

F
Famine, 3, 6, 19, 38, 98, 106–108, 114, 120, 128, 129, 131, 145, 160, 201, 202
Food, 10, 24, 43, 52, 53, 56, 82, 106, 108, 113, 126, 169, 183

G
Games, 93, 200
Garciones, 49, 68, 69, 173
Guardian, 19, 36–43, 45, 51–54, 56, 57, 80, 84–86, 88, 90, 95, 119, 124–128, 130–140, 142, 144, 147, 150, 157–159, 162, 164–166, 169, 172, 173, 183, 184, 201, 202, 204

H
Heriots, 40, 43, 64, 79, 86, 95, 98–104, 108, 144, 145, 158

I
Infant, 4, 6, 82, 105, 109, 148, 167, 189, 198
Inheritance, 18, 20, 36, 37, 40, 42, 43, 53, 54, 56, 57, 62, 63, 80–87, 89, 90, 92, 103, 104, 106, 119, 120, 122, 123, 125–128, 130–132, 135, 136, 138–143, 146, 159, 160, 162, 163, 166, 167, 176, 182–184, 186, 187, 198, 201, 203
  custom, 18, 27, 63
Inventories, 87, 90, 91, 93–98, 111, 112

L
Literacy, 174, 179, 181, 182, 192
Livestock
  Horses, 96, 101
  Oxen, 96, 100
  Pigs, 101, 102, 170
  Sheep, 96, 101, 103, 170
Lordship, 5–7, 21, 57, 86, 98, 104, 130, 136, 142, 147, 148, 175, 178, 182, 203

M
Manor court, 18, 20, 26–28, 44, 46, 53–55, 58, 66–70, 72, 73, 79, 82, 109–111, 124, 129, 131, 146, 176
Market, 5, 20, 27, 36, 81, 111, 147, 169, 197
Marriage
  arranged, 162, 163, 166, 167
  licence (merchet), 65, 144, 152, 160, 162–166, 175, 191
Merchet. *See* Marriage
Mutuality, 7, 158, 172, 182, 184, 201

R
Revolt, 58, 67, 68, 71, 110, 141, 151, 175, 181, 191
Rituals, 33, 49, 59, 79, 130, 136, 179

S
School, 6, 21, 60, 174–182, 190, 191, 193
Schooling, 174–178, 181, 191, 200, 203
Scotale, 50, 51
Service, 13, 20, 22, 34, 36–39, 41, 45, 46, 49, 51, 54, 55, 63, 65, 68, 84, 86, 107, 133, 171–173, 189, 197, 203

Siblings
by blood, 125–127
half-siblings, 125, 131, 140
step-siblings, 126
Smallholders, 81, 99, 105, 108, 160, 161, 175, 202, 203
Step-parents, 124, 125, 131, 138, 140, 157, 160, 203

T
Tenement, 17, 34–37, 39–41, 43, 44, 47, 55, 56, 62, 86, 88, 102, 104, 106, 108, 110, 120, 124, 130, 133, 142, 143, 163, 178, 186
Tools, 11, 59, 92, 95, 96, 107, 164, 167, 171
Toys, 5, 14, 93, 95, 112

V
Villein, 7, 17, 33, 36, 41, 51, 56, 58, 63, 65, 79, 81, 85, 90, 98, 104, 123, 125, 126, 141, 142, 144, 158, 164, 175

W
Wages, 41, 45, 47–49, 52, 69, 143, 152, 169, 173, 174, 198, 203
Weaning, 5, 14, 25, 82, 109
Work, 3, 7, 15, 23, 25, 34, 38, 46, 54, 68, 81, 92, 93, 112, 120, 121, 147, 152, 157, 166, 167, 170, 189, 191

The manufacturer's authorised representative in the EU is Springer Nature Customer Service Centre GmbH, Europaplatz 3, 69115 Heidelberg, Germany. If you have any concerns regarding our products, please contact ProductSafety@springernature.com

Printed and bound by CPI Group (UK) Ltd, Croydon, CR0 4YY

30/09/2026

02225228-0001